the 7 KEYS
to EFFECTIVE
WEB SITES

Prentice Hall PTR
Upper Saddle River, NJ 07458
http://www.prenhall.com

DAVID SACHS
HENRY STAIR

Editorial/production supervision, interior design: *Camille Trentacoste*
Composition/layout: *Joanne Anzalone* and *Patti Guerrieri*
Art Direction: *Meg VanArsdale*
Icon design: *Don Martin*
Cover design director: *Jerry Votta*
Cover design: *Deesign Source*
Manufacturing manager: *Alexis R.Heydt*
Acquisitions editor: *Mary Franz*
Editorial Assistant: *Noreen Regina*

The publisher offers discounts on this book when ordered in bulk quantities.
For more information, contact:

>Corporate Sales Department
>Prentice Hall PTR
>One Lake Street
>Upper Saddle River, NJ 07458
>Phone: 800-382-3419 Fax: 201-236-7141
>E-mail: corpsales@prenhall.com

Printed in the United States of America

10   9   8   7   6   5   4   3   2   1

ISBN 0-13-490087-1

Prentice-Hall International (UK) Limited, *London*
Prentice-Hall of Australia Pty. Limited, *Sydney*
Prentice-Hall Canada Inc., *Toronto*
Prentice-Hall Hispanoamericana, S.A., *Mexico*
Prentice-Hall of India Private Limited, *New Delhi*
Prentice-Hall of Japan, Inc., *Tokyo*
Simon & Schuster Asia Pte. Ltd., *Singapore*
Editora Prentice-Hall do Brasil, Ltda., *Rio de Janeiro*

Dedication

The Seven Keys to Effective Web Sites is dedicated to my wife, Linda Shackelford, whose continued commitment to the Appalachian Service Project (ASP) for the past three years has enriched so many lives. Linda's energy and enthusiasm have made it possible for the many participants in this program to create a world that is warmer, safer, and drier for those less fortunate than they. I continue to remain in awe of her dedication to this project and of the inspiration and joy that she provides so willingly to so many others.

David Sachs

This book is dedicated to my wife, Lorrine, and to four wonderful people whom I once called my children. I am now privileged to call them my adult friends. It is also dedicated to my co-author Dr. David Sachs. David continues to be the guidance and stimulation of our partnership.

Henry H. Stair

About the Authors

David Sachs is Professor of Office Information Systems and Assistant Dean in Pace University's School of Computer Science and Information Systems in New York. He has been actively involved in developing and teaching computer science courses since 1984. He has co-authored *Discovering Microsoft Works, Hands-On Internet, Hands-On Mosaic, Instant Internet,* and *Hands-On Netscape.* He frequently presents workshops and courses about the Internet and the World Wide Web to corporate clients around the world, and participates actively in the Internet World conferences sponsored by Mecklermedia. Dr. Sachs is particularly interested in the field of telecommunications and its impact upon our world. His interests include racquetball and downhill skiing. He can be reached at `dsachs@ibm.net`

Henry (Pete) Stair is President of Mycroft Information, LLC New Canaan, Connecticut. Mycroft specializes in client consulting for high-performance global Internet and telecommunications networks. He co-authored the post-graduate textbook *Megabit Data Communications* as well as *Hands-On Internet, Hands-On Mosaic, Instant Internet,* and *Hands-On Netscape.* He is a registered professional engineer (CA) and a member of the IEEE and the Internet Society. He frequently presents workshops and courses about the Internet and the World Wide Web to corporate clients around the world, and participates actively in the Internet World and World Wide Web conferences. His interests include demystifying technology, cross-country skiing, consciousness research, wine, and classical music. He can be reached at `stair@mycroft.com`

As always, we are grateful for the help and support that we have received during the past few months from the personnel at PTR Prentice Hall and others. Even with all of this help, we and we alone, are responsible for any remaining goofs, glitches and gaps. Please be sure to let us hear from you if there are any suggestions about how to make the next edition of this book even better.

Contents

4.   Key 2 — Valuable, Useful, or Fun   61

5.   Key 3 — Current and Timely   97

6.   Key 4 — Easy to Find and Use   135

8.   Key 6 — Involve the Visitor   207

9.   Key 7 — Responsive To Its Users   243

Acknowledgments

The Seven Keys to Effective Web Sites is the product of many hands. Our gratitude goes out to all who have been so supportive and encouraging. There have been several individuals who deserve special thanks.

At PTR Prentice Hall, our executive editor, Mary Franz, continues to be an inspiration. Mary knows her subject, understands the software, and has willingly committed herself to the support that goes above and beyond the call of duty. We have been privileged to have worked with Mary since 1993, and look forward to many more opportunities to do so. In fact, it was Mary's suggestion at Fall Internet World '95 in Boston that led to our turning a seminar entitled "Seven Habits of Effective Web Sites" into the book that you now hold in your hands.

Camille Trentacoste, our production editor, has a magical way taking our prose and screen shots and transforming them into the book you now hold in your hands. Gail-Cocker Bogusz, Meg Van Arsdale, and Don Martin have created a set of graphics that does a wonderful job of enhancing our prose. We are most appreciative.

Martha Williams, our copy editor, always has many important and useful suggestions to add to our writing. Martha's attention to detail is impressive, and she adds that special touch that causes our prose to be tighter, clearer, and more readable.

There were a number of technical reviewers of *The Seven Keys to Effective Web Sites*. We are extremely grateful to them for the time and attention that they paid to early drafts of this manuscript. Their support of the concept was appreciated, and their suggestions for improvements have, hopefully, been incorporated into the text.

As always, we are grateful for the help and support that we have received during the past few months from the personnel at PTR Prentice Hall and others. Even with all of this help, we and we alone, are responsible for any remaining goofs, glitches and gaps. Please be sure to let us hear from you if there are any suggestions about how to make the next edition of this book even better.

David Sachs   `dsachs@ibm.net`
Pete Stair   `stair@mycroft.com`

Introduction

What Are The Seven Keys to Effective Web Sites?

We believe that there are certain characteristics or *keys* that help to define effective Web sites. In our judgment, for a Web site to be effective, it must incorporate as many of the following keys as possible.

Key 1: A site must be visually appealing.

Key 2: A site must be valuable, useful or fun.

Key 3: A site must be current and timely.

Key 4: A site must be easy to find and use.

Key 5: A site must have intuitive on-page navigation.

Key 6: A site must involve the visitor.

Key 7: A site must be responsive to its users.

Reviewing thousands of Web sites has led us to conclude that sites that attend to these seven keys are, for the most part, highly effective. Such sites cause us to pay attention to what they have to say, and to how well they say it. They invite us in and cause us to stay longer than we might have originally intended. Effective sites pay attention to our needs and interests, and provide us with information or resources that we might otherwise be unable to find. They enable us to do our work more quickly or efficiently. Effective Web sites continually recreate themselves, and continuously shape themselves to our very personal needs. In addition, we tend to return to these sites, either to obtain new information, or to make additional purchases. As you will see in the many examples that are provided in the following chapters, effective sites serve their sponsoring organizations well. They are clear about the business that they are in, whether it is education, not-for-profit, or profit-oriented, and they provide information, or services, or facilities that would not be available any other way.

For Whom Is This Book Intended?

The Seven Keys to Effective Web Sites is intended for three audiences: those who create Web sites— often known as Webmasters; those who are responsible for Web sites; and those who are thinking about the development of Web sites. Webmasters should find this book to be quite useful. When the concepts in *The Seven Keys to Effective Web Sites* have been presented in seminars, they have been well received, and Webmasters have told us that the examples are helpful and the technical information is valuable. In addition, there are those who are responsible for Web sites, although they may not actually be constructing them. Attendees at our seminars have indicated that information about, and examples of, effective Web sites help them to ask better questions about their own sites, and to think more clearly about the goals and objectives of their particular sites.

Finally, beginning Webmasters have also told us that these examples and insights are helpful; there are lots of marketing issues affiliated with all the technical ones, and beginners have appreciated the opportunity to think about all these perspectives simultaneously and in advance of their actual work. The examples presented in *The Seven Keys to Effective Web Sites* are readily available at Prentice Hall's Web site: `http://www.prenhall.com/7keys` They should provide a good introduction to state-of-the-art sites that have been developed by a wide array of companies and organizations.

Those who are contemplating the establishment of a Web site would do well to look at all of the examples that are included, and to think about the various issues, both technical and conceptual, that are presented, before committing significant time, energy and money to the establishment of their own sites.

How Is This Book Organized?

Chapter 1 provides a brief review of the origin and components of the World Wide Web. Readers who are already familiar with this information may wish to skip ahead to Chapter 2. For those for whom this is new information, the chapter provides a context within which to understand the phenomenon known as the World Wide Web.

Chapter 2 provides a detailed discussion of the Seven Keys to Effective Web Sites. Web site success is defined, and seven guiding questions are presented for those who are thinking about when sites are most clearly effective. A definition of each one of the seven keys is offered, followed by a brief discussion about what it is that makes the World Wide Web so different from other media.

Chapter 3 presents examples of Web sites that do an excellent job of demonstrating Key 1, which is to be Visually Appealing. Technical points and tips about how to provide visually appealing sites are offered, including a brief discussion about bandwidth, graphics sizes, background colors, thumbnails, transparent GIFs, Java applets, and sound and movies. Examples follow, including a discussion of the strengths and weaknesses (if any) of each one of the sites that is presented.

Chapter 4 focuses on Key 2, sites that are valuable, useful or fun. "Valuable" and "useful" are defined with regard to the functions that they perform or the content that they provide. Also, some concerns are delineated about the need to maintain the credibility and currency of sites. Excellent examples of valuable and useful and sometimes funny sites are provided, along with detailed discussions about their technical strengths and weaknesses and suggestions about how to improve any weaknesses.

Chapter 5 focuses on Key 3, sites that are current and timely. We define what we mean by current and timely, and then detail some of the technical concerns that go into keeping sites that way. A wide array of excellent current and timely sites is offered. We discuss the information or services that they provide, the technical considerations that must be taken into account, and any possible pitfalls that we have observed. Some of these sites represent outstanding examples of how the new and emerging technology of the World Wide Web is forever changing our perception of the speed with which we access news and information.

Key 4, sites that are easy to find and use, is the focus of **Chapter 6**. The amazing proliferation of Web Sites in the past three years means that it is imperative for sites to be easily found and used. A discussion of the technical aspects of the Web domain name system is offered, after which outstanding examples are presented, showing sites that have attended carefully to this important issue. The increasing number of sites means that those using the Web are finding it harder and harder to find the information and resources that they desire. Therefore, it is incumbent upon those who develop sites to make sure that they are found quickly and easily by all of the major search engines and directory trees that exist. As well, once a visitor finds a site, it is critical that navigation throughout the site be intuitive and fluid. The examples we have chosen do an exemplary job of making it easy for visitors to find what they want, when they want it.

Intuitive on-page navigation, Key 5, is the focus of **Chapter 7**. The technical discussion focuses on navigational icons, image maps, alternatives for navigation, the IMG ALT parameter, and the need to test a Web site continually with a number of different browsers. The examples in this chapter typify sites that have made it intuitively obvious to their visitors how to navigate through their sites. As sites grow larger and more complex, it becomes increasingly important that creators focus carefully on the navigational aspects of their creation. There is no point in having very valuable or useful information at a site if visitors are unable to find it. The examples provided represent the best of the breed. Occasionally there is a minor pitfall, in which case we offer a possible fix.

Key 6, which is to involve the visitor, is the focus of **Chapter 8**. These sites are aware that they must involve their visitors actively in various activities once they arrive, or else they will leave. The technical discussion notes that the involvement really has two aspects to it; the first one focuses on involving visitors to make them feel at home, while the second one focuses on involving visitors to develop a customer list or client base. Many excellent examples are provided of sites that do an outstanding job of involving their visitors.

The focus of **Chapter 9** is on Key 7, sites that are responsive to their users. These are sites that do an outstanding job of actively seeking to learn more about those who come to visit. Using feedback forms, questionnaires, a set of questions, or a registration form are just some of the methods sites are employing to do this. The technical discussion focuses briefly on the strengths and weaknesses of text-only and graphics options and then explores in detail some of the issues surrounding the use of various feedback mechanisms. The examples in this chapter are quite varied, and offer a good set of possible options for others to emulate.

Chapter 10 focuses on the new and emerging options that Webmasters are beginning to confront. The technical discussion focuses on the strengths and weaknesses of the features that are being offered. Following that are examples of eight new and emerging features that appear to be promising.

Conventions Used Throughout The Book

Chapters—As noted, there are 10 chapters. The first one provides a brief review of the World Wide Web, the second one defines the seven keys, and chapters 3–9 present the seven keys in detail. Chapter 10 provides a hint about the new and emerging features that Webmasters are likely to confront in the immediate future.

Technical Points—Each chapter contains an initial section on the technical points related to the particular key being discussed. Knowing that our audience will vary, we have tried not to make the technical discussion too complicated, but we have attended to the important issues that Webmasters and others should consider as sites are being developed.

The goal of this book is not to show Webmasters "how to do" something, but rather to detail all the issues that need to be addressed at a macro level in order to assess a Web site and its potential. This sounds simple, but it is important to emphasize that diving headlong into the technical solutions that go into creating a Web site may not be the best answer. We would urge Webmasters to take some time to think about the many issues presented in this book; these issues are just as important as (or some would say more important than) the technical solutions. If a Web site is to be effective, it is imperative that those who are responsible for it take the time to think about the user and the many issues that are discussed in the following pages.

Examples—Chapters 3–9 each contain at least 15 examples of Web sites that illustrate the particular key being discussed. The examples, presented in alphabetical order, are current as of mid-1996, and are accompanied by screen shots using Netscape 2.01 running on Windows 95.

Key Feature—For each example, we have denoted the key feature (or features) that make this particular site so exemplary.

Pitfall—Even good sites occasionally have some room for improvement. Where this is true, we point out the pitfall (or pitfalls) that could be improved on an already outstanding site.

Fix—Where pitfalls exist, so do solutions. Wherever a pitfall has been presented, we also present the fix that might be used to improve it.

How To Use This Book

If you are brand new to this whole topic, then we would urge you to read all the chapters in the book in the order in which they are presented. If you are conversant with the World Wide Web, then you can skip to Chapter 2, where we define the seven keys in greater detail. You may wish to read the chapters in the order in which they are presented, or you may wish to focus on the topics that interest you the most.

The Seven Keys to Effective Web Sites is intended to help you to make your Web sites stronger and more successful. Be sure to let us know how this book helps you to do that. As well, be sure to let us know if there are ways in which future editions of this book can be improved.

David Sachs   dsachs@ibm.net
Pete Stair   stair@mycroft.com

Chapter 1

World Wide Web Review

World Wide Web Review

NOTE

What follows is a brief review of the origin and components of the World Wide Web.

Readers who are already familiar with the Web may wish to skip ahead to Chapter 2, "The Seven Keys to Effective Web Sites."

The Web

The World Wide Web, although invented in 1989 by Tim Berners-Lee, really burst upon us in 1993. That was the year of Mosaic, the first truly popular graphic Web browser. Its explosive growth since then is shown on the facing page with the statistics courtesy of the Internet Society.

The Web, as we will call it throughout this book, has four components. They are, in no particular order,

- The global Internet—to carry the information

- Attached Web servers—hold the information

- Web Browser software—show the information

- A universal addressing scheme—to find the information

Let's look at each component in turn and see how it contributes to this thing called the Web.

Web Traffic in Megabytes

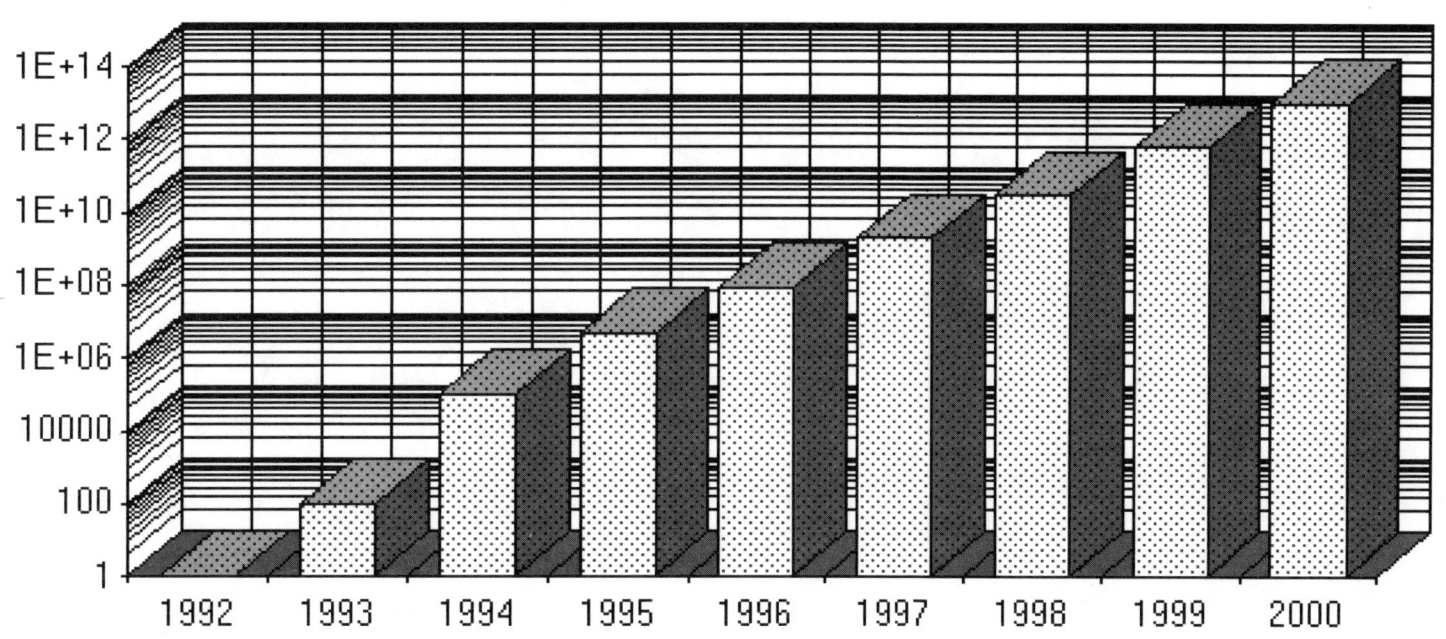

The Global Internet

First we need an electronic system or network or collection of computer networks. It needs to be just about everywhere and easy for people to access. The global Internet, around for over 25 years, is just such a collection of networks. Because the Internet originated during the Cold War, no single person or group or country is in charge, but it's there and it works. (There are some very enthusiastic people around the world working hard to improve it.) Many good books tell the tale of the Internet and all its details if you really want to know.

The Internet is there and it's getting easier every day to gain access from home, work, or school. All you need is a computer, some Internet access software, and a network connection. The net connection may be by dial telephone and modem or by a local area network (LAN) and a device called a router hooked up to the Internet. The map on the facing page shows global Internet connectivity as it stood when we wrote this.

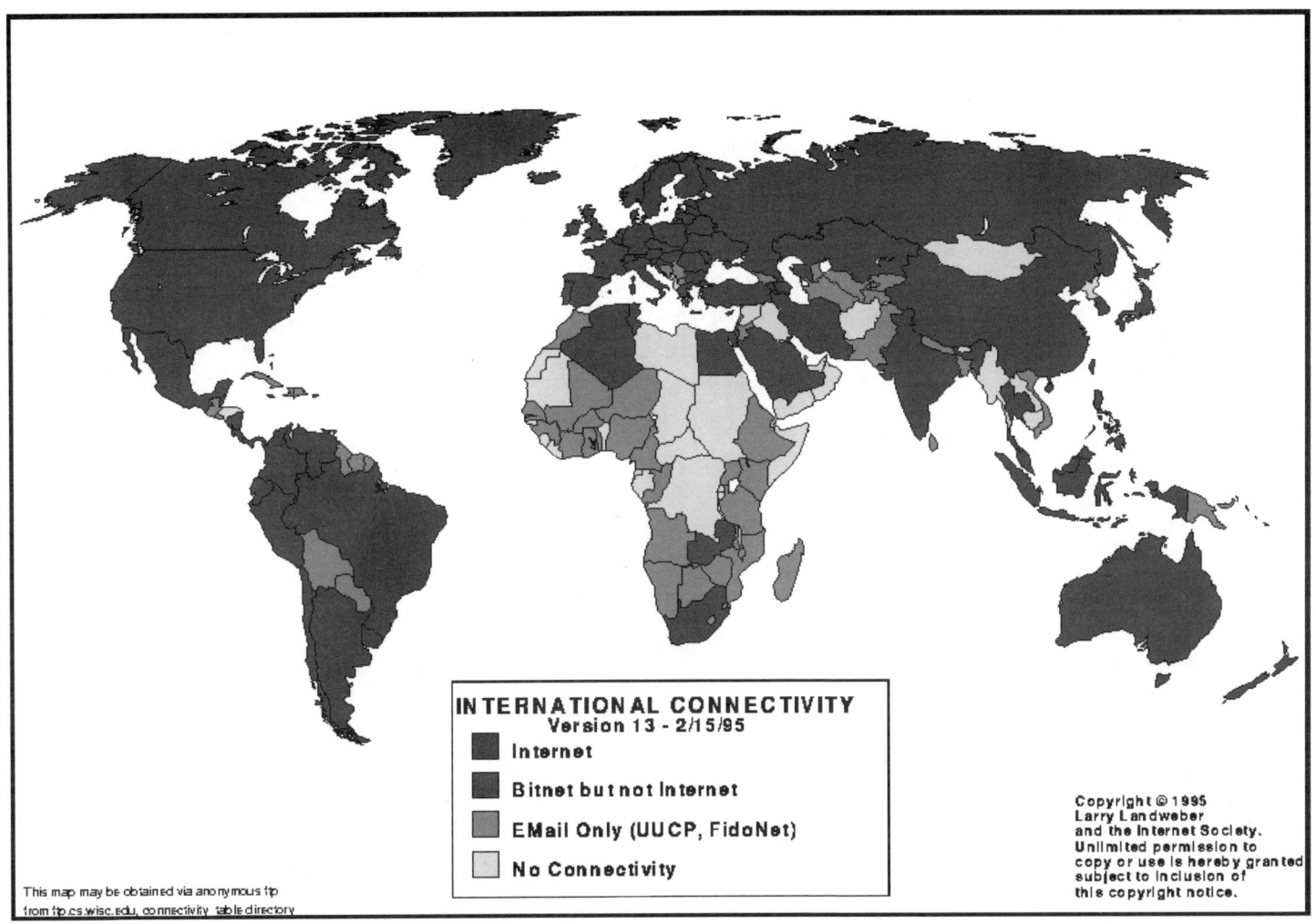

INTERNATIONAL CONNECTIVITY
Version 13 - 2/15/95

Internet

Bitnet but not Internet

EMail Only (UUCP, FidoNet)

No Connectivity

This map may be obtained via anonymous ftp
from ftp.cs.wisc.edu, connectivity_table directory

Web Servers

These computers are connected full time to the Internet and are waiting to be asked for information. Information on the Internet used to be pretty much text only. As we will see on the next page, graphic browsers changed all that. Now information is text and pictures and games and movies and sound and programs brought across the Web to run on the local or "client" computers.

Server computers can range from small PCs to huge water-cooled mainframes. The only requirement is that they always be connected to the Internet, as they never know when some browser will call. Of course, they must have the right software (known as Web server software) to talk to the Internet. As you can see on the graph, a lot of companies, schools and Internet providers are joining up. They do this by setting up a *domain name*. It's like naming your stop on the Internet and it must be different from all others. We will discuss domain names in greater detail in Chapter 6.

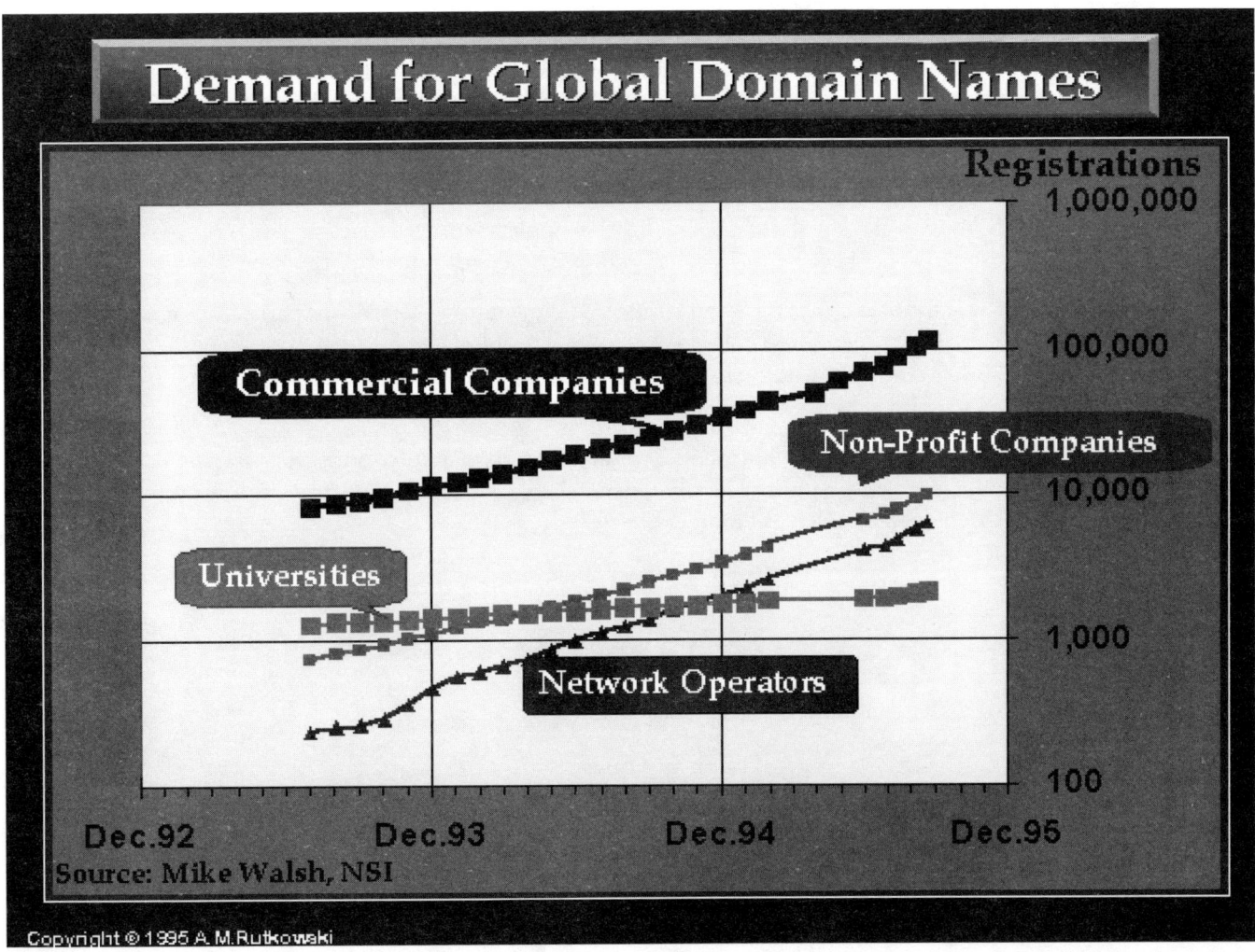

Demand for Global Domain Names

Source: Mike Walsh, NSI

Copyright © 1995 A.M.Rutkowski

Web Browser Software

The earliest Web browsers showed only text, but Mosaic changed all that forever in 1993 when NCSA Mosaic was given away for free to everyone on the planet by the University of Illinois National Center for Supercomputer Applications. It had already been paid for with tax money. Shortly after Mosaic's astounding success, many of Mosaic's developers, under Marc Andreesen, moved to Silicon Valley and they now produce a browser known as the Netscape Navigator. Netscape's browsers show text, graphics, sounds, movies and small software application applets written in Java or JavaScript. Java, from Sun Microsystems, has become the new programming "lingua franca" of the Web.

The key to a graphic browser's success is—no typing. When you see a "screen," or part of a "page," you will see one or many *hyperlinks*. These colored, underlined, or bordered bits of text or graphics hide the addresses of other resources. And those other resources can be anywhere on the global Internet. Click on a hyperlink with a mouse and you go there.

Not all browsers, however, show the information quite the same way. Text-only browsers, such as Lynx, show just the text—no graphics. The facing page shows the Yahoo Web site as it is viewed using Lynx, America Online, Netscape, and Prodigy.

Yahoo!

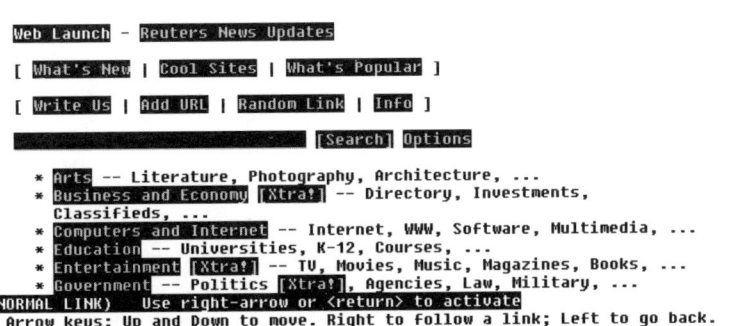

```
Web Launch - Reuters News Updates

[ What's New | Cool Sites | What's Popular ]

[ Write Us | Add URL | Random Link | Info ]

                                [Search] Options

   * Arts -- Literature, Photography, Architecture, ...
   * Business and Economy [Xtra!] -- Directory, Investments,
     Classifieds, ...
   * Computers and Internet -- Internet, WWW, Software, Multimedia, ...
   * Education -- Universities, K-12, Courses, ...
   * Entertainment [Xtra!] -- TV, Movies, Music, Magazines, Books, ...
   * Government -- Politics [Xtra!], Agencies, Law, Military, ...
(NORMAL LINK)   Use right-arrow or <return> to activate
 Arrow keys: Up and Down to move. Right to follow a link; Left to go back.
 H)elp O)ptions P)rint G)o M)ain screen Q)uit /=search [delete]=history list
```

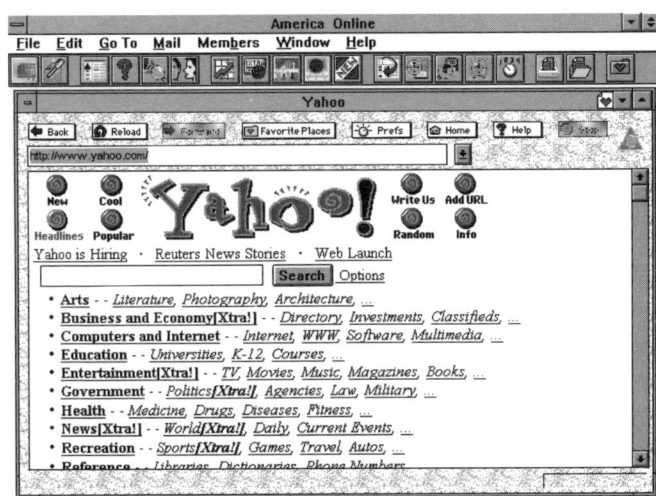

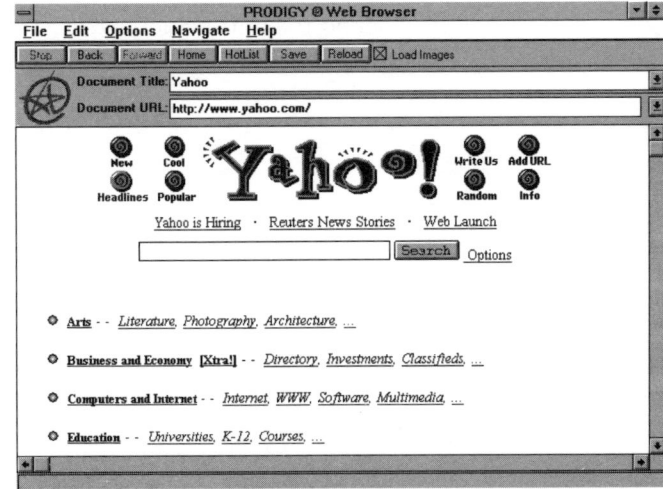

Web Addresses

A scheme of addresses we call *Uniform Resource Locators* or URLs (pronounced *you are ellz*) allows our Web browsers to find Web servers over the global Internet. Although URLs look complex, most of the time you don't need to know them. Remember, the browser hides them from you.

Here is a sample URL: `http://www.pace.edu`

Here is how URLs are constructed.

The part to the left of the `://` is the Internet tool or protocol. Most Web sites use hypertext transport protocol or http, but a URL may also be used for protocols such as telnet, ftp, gopher, or several other older Internet tools.

After the `://` comes the Web server's address in Internet form where `.com` means commercial, `.edu` means educational, `.ca` means Canada, `.fr` means France, and so on.

Finally, there may be a computer directory (folder for you Mac users) and a file name. This directory and file contain the information toward which your hyperlink URL is pointing. Click once on the hyperlink and your browser sends a request for the information to that URL.

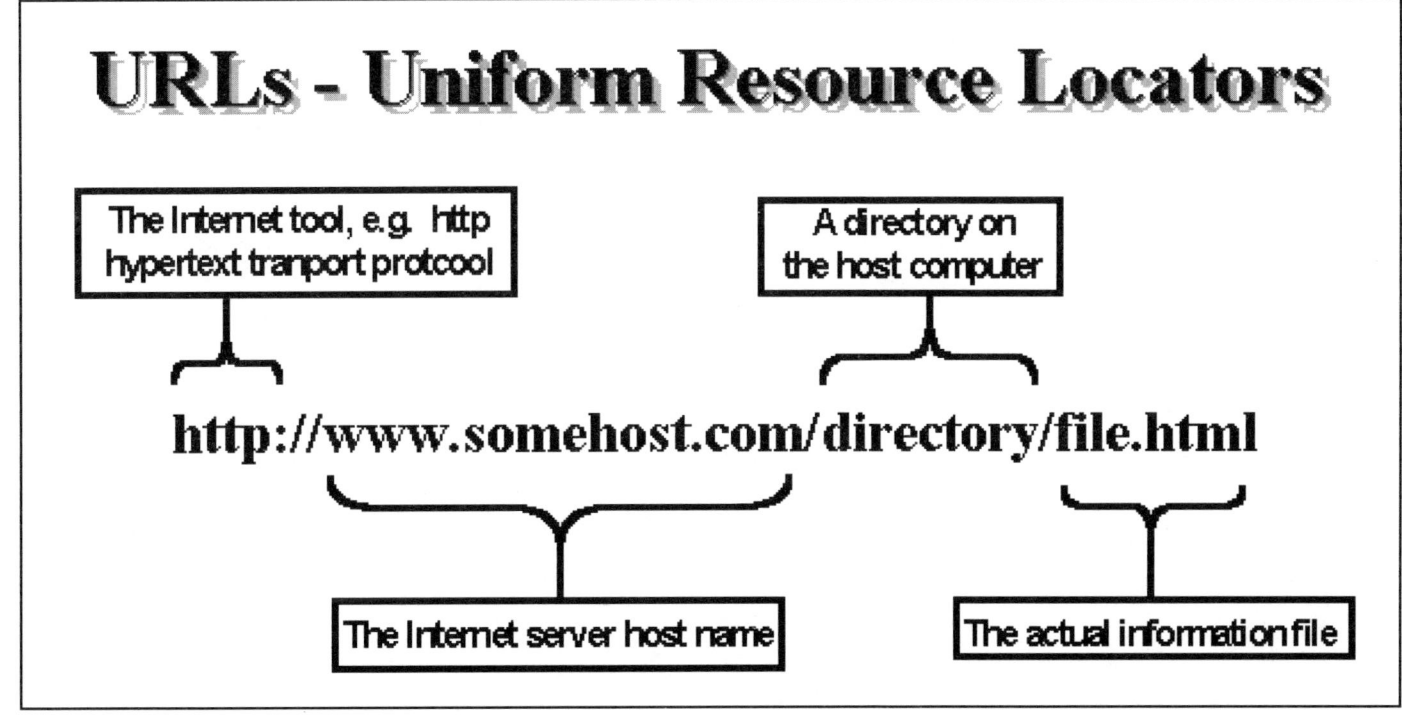

Chapter 2

What is an Effective Web Site?

What Is an Effective Web Site?

Many Web awards are given for "Best," "Top," "Most Visited," or "Cool." We are not going to do that. It is our firm belief that Web sites are effective only when they further the interests of their sponsoring organizations. That is, an effective Web site is yet another powerful tool to help achieve the goals of the enterprise. The enterprise can be a business, a school, a government agency, or an individual. It doesn't matter who sponsors the Web site; the Web site should be viewed as a key new tool and must play its team role.

Web site success, for us, is furthering the goals of the business, school, government, or individual. Success is not, necessarily, being a cool site or a most visited site. These are nice side benefits, of course, but they should not be goals in themselves. If you are trying to reach plastics resin buyers, being visited too often by students may overload your site. Imagine your Web site as your showroom or your customer care center or your service center. You want customers, constituents, prospects, business partners, and employees at your site, not just a curious world passing through.

When you think about the effectiveness of your Web site (or your proposed Web site), we strongly recommend that you ask yourself seven questions.

1. What are the objectives of your enterprise?

This question should be the starting point when you create or remodel your Web site. All organizations have some formal or informal advertising, marketing, sales, fulfillment, and customer support or service activities or goals. These involve the customers, vendors, partners, prospects, constituents, employees, management, teachers, administrators, and students along with all the others who are stakeholders in the enterprise.

2. With this in mind, what are your Web site objectives?

How does or will your Web site coordinate with these activities and the goals of your enterprise? How can it better these activities, make them faster or more effective or less expensive?

3. Who are the visitors you wish to attract and serve?

A Web site may be an Intranet that is visible only inside the enterprise or it may be on the Internet's World Wide Web. You may want to think about how your site can expand the outside reach of your enterprise or attract new prospects or constituents. Or you may want to limit it to the Intranet. Are there ways that an Intranet Web site and an outside Web site can synergize?

4. How do you get visitors to find your Web site?

A wonderful Web site is useless if no one knows it's there. You should put your site address on your stationery, fax forms, business cards, and all your publications. You should think about aligning your site with your marketing, sales, customer, or client public relations and advertising. You will want to register your site where it can be found easily and intuitively.

5. What do visitors want to accomplish when they visit?

Is your site a billboard, a catalog, a product or service delivery center, a technical manual, a showroom, a classroom, a support center, a public service, a fun and wacky place to visit, or some or all of the above? Or is it something completely new and different?

6. How can you get visitors involved so you know who they are?

The visitors have arrived, but as the Web saying goes, "you're only a mouse click away from obscurity." What will you do to intrigue or interest a visitor? Can you get the visitor to leave some information about themselves for follow-up or a next visit?

7. How do you get visitors to return to your site?

Bookmarking is now common with almost all Web browsers. What will you do to get your desired visitors to bookmark your site and return? What fun or services or information or whimsy will bring them back? How do you build visitor loyalty?

The Seven Keys to Effective Web Sites

We believe that there are certain characteristics or "keys" that define effective Web sites. In our judgment, the seven following keys are crucial.

1. A site must be *visually appealing*.

It should be inviting and informative, with constant re-invention.

2. A site must be *valuable, useful or fun*.

It should be immediately useful, giving users reasons to bookmark it.

3. A site must be *current and timely*.

The content should always appear fresh, giving users reasons to return.

4. A site must be *easy to find and use.*

It should be easy to find, widely registered, and have well-chosen keywords.

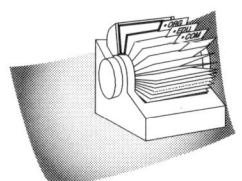

5. A site must have *intuitive on-page navigation.*

It should have easy on-page hyperlinks with good signposts and returns.

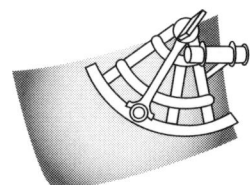

6. A site must *involve the visitor.*

It should invite the visitor to come in, register and stay a while.

7. A site must be *responsive to its users.*

It should be friendly to text browsers, slow communications lines, multiple languages, and open and responsive to visitor suggestions. It should encourage its desired visitors to provide feedback.

These seven keys are not dependent on Web or browser technology. They represent ways of interacting with people. Technology can help us make a site better, but first we must understand that it is a people-oriented new medium. In this book, we will look at people interactions and Web technology.

What Is New about the Web?

As we go through the seven keys, we hope to point out a few reasons why we all must use new thinking. New thinking is needed because the Web is unlike anything that we have seen or used before.

It offers singular new options that we are only now beginning to explore. As we start to take advantage of the Web's unique aspects, we will change many of the ways we do things. The table below gives a few examples of how the Web differs from other mediums we interact with.

Medium	Scheduled	Immediate	Intrusive	Interactive	User Controlled
Newspapers	yes	yes	no	no	no
Radio and TV	yes	yes	yes	no	no
Movies	yes	no	no	no	no
Video Games	no	no	no	yes	yes
The Web	no	yes	no	yes	yes

The Web looks like a mass medium, but it is really a personal medium. People can interact with and choose what they visit and view. They choose when and where they wish to visit. They interact and control what happens next. Users make the choices, not editors and producers.

This means that a Web site must be designed and constructed for Web users, not newspaper readers or TV viewers. The seven keys will lead us to serve these people in this new medium.

Our Illustrations of the Seven Keys

In the chapters that follow, we select certain Web sites that we feel illustrate each of these keys best. Although no site is listed more than once, we hope you will see that many sites incorporate a number of the keys. The sites we have chosen are for illustration only; we are not in the award business. There are many other worthy sites we could have chosen for each key. We hope you will see these keys reflected in your own sites and in those that you visit.

A current file of the URLs for these sites may be found at

```
http://www.prenhall.com/7keys
```

Chapter 3

KEY 1:

Visually Appealing

Introduction to Key 1—Visually Appealing

The first key to an effective Web site is for it to be **visually appealing**. This is easy to illustrate but very hard to prove. What makes it hard to prove is that we all have different standards of what we find to be appealing. Visually appealing is indeed the most subjective of the seven keys, but we believe that the pages which follow illustrate the concept well. While not all of the sites may appeal to you, remember that the site's intent is (as it should be) to appeal to a specific set of visitors. These viewers are the customers and potential customers of the organization that is presenting the site. They may also be the vendors, business partners, competitors, employees, bankers, stockholders, and others who form the whole set of target patrons.

As we noted in the previous chapter, an effective Web site conveys the goals of the organization to these patrons. It's also nice to appear on a "Top 5%," or a "Top 250," or someone's "cool site" list. But that may not be part of the objective. In later chapters we will show some relatively "plain" sites that meet their patrons' needs exactly.

Technical Points and Tips

Size and number of graphics

As you will see in a moment, there are some really appealing sites in this chapter. And you will discover that many of them have graphics that are very large. There will always be many people who have very slow connections trying to look at these sites. To give you some idea of how slow is slow, we present the graph on the next page.

The three lines on the graph represent, from bottom to top,

1. An older modem running at a speed of 9,600 bits per second

2. The fastest currently available modem running at 28,800 bits per second

3. A T1 carrier running at 1,544,000 bits per second

Very few individuals have T1s and the enterprises that have them share them among many users. The net effect is that most people will view sites at roughly the speed of the middle line. This means that for many visitors, a 30,000-byte graphic file will take approximately 30 seconds to download.

As we look at the examples in this chapter, we will indicate some of the approaches that sites use to get the graphics to download faster. In the next section we will discuss some others.

Download Times versus File Size and Link Speed

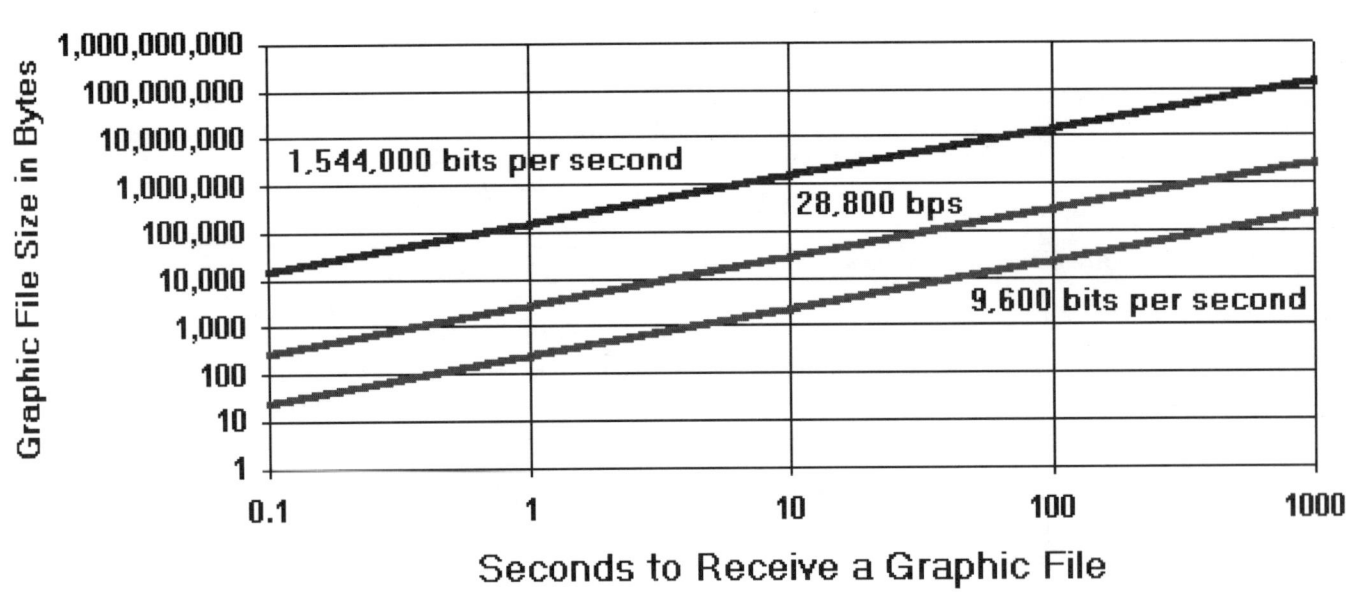

Large Graphic Alternatives

The first and most important tip when putting graphics on your page is to use the HTML IMG ALT parameter. Every image in an HTML (HyperText Markup Language) file should have the ALT parameter specified with a word or phrase. It should look something like this for a photo:

<img src= "photo.gif" alt="[Photo]">

Visitors without graphic browsers, or those who have turned graphics off, will see the text word [Photo] instead of nothing. The HTML ALT parameter should always be used with images.

GIFs versus JPEGs

Many Webmasters use JPEG (Joint Photographic Experts Group) graphic files instead of GIF (CompuServe's Graphic Image Format) files. More and more browsers now have the ability to display JPEGs directly, but *all* graphic browsers can display GIFs. If you are not sure, stick with GIFs.

Number of Colors and Size in the GIF

Another way to reduce the size of graphics files is to reduce either the size of the image or the number of colors being used (or both). If you reduce each side of a color image by 50 percent, then you will reduce the size of the color image to 25 percent of its original size. For example, a 2-inch by 2-inch color image with 256 colors and a file size of 28,000 bytes becomes 6,500 bytes by reducing the size to 1 inch by 1 inch. You should also realize that you will often lose little by reducing either the size or the number of colors being used.

Background Images and Colors

Browsers like Netscape's Navigator allow the use of background colors and background images controlled by the HTML file. First, you must recognize that not all browsers will respond to these HTML options. However, if you do choose to use background colors and images, be sure to test them and get comments from your users and designers. Many background colors and images make it difficult to read the text on your page. More information on background images can be found at

http://home.netscape.com/assist/net_sites/bg/backgrounds.html

Background colors may be specified in the BGCOLOR attribute of the HTML BODY tag. It is expressed as a simple triplet of Red Green Blue in hexadecimal numbers from 00 to FF.

The tag would read

<BODY BGCOLOR="#XXXXXX">

where XXXXXX represents the Red value followed by the Green value followed by the Blue value.

Here are a few values of background colors for various XXXXXXs:

Red = "#FF0000" Green = "#00FF00" Blue = "#0000FF"

Black = "#000000" Gray = "#C0C0C0" White = "#FFFFFF"

You may experiment with values in between to achieve your desired color. Remember to test your results with multiple browsers.

Use of Thumbnails

A small-size image in the range of about 1 inch by 1 inch (or under) is often called a *thumbnail*. A popular method of having a large graphic but sending it out quickly is to first send out a hyperlinked thumbnail. The visitor sees a small representation of your graphic and has the choice of asking for the full-size one. The choice is now up to the visitor. (A good example of this will be presented in Chapter 4 when we look at the Wild Dunes site.)

Use of Transparent GIFs

A transparent GIF allows the background color of the page to show through the blank parts of the images. This is handy for logos and line drawings, as not everyone keeps the default browser background of light gray.

Use of Sound and Movies

Graphics files are large, but QuickTime movies and AU sound files are gigantic! Where they are offered, file sizes or download estimates should be shown. *If* someone wants to download a 5-million-file, then they should know that it's 5 megabytes before they begin downloading it.

Use of Java Applets

As Java works its way onto the Web, it will be possible to make attractive Web pages with it. However, it is important to remember that many visitors cannot use Java with information services browsers, Windows 3.X, or older Mac browsers. As we write, Java needs browsers which run under newer operating systems, but it will be some time before most people have migrated to the new operating systems. Keep this in mind and be sure that your pages make sense to users with both Java- and non-Java-enabled browsers.

Testing Appearance and Features on the Popular Browsers

If you are in the Web page creation business, be sure to test your pages with all the major browsers. Things look different in Netscape, Mosaic, Web Explorer, and so on. Remember to test everything with graphics turned off or with Lynx, the text-only browser. If your potential audience is on America Online or Prodigy, check your appearance here also. Testing with various browsers is a simple matter of running each browser (for AOL, Prodigy, and so forth, this means getting an account) against your site page URLs. You won't know what your site looks like on each until you actually try them.

Involvement of Design Professionals

A final tip: Involve your professional design people in Web page design. Web page creation is new to all of us, but the basics of good design have not changed. Design professionals may not know the Web, but they will want to learn and they bring with them knowledge of tasteful design principles.

Now let's look at some sites that exemplify the key to making a site visually appealing. For each site on the pages that follow, we will explain why we believe the particular page has appeal. We will also discuss some of the technical considerations that must be taken into account.

Before we begin, a word about "metaphor." Many of the sites we will see use a *metaphor*, that is, a suggestion of a likeness to something else. We have discovered that many of the most appealing sites use a metaphorical likeness to draw us in. We are comfortable with the images that we encounter because we understand (even if we don't recognize) the metaphor that is being used.

For each site we will also point out a key feature. For many, we will also list a few pitfalls and perhaps some fixes. The sites are presented in alphabetical (not rank) order and they should all be viewed as examples of sites that are visually appealing. The illustrations and our comments on them are current as of 1996. The browser used is Netscape 2.0 for Windows 95.

As Web pages and sites are constantly changing, you will most likely see some differences when you visit each page. Our comments are based on the site's appearance as we write this.

Classroom Connect

URL: `http://www.classroom.net/classroom/default2.html`

This is not actually Classroom Connect's initial page. On that page (http://www.classroom.net), the visitor is offered a choice of destinations based on their connection speed. The two choices are

> I have high-speed access (28.8 modem, ISDN, 56k, T-1, Ethernet).
> I have low-speed access (14.4 or slower modem, AOL, Prodigy, CompuServe).

We have selected the high-speed option and the resulting screen is shown on the opposite page. An important point to note, however, is that the choice is offered on the very first page. That page contains very limited graphics and is only intended to direct visitors. This option allows Classroom Connect to have the best of both worlds: visually attractive graphics for those who have the capability to view them and quick information for the others. In addition, they let the user make the choice.

This full-color graphics version of the Classroom Connect page is well designed, with crisp, clear choices being offered to the visitor. You naturally want to explore this site in greater detail and it is easy to do so. Each graphic image uses a familiar metaphor to illustrate its purpose and together they form an inviting whole.

Key Feature

An attractive full-color graphics version is offered to those who want to wait for the graphics to be downloaded. Visitors to this site are immediately offered a choice as to whether or not they want to be presented with graphics and the words for those choices are clear and to the point. Many other sites fail to provide such choices at all, or hide the text-only option at the bottom of a screen, or present the text-only choice only after you have already waited for a large full-color graphics screen to be downloaded.

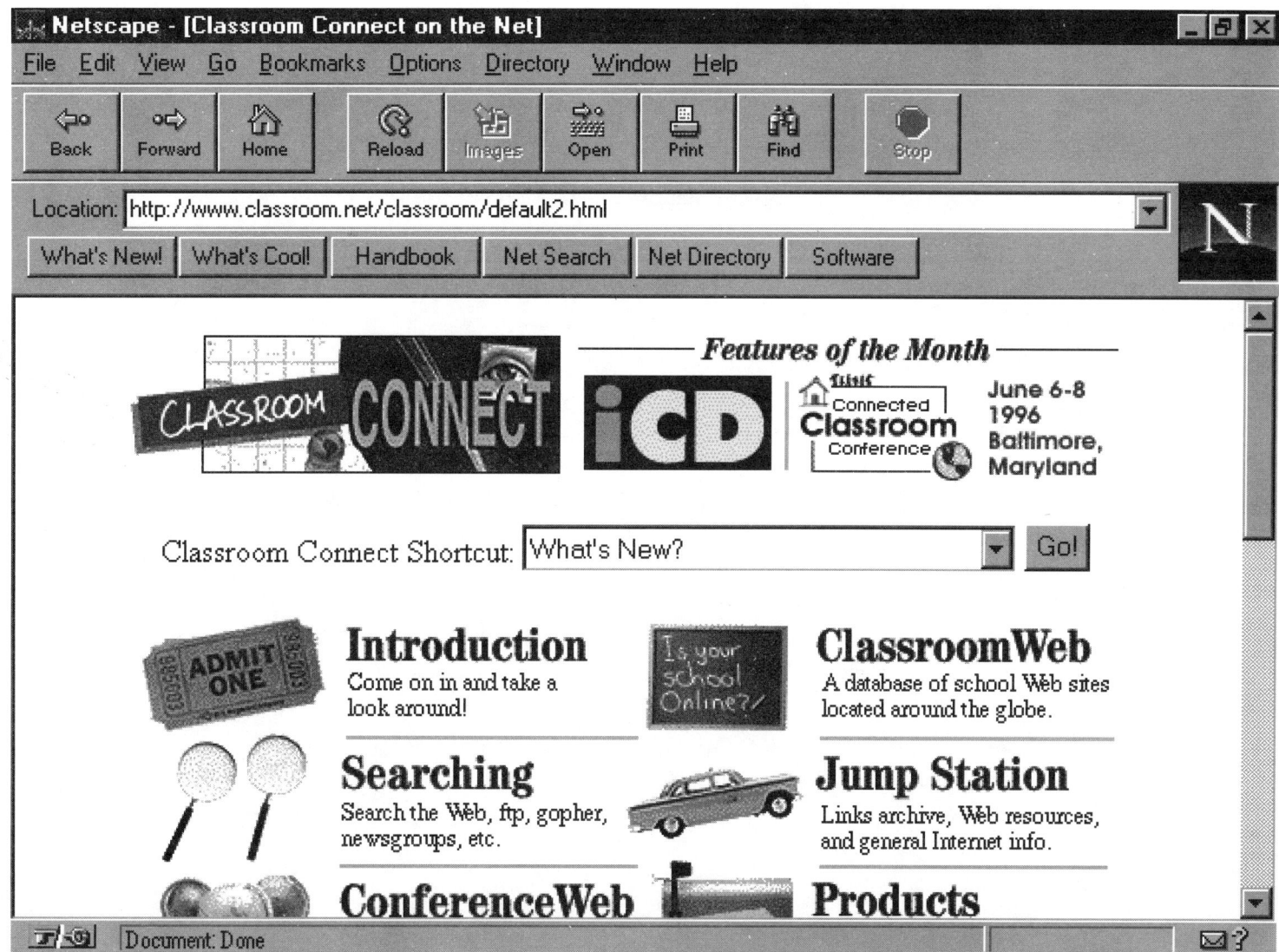

Condé Nast Traveler

URL: `http://www.cntraveler.com`

The Condé Nast Traveler magazine pages reflect the metaphor of a colorful magazine. This is quite understandable, as this is the product Condé Nast produces. The covers represented on their Web pages are designed to entice you into traveling and buying their magazine. They offer extremely colorful photographs of desirable scenes and places for travel. This is a first-rate example of both visually appealing and meeting the objectives of the parent organization.

Key Feature

This is a page of stunning colors and topic- (travel-) related scenes. Clear directions ("CLICK HERE TO ENTER") are provided on the color graphic. In addition, visitors are provided immediately with an obvious "TEXT-ONLY HOME" option at the top of the initial screen. In addition, viewers are told quite clearly that the site is kept current; the day's date appears on the initial screen, implying that someone is paying close attention to the information that is presented here.

Pitfalls and Fixes

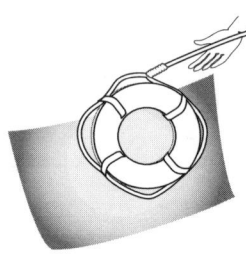

Pitfall: As we mentioned in the Technical Points and Tips section, large color graphics are big files and take many seconds to fill browser screens on slower connections. This can often frustrate users with slow modem lines.

Fix: Images could be divided into several smaller groups. Not only would the time to load the total screen be shorter, but it would also appear to load more quickly as the images "pop" in somewhat independently.

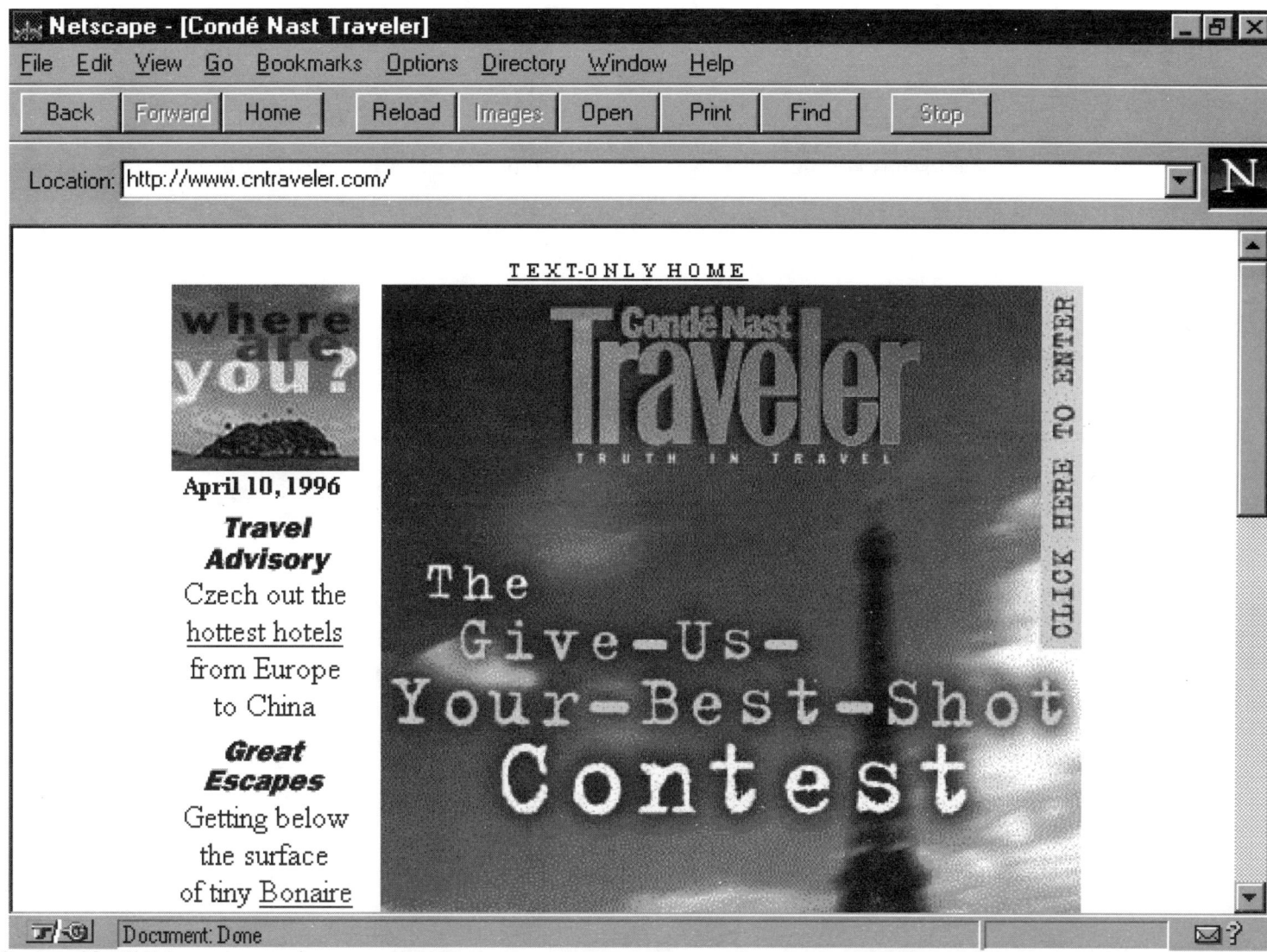

Cybertown Home Page

URL: `http://www.cybertown.com`

Cybertown is a complete fictional creation of a futuristic city. As in a real city, there are a myriad of things to visit, see, and do. Notice that on one screen, this site offers us several ways to proceed. We can click on the objects in the main map or we can use the hypertext links below the map. For first-time visitors, the hypertext links are more explanatory, but for those returning, the map icons are faster. This is a very good example of a site that is visually appealing and one that adds the benefit of easy navigation as well.

Key Feature

This brilliantly colored futuristic 3D city view (a bit-mapped image) is quite inviting.

Pitfalls and Fixes

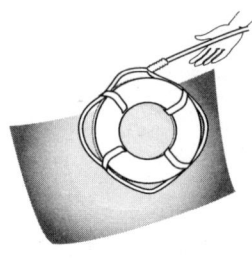

Pitfall: There is a tendency to try to click on what appear to be icons (Education, Library, Town Hall, TV Station, Entertainment, Info, Mall, and Activities) on the right below the map. However, they are really map legends, not hyperlinks.

Fix: Since the visitor's tendency is to try to click on these pseudo-icons, perhaps they should be made into hyperlinks. If it looks like a hyperlink, make it a hyperlink.

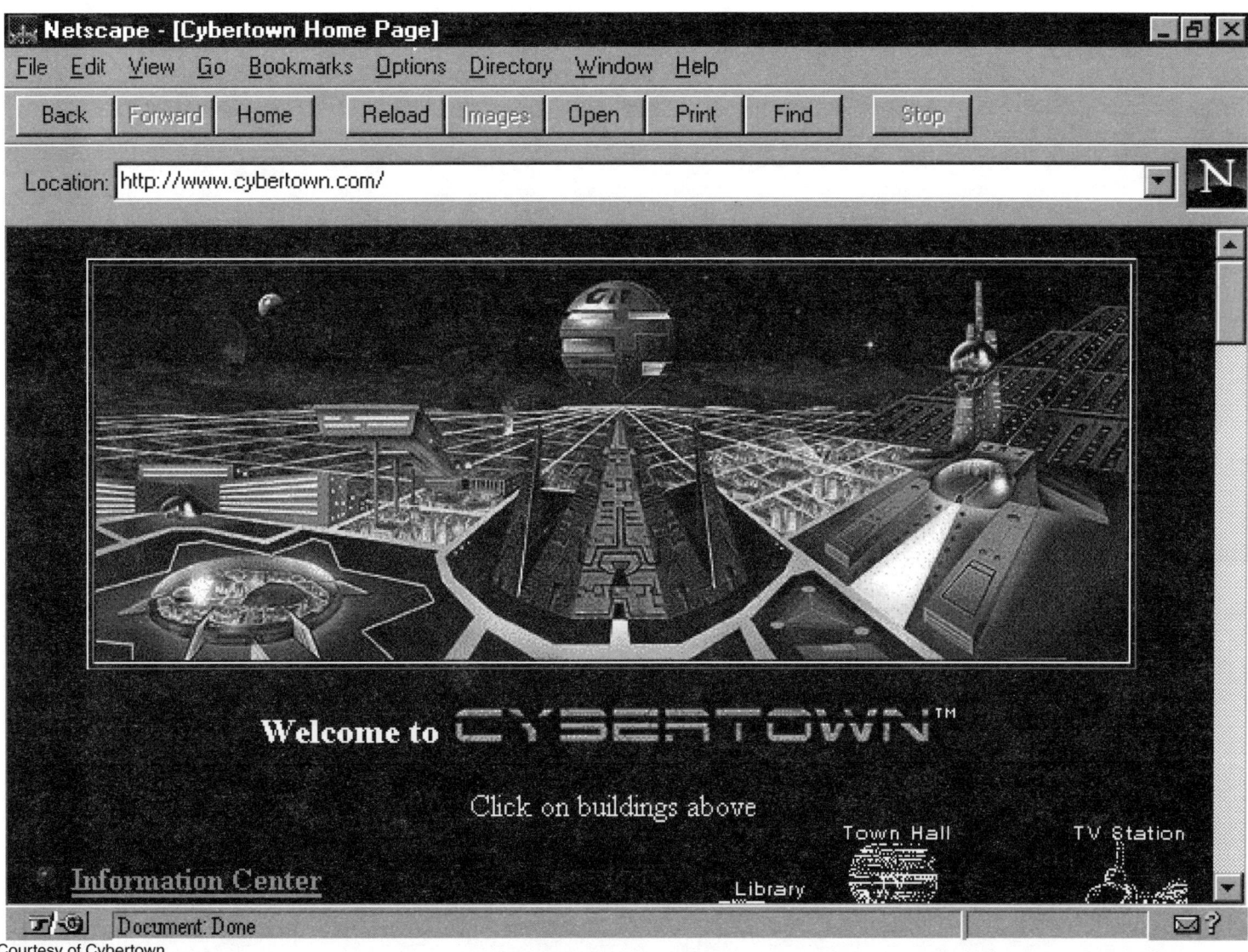

Interactive Imagination's Riddler

URL: `http://www.riddler.com`

While the main graphic appears to be huge, it is actually under 30,000 bytes. Interactive Imagination has presented a natural metaphor—a board game. The dark background draws the eye to the game board. Like some of the other graphics you will see elsewhere, this graphic is an image map. The image is quite alluring and gamelike in its look and feel, which is entirely appropriate given the company it represents. Here text links may hold less importance and the target clients are most likely to want the full color and graphics of games. In addition, this is a very focused home page that offers viewers one (and only one) hyperlink choice. Below the full-color graphics shown on the opposite page appear several sentences, all of which encourage the visitor to register. "The games begin in April. Pre-register now and receive twice as many Riddlets as those who register at a later date. What is a Riddlet? Let's go register and find out." Since the one and only hyperlink is the word "register," a visitor to this site has only one thing to do!

Key Feature

This vividly colorful game board provides viewers with a forced choice option; the viewer must click on the word "register."

Pitfalls and Fixes

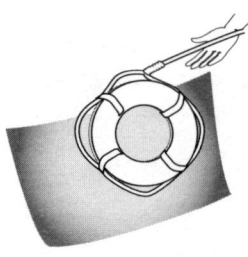

Pitfall: This is the first page we have come to that requires a free registration (it won't be the last). As mentioned above, there is a registration hyperlink at the bottom of the screen which is where you start. The registration page provides us with a great deal of information about Riddler, as well as an opportunity to register with them. However, it should be noted that some people feel that registration is a bit of a hassle and are annoyed by having to do so (and, it is hard to remember all of the various user ID and password combinations that we have to create).

Fix: Certainly, if registration is perceived by some to be annoying, one simple way to fix this would be to remove the need for visitors to have to do so.

Courtesy of Interactive Imagination

NASA's Jet Propulsion Lab

URL: `http://www.jpl.nasa.gov`

NASA's Jet Propulsion Lab (JPL) is the focus of the United States' efforts to explore our universe. The page is a composite of planets from our solar system rendered in rich colors. The overall effect is very impressive and tells you quickly of JPL's interest in the planets. This is a highly visited site, currently due to the Galileo spacecraft's activities near the planet Jupiter. Here NASA's objectives are met: U.S. taxpayers (and others) can see where some of their NASA money is going.

Key Feature

Colorful composite planetary close-ups make up this relatively small (37K) initial graphic that downloads quickly.

Pitfalls and Fixes

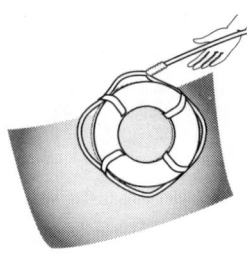

Pitfall: While it is a gorgeous composite, the graphic (which looks like a hyperlink) leads nowhere. It is not a clickable image map as are others that we will see, but the entire graphic is a hyperlink that does point to another host site. (When we tried it, we were unable to get to the site to which the large graphic points.) Many useful hyperlinks (and there are lots of them) are all listed below the large graphic.

Fix: One possible solution would be to make this into an image map that does include a number of hyperlinks. Another solution would be to remove the hyperlink information that is now included with it, since it does not seem to work anyway.

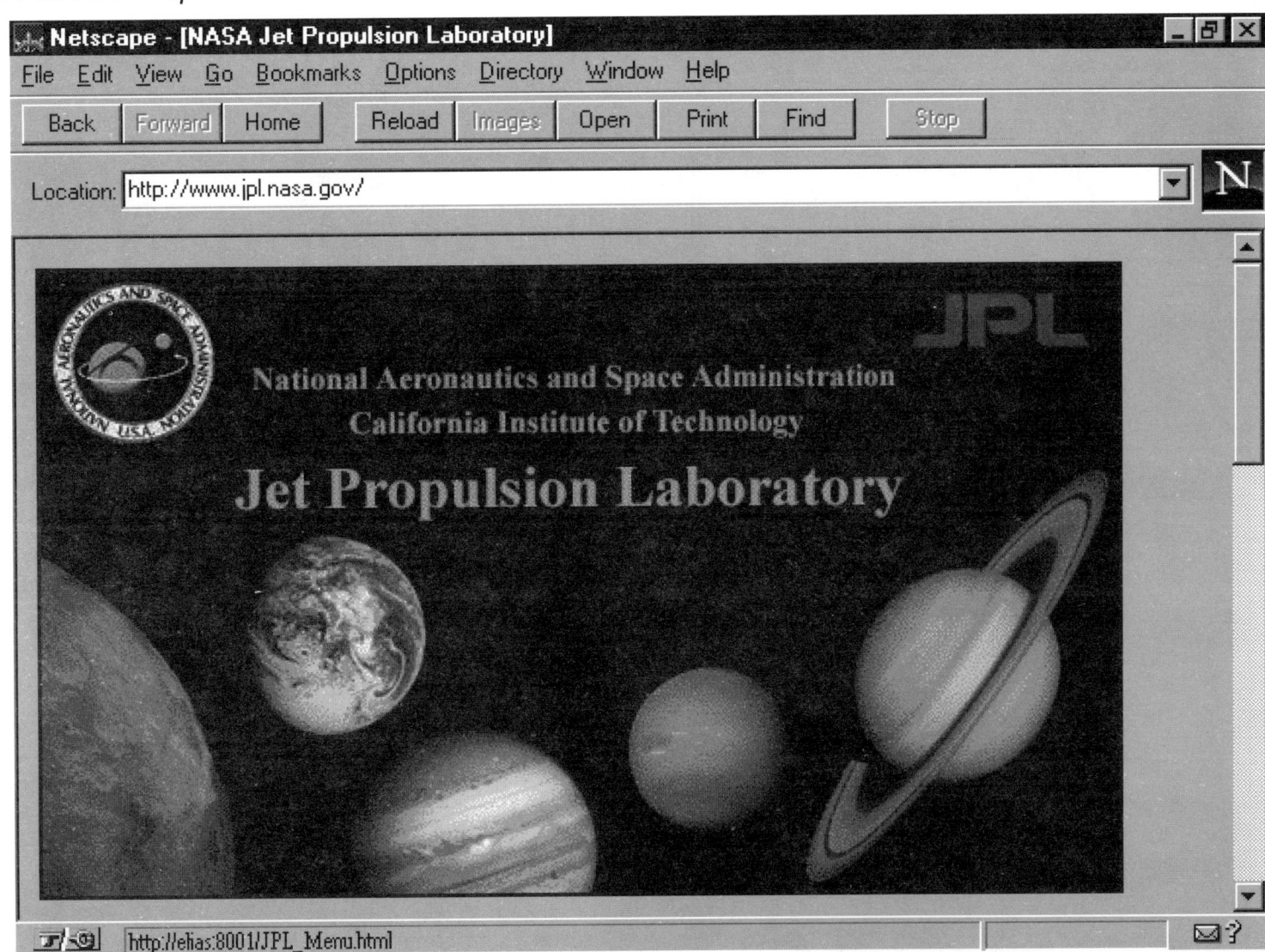

Courtesy of Jet Propulsion Laboratory

Mecklermedia's iWorld: Internet News & Resources

`URL: http://www.iworld.com`

Mecklermedia is the publisher of a number of Internet and Web-related publications and is also the sponsor of the Internet, Web, and VRML trade shows. The iWorld: Internet News and Resources page is a visually appealing graphic that downloads quickly. However, it is important to note that viewers are instantly provided with a text-only hyperlink, and the hyperlink for making this selection has been placed in an extremely obvious position. iWorld is focused on providing Internet news and resources and this information is keyed to the wide array of Mecklermedia publications, including *Internet World, Web Week,* and *Web Developer.* This initial page provides a good blend of current news about the Internet (netday news); useful resources including The List, Internet Shopper, Electronic Commerce Guide, and WebPointer (net resources); links to Mecklermedia publications (newsstand); information about their upcoming trade shows (events); useful search tools (search); and information about Mecklermedia and some of its services (corporate).

Key Feature

This is a good, clear page with a pleasing use of color. The iWorld: Internet News and Resources Home Page provides a lot of choices in a relatively small space. The initial graphic downloads quickly, and viewers who choose to do so may select to have all succeeding pages presented as a text-only version. The hyperlink for making this selection is as obvious as one could ask for.

Pitfalls and Fixes

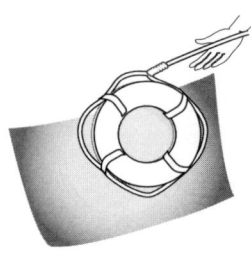

Pitfall: There is a curious phenomenon associated with the colorful graphic at the top of the iWorld page. In addition to being visually appealing, it is also a hyperlink that is designed to take viewers to a form called feedback.html. This feedback form, which is quite well done and quite extensive, is not mentioned anywhere else on the page, nor is it at all obvious that clicking on the initial graphic takes you there.

Fix: An obvious fix would be to label the graphic, or, since this might detract from its visual appeal, to put a hyperlink elsewhere on the page that would let viewers know they could provide feedback to iWorld. The feedback form is clear and well designed; it would be a shame if more visitors to this site did not know about its existence.

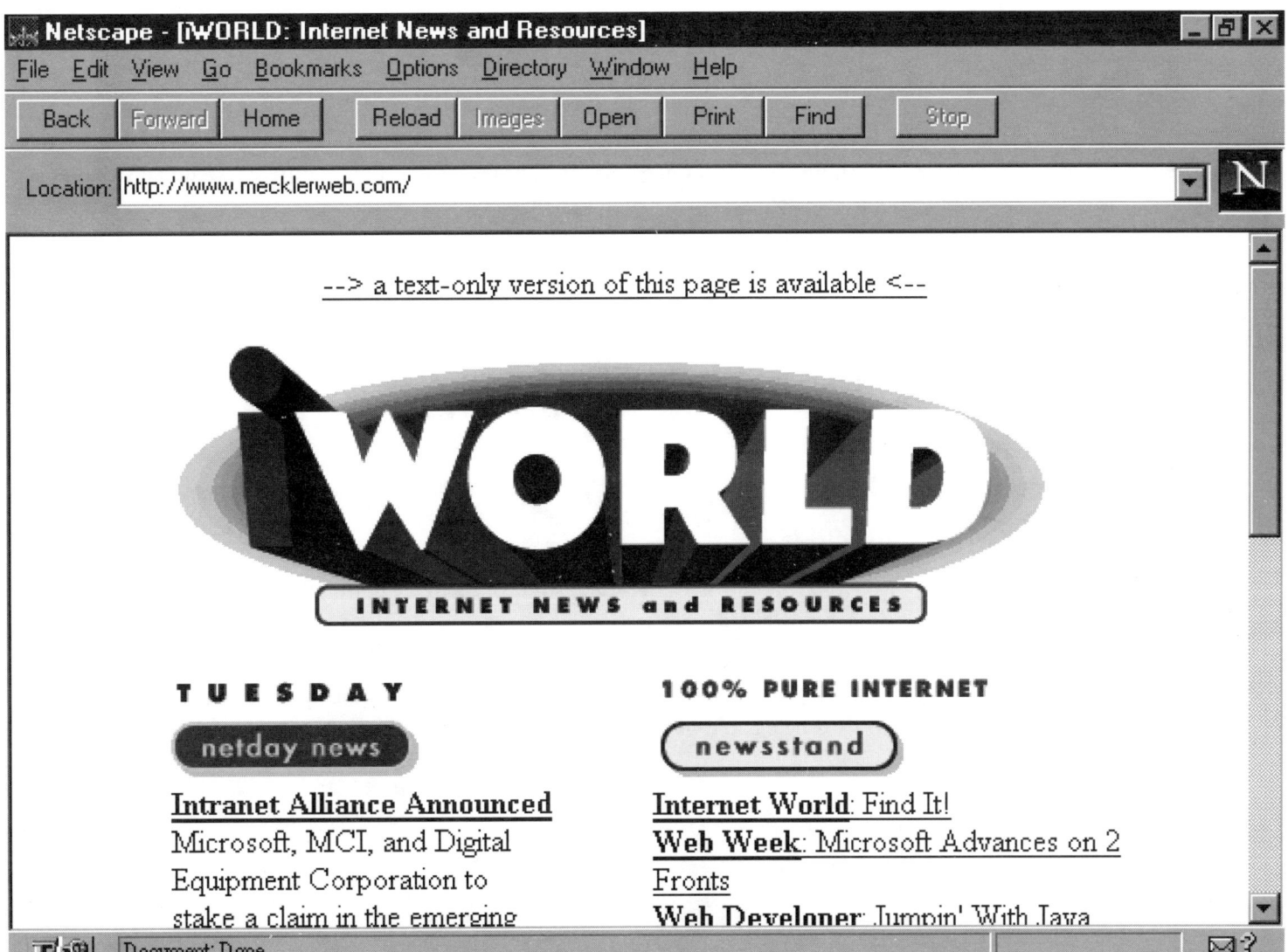

Metaverse

URL: http://metaverse.com

Budweiser, in conjunction with On Ramp, Inc., has created a slightly different fictional city that is viewed through a welcoming entry gate. Here the metaphor seems to say "Please come in to our site." The main page centers on the gateway which is the main hyperlink to what lies beyond. The main advantage here is a consistent first-page theme with the ability to change what is inside.

Key Feature

There is a main entry gate to draw in the visitor to what is waiting behind it. The image is somewhat mysterious, but the two open doors make it very inviting.

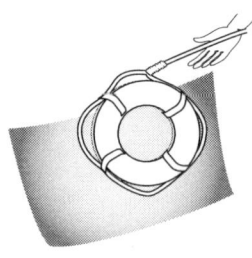

Pitfalls and Fixes

Pitfall: Many graphics are involved here, and some of them are up to 30,000 bytes. The full page takes quite some time to download.

Fix: As we pointed out at the beginning of this chapter, there are ways to reduce the size of graphics, which in turn make it possible for one to download them more quickly. Reducing the file size of the graphics being used here could be of some help.

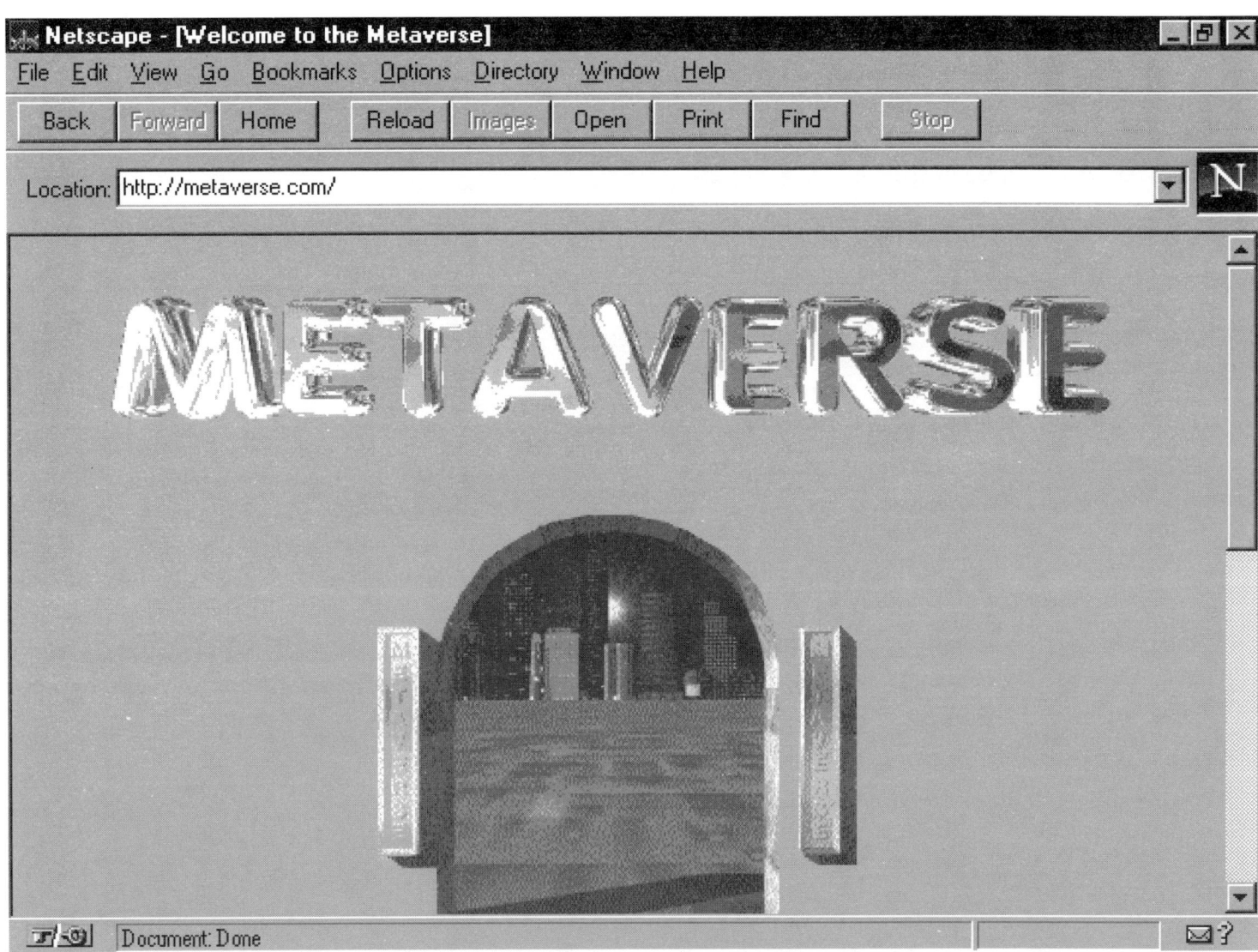

Courtesy of On Ramp, Inc.

NetManage Corporation

URL: `http://www.netmanage.com`

NetManage provides Internet- and Web-related software and uses the color-changing Chameleon as their corporate logo. Here the Chameleon enhances their pages with its color and draws your eye to what the Chameleon is saying (in this case, the announcement of free software.) Within the same first screen, we can also see colorful smaller images which highlight nine other places to go on the first jump. While each image appears to be independent, in actuality they all form a colorful whole with the Chameleon. The overall image map is about 56,000 bytes.

Key Feature

The NetManage Chameleon software is well-known TCP/IP software. The Welcome to NetManage page provides an effective use of their colorful corporate logo; it is quite visually appealing.

Pitfalls and Fixes

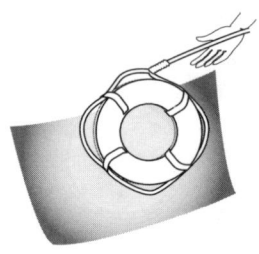

Pitfall: The page is one large image map (56,000 bytes). This can take some time to download (almost a minute) for users with 28.8 modems, and even longer for those with modems that are not as fast.

Fix: The same page could be constructed from ten or more smaller images which would download and appear much more quickly.

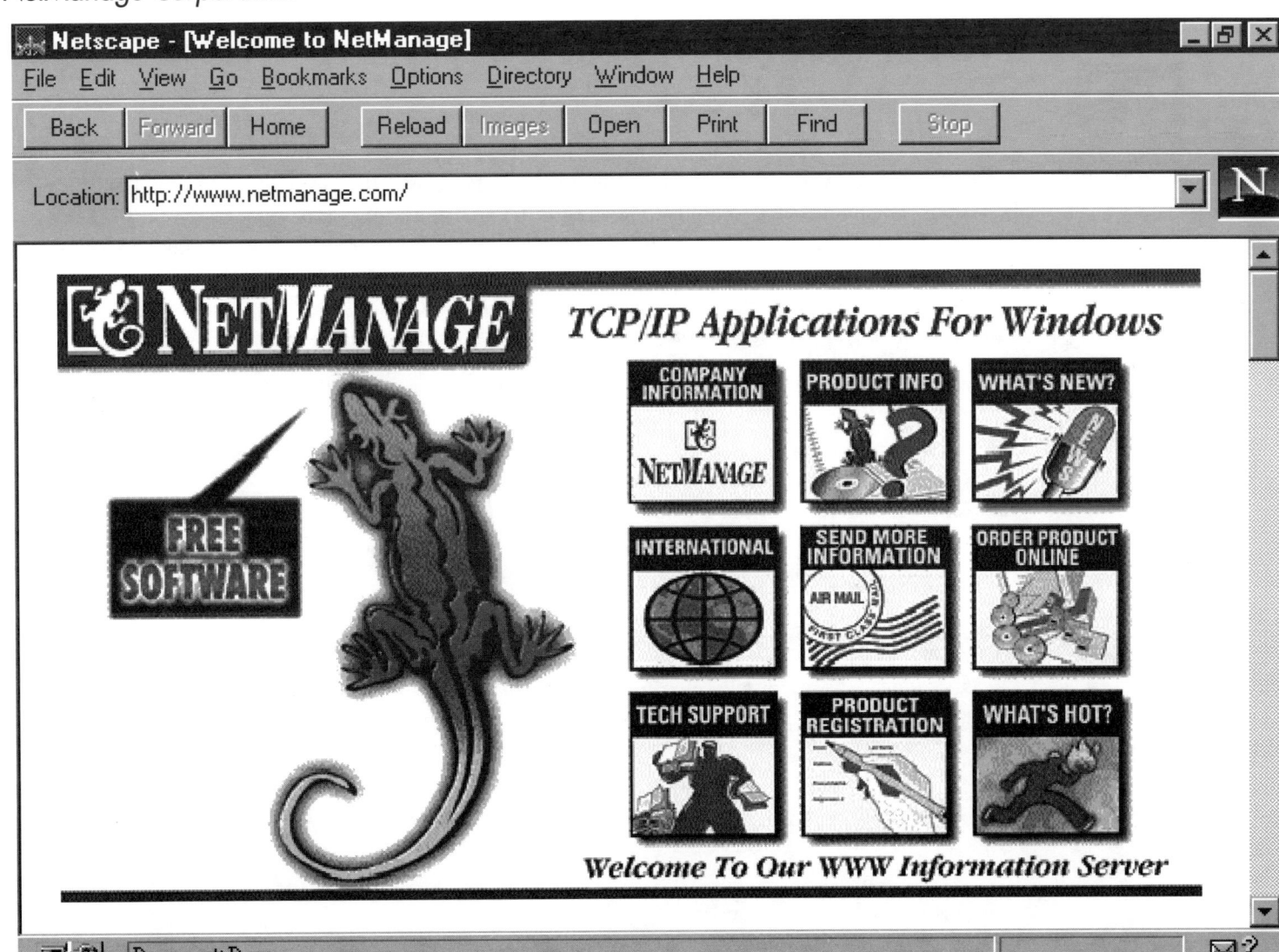

Novell World Wide: Corporate Home Page

URL: http://www.novell.com

Novell has long used the icons with great effect. In earlier pages, they were like reference books on a bookshelf. The bookshelf metaphor evolved into the eight buttons you now see at the bottom of the page. The buttons themselves retain the characteristic color and to some degree the look and feel of the original books. Most people used to the Web are comfortable with a "press the button" metaphor. To keep the main graphic smaller, they used just a few colors, mainly black and red, very effectively. In addition to being appealing, this page also offers several ways to begin on-page navigation.

Key Feature

The careful use of limited colors does a good job of reducing image file size. They also provide good and clear navigation directions all over the image map. And, they provide a "Text-Only" option at the very top of their screen for those who are interested in just seeing the information that this site contains. Finally, the April Promotions hyperlink is clever; this hyperlink changes monthly, sending a clear message to viewers that the site is current and well maintained.

Pitfalls and Fixes

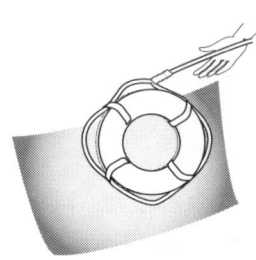

Pitfall: Not necessarily a pitfall, but a concern. This is our second black background. Some people find black backgrounds to be disconcerting. And recently, black backgrounds have become associated with "protest" pages.

Fix: Explore your visitor's reaction to, and appreciation of, unusual background colors.

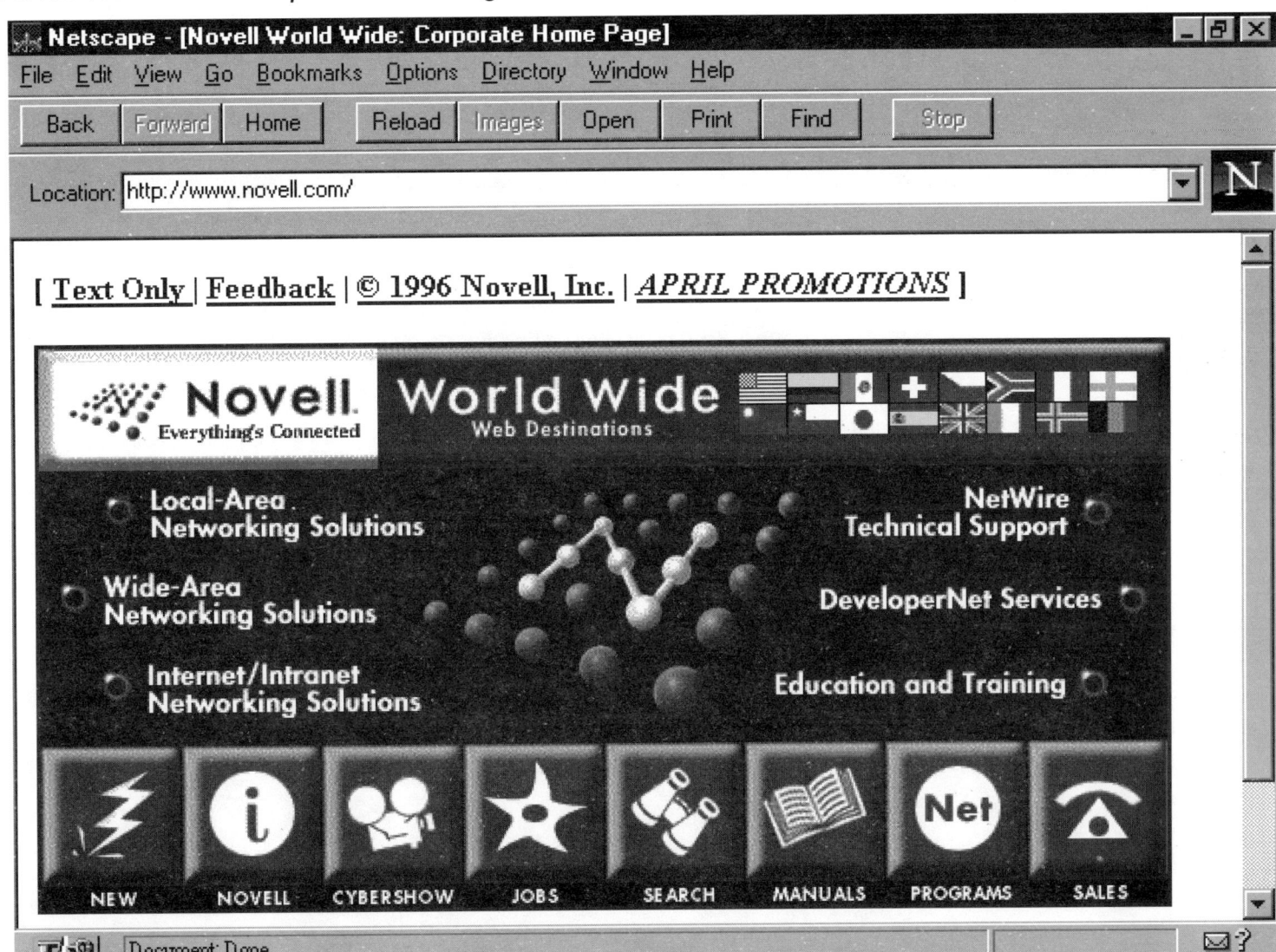

Sprint

URL: `http://www.sprint.com`

The image map used for the Sprint Home Page is large but is also quite beautiful. With the image of the clouds extending into the horizon and the open door, it is quite inviting. There are nine choices provided on this initial page: For Home, For Work, For College, Products & Services, Special Offers, Sprint News & Info, Customer Service, Cool Stuff, and Search/Map. Each choice is presented twice, once as part of the image map, and once as a text choice at the bottom of the page. A clever feature is the use of the three red "Click!" buttons on the image map. Sometimes, it is not obvious where one should click on an image map. And they have avoided the dreaded "click here" phrase.

Key Feature

This page is a large image map (61,000 bytes) with nine repeated choices. The initial graphic is peaceful and pretty, and the open door is welcome and inviting. A limited use of colors (primarily red, white, blue, and black) speeds up the downloading time somewhat.

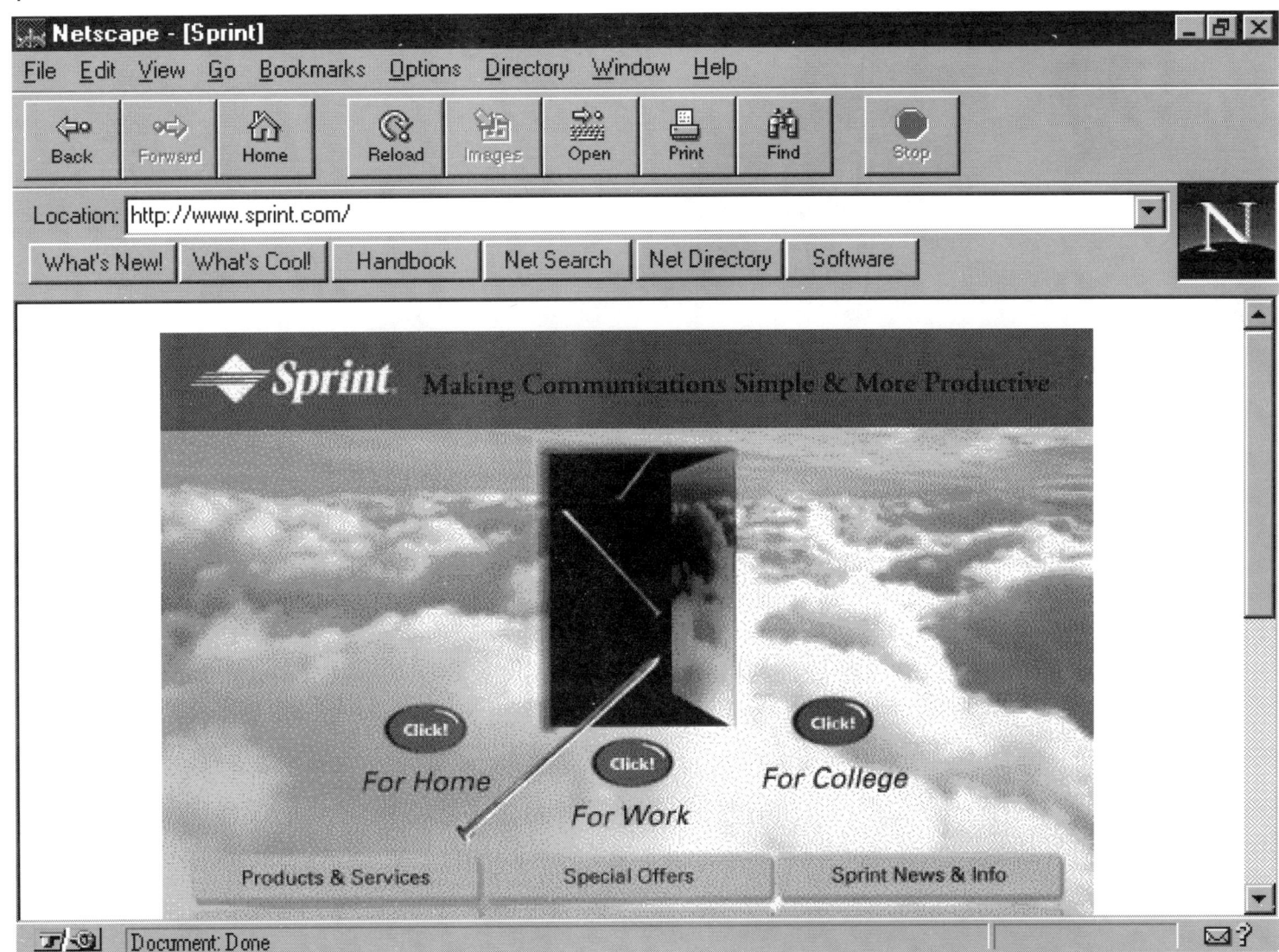

Courtesy of Sprint Communications Company

The Smithsonian Institution Home Page

URL: `http://www.si.edu`

Everyone who has visited the Smithsonian museum complex in Washington, D.C. remembers "the Castle." The Smithsonian Institution Home Page uses images of the Castle very effectively. Both the center picture and the four surrounding icons represent the Castle. The picture evokes a warm summer day and invites us to select from the nicely limited menu. menu. Behind this simple yet elegant page there is a wonderful world of treasures.

Key Feature

This is a very effective use of a readily identifiable landmark and extremely clear navigational aids. Visitors are presented with ten choices, each of which is clear and informative, as well as being visually appealing.

Pitfalls and Fixes

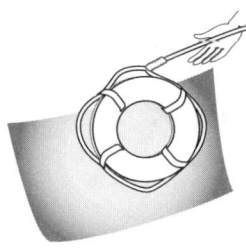

Pitfall: This is a large image map (46,000 bytes), causing wait time for many visitors.

Fix: One possible solution might be to reduce the size of the image file by reducing the number of colors being used.

Stanford University

URL: http://www.stanford.edu

Many universities around the world have excellent home pages and we have had to make a difficult choice. We have selected Stanford as a very good example from a very large set. Many universities, like Stanford, have extremely attractive buildings and grounds and they choose to feature these. It is a good choice and could also work well for other kinds of enterprises. Here, Stanford shows us part of its typically Spanish-California style campus. But the palm trees and blue sky give an implied subliminal message—clear skies, warm weather. As you can see, not everything on a page need be explicit to give an appealing message.

Key Feature

This site does a wonderful job of providing an appealing use of Stanford's architecture and natural surroundings. The Stanford University Home Page is inviting and visually very appealing.

Pitfalls and Fixes

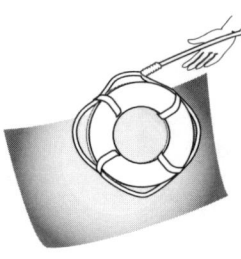

Pitfall: The image map is 52,000 bytes and this will mean that some who visit this site will wait a short while until the file has been downloaded.

Fix: It might be possible to speed up the download process by limiting some of the colors that are used in this image. However, one would certainly want to be careful not to detract from the beauty this image currently presents.

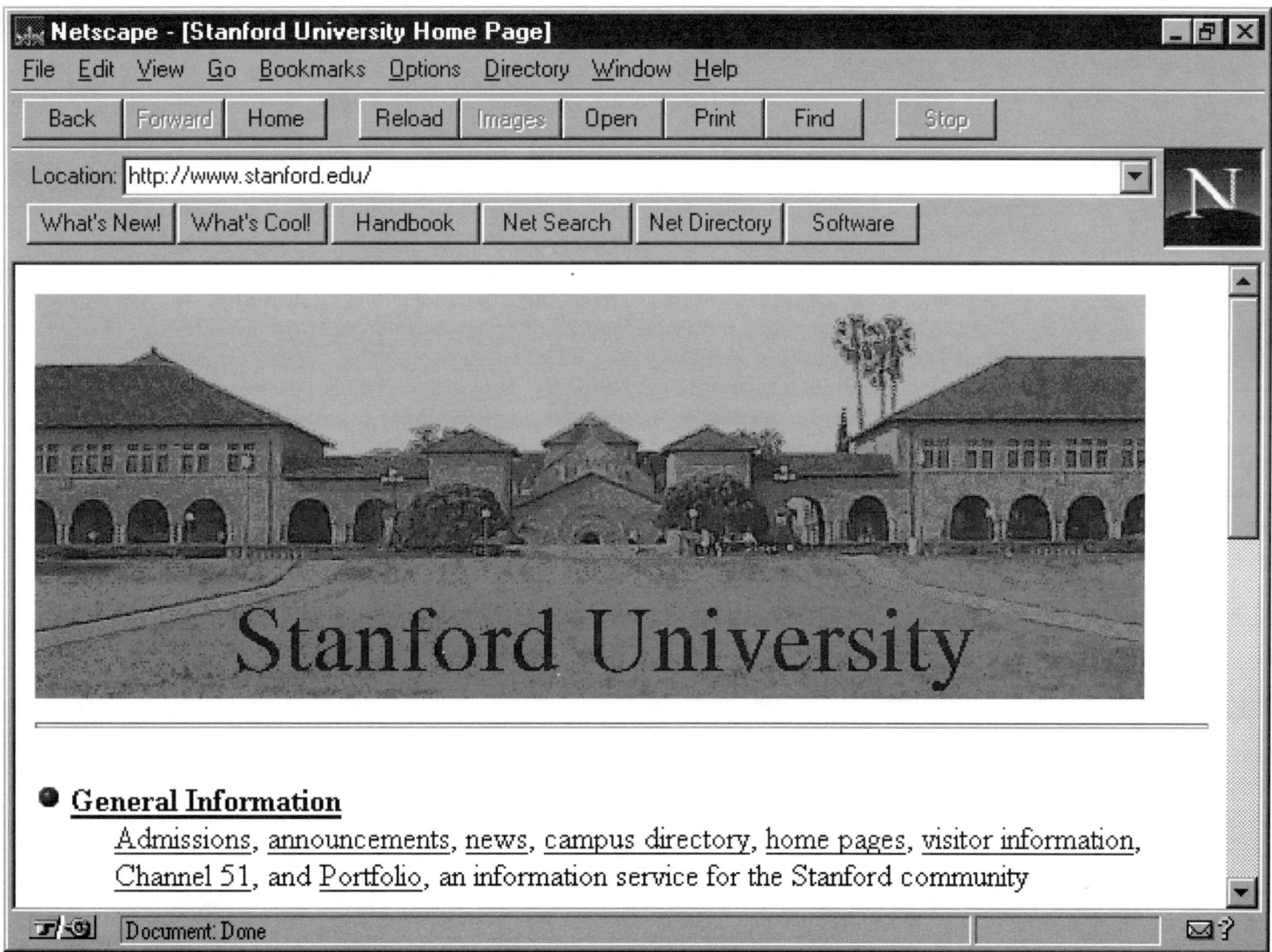

Pathfinder Travel

URL: `http://www.pathfinder.com/Travel`

Like Condé Nast Traveler presented earlier in this chapter, Time Warner's Pathfinder invites us to consider travel. But here we are presented with small whimsical images such as parachutes, balloons, and old-fashioned baggage. Rather than showing us destinations, they seem to be saying that we should imagine the romance of travel. Each part of this page is also clearly labeled with pointers to a potential next jump. Not only is this an attractive site, but it is also one that offers us some free travel-related extras. We can look at current weather, get currency exchange rates, or learn just enough of one of 16 languages to travel. They have done an excellent job of making this site visually appealing. The site also provides some valuable and useful information (which we will discuss in greater detail in Chapter 4) and also engages the visitor in a number of activities (which we will explore in greater depth in Chapter 8.)

Key Feature

Pathfinder Travel does an excellent job of providing the romance of travel in a whimsical setting.

Pitfalls and Fixes

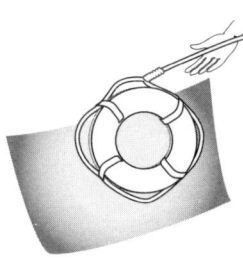

Pitfall: Although the hyperlink for "see our table of contents" is placed in a very obvious position, it is not clear that this is a way for visitors to be taken to the text-only version of this site.

Fix: Most Web visitors have become used to the phrases "text only," "text version," or "limited graphics." Following these conventions would reduce visitor confusion.

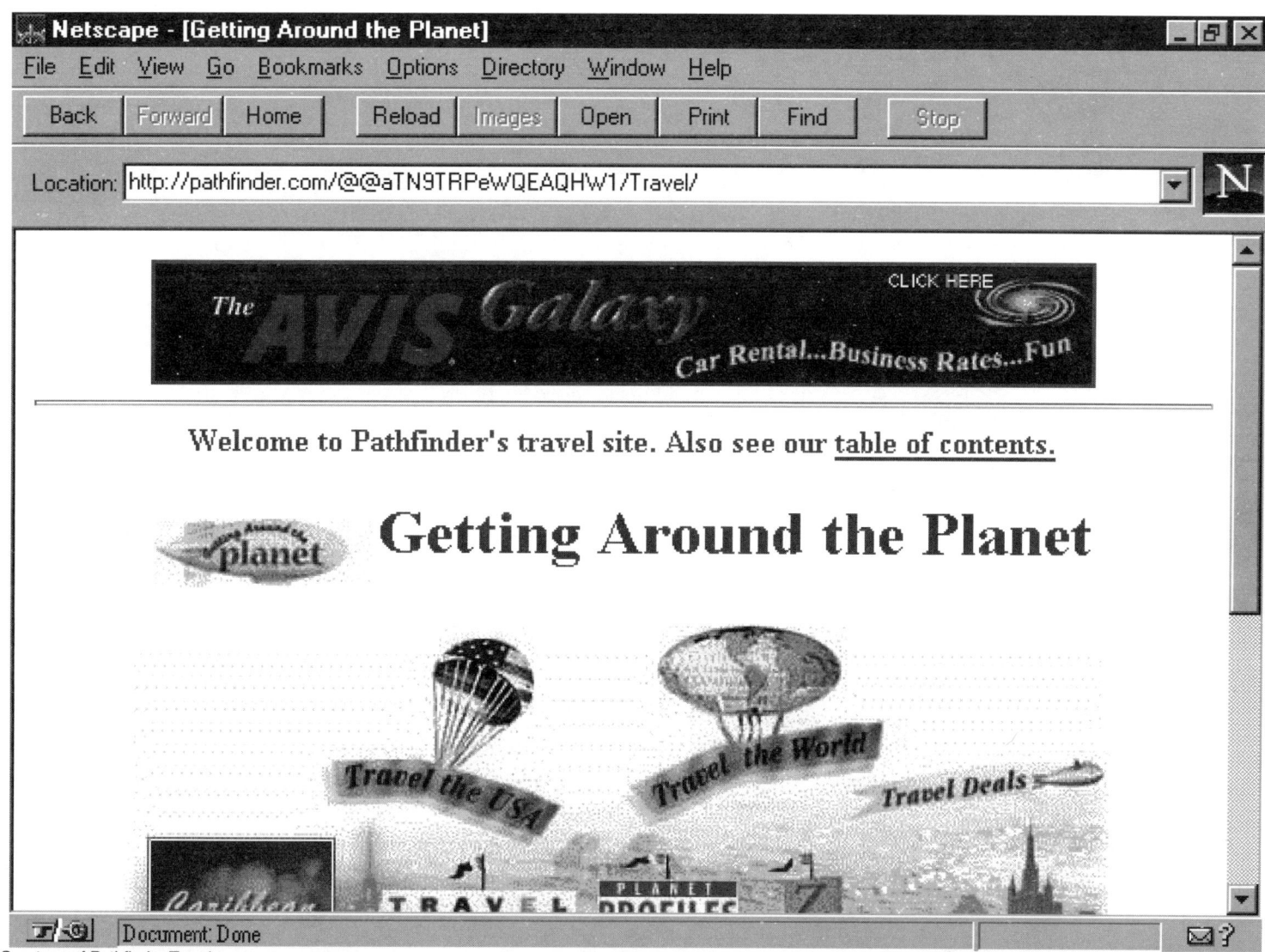

Paramount Voyager

URL: `http://voyager.paramount.com`

Paramount presents us with perhaps one of the most visually appealing pages on the Web. This is an image worth studying as much is revealed only upon close inspection. Start with the brick forecourt and move to the red-tiled roof (California-Spanish architecture). Now go to the intricate and ornamental iron gate with "Paramount Pictures" above. Imagine the great movie stars and directors who have passed this way! Now look beyond the gate at the mountain that is seen in the openings of Paramount movies. Don't miss the fluffy clouds against the rich blue sky. It may all be imaginary, but that is the business of the movies. Here is a marvelous, if fictional, creation to put us in a movie mood. Now look at the featured pictures on either side of the gate. Done in the style of movie posters, they also remind us of the movie metaphor.

Key Feature

This is a colorful, complex and compelling site that has been created by Paramount. Complementing the large colorful image at the top of the page is a bit-mapped image containing hyperlinks to five current Paramount movies.

Pitfalls and Fixes

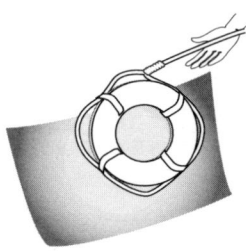

Pitfalls: It takes big images to do this good a job and this one is 93,000 bytes. Several other images on the page are also somewhat large. Obviously, this means that this page will download slowly for those with modem connections. In addition, they have chosen to use a black background for the page as a whole. This is not a problem for the colorful image on the top of the page, but the black background does make it hard to read the blue text hyperlinks presented at the bottom part of the page (not shown).

Fix: One choice would be to limit the number of colors that are used in this image. Another option would be to see if it would be possible to create a similar image using a number of smaller files that would download more quickly. The text hyperlinks would be far easier to read if the black background were changed to a color that would provide more contrast.

The White House

URL: `http://www.whitehouse.gov`

Almost everyone in the world has seen pictures of the United States White House. It represents more than just a president's home and office. It is a symbol of America. When the first White House page appeared several years ago, it quickly became one of the most popular sites on the Web. It featured a grand picture of the White House surrounded by hyperlinks. This redesigned site offers us a new metaphor: an invitation to the White House looking as it might if we received it personally. One nonobvious feature of this attractive new page is the greeting that changes during each day to match Washington's local time (Good morning, Good afternoon, and so forth). In addition, the image of the White House changes to match the time of day. Fluttering American Flags are visible to those with Java-capable browsers. Notice the properly placed "Text version" hyperlink in the upper left.

Key Feature

Elegant and impressive, this page provides a personal invitation and an effective (timely) changing of images.

Summary

As we have shown you in this chapter, there are lots of visually appealing sites on the World Wide Web and a variety of techniques have been used to make them that way. Clearly, one challenge for Webmasters is to be sensitive to the speed with which their potential visitors can access the information that will be presented to them. As we have seen, some sites have figured out clever ways to provide visually appealing information, while at the same time not overwhelming their visitors. It is also important to remember that some visitors might always prefer to access the information that the site provides and to forego the visual images; providing text-only or limited graphics links early on is quite useful.

Chapter

4

KEY 2:

Valuable, Useful, or Fun

Introduction to Key 2 — Valuable, Useful, or Fun

Web sites that are valuable, useful, or fun become an integral part of our lives. We refer to them often for the information that we need, when we need it. Typically, we turn to these sites for one of two reasons: They perform a particular function or they provide particular content that we must have. The function-driven sites are those that permit us to do something, such as searching for information on the World Wide Web, in a quick and easy fashion. Since they provide a valuable function for us, we tend to return there often to perform that function. As you will see once you get to them, DejaNews, InfoSeek, The List, NewsPage, Starting Point, and WebLint are all good examples of function-driven sites. The content-driven sites are those that contain particular information that relates to our specific area of interest or expertise. Some good examples of content-driven sites are the CIA World Fact Book, City.Net, GE Plastics, Hoover's Online, and the Goodyear Tire and Rubber Company.

Once these sites have been identified as ones that perform the functions we require, or provide us with the information we need, they frequently become our key bookmarks to which we return frequently. If these are functions we perform every day, such as searching for information on the Web, then we will return there every day. If this is content that pertains to our personal or professional lives and it is important, then we will return frequently to make sure the information we have is current and useful. Obviously, good function-driven and content-driven sites also lend themselves easily to becoming locations where advertisers might be likely to spend their money. As you will see in the following examples, these sites vary in their objectives or scope, but their continued attention to being valuable, useful, or fun sets them apart from many other sites on the World Wide Web. We will take a look in a moment. First, let's stop to consider a few technical points.

Technical Points

Value

If a site is seeking to be valuable, then credibility and currency must be maintained. Such sites actively seek out corrections and updates from their visitors and freely admit problems and mistakes when they occur (we all make them).

Value also means continuing to be more (or at least as) valuable than competing sites. If a site performs a valuable function such as searching and it does it very well, then we will use it often. However, as has clearly been the case with search engines on the Web, value invites competition and these sites must continuously watch for existing and new competitors.

Useful

Usefulness is often easier to provide to a narrow target set than to the whole Web audience. Many of the examples you are about to see have selected a particular topic to cover (finding an Internet service provider) or a set of visitors (those who are interested in plastic resins) and directed their focus to this set. Obviously, this makes them very useful to those who need that particular information, and less useful to those who do not.

Fun

Fun must be kept fresh for old and new visitors alike. This is perhaps the most difficult requirement of all. Fun can be any type of entertainment. Some jokes, acts or routines are always funny; some are funny once and must constantly be replaced. Some of the sites you will see in this chapter have found just the right way to do this.

Responding to the Needs of Your Visitors

As we will discuss in much greater detail in Chapter 9, some sites do an excellent job of responding to the needs of their users. In particular, some sites modify themselves to those who are visiting in an attempt to serve them better. If the goal of a site is to be function driven and the site can provide its given functions better and better, then visitors are likely to return frequently.

A good example of a function-driven site is the Starting Point site: Notice their tag line—"Everything You Need To Work The Web. Every Day. Here's How." The hyperlink "Here's How" takes the visitor to a set of instructions that teaches them how to install Starting Point as the default URL for their browser. This is a clever thing to do since it means that more people will visit Starting Point. Providing information about how Starting Point might be installed as the initial URL makes Starting Point more useful for visitors who might not have known how to do this.

As you will see in a few moments, a good example of a content-driven site that is making itself more and more valuable is provided by City.Net—their current listing of 2,076 cities and 769 other online destinations is significantly higher than it was only a few months ago. Their goal is to be a premier content-driven site, and by continually increasing the amount of content one can find there, they will continue to increase their value to their visitors. The site was good to begin with; now it is even better!

Now let's look at some sites that are valuable, useful, or fun. For each site on the pages that follow, we will explain why we believe the particular page is one or all of these. For each site we will point out one or several key features. For many, we will also list a few pitfalls and perhaps some ways to fix them.

Note: The sites in this chapter appear in alphabetical (not rank) order and should all be viewed as examples of valuable, useful, or fun. The illustrations and our comments on them are current as of 1996. The browser used is Netscape 2.0 for Windows 95.

CIA's World Fact Book

URL: `http://www.odci.gov/cia/publications/95fact/index.htm`

The World Factbook, provided to us by the United States government's Central Intelligence Agency, is a wonderful repository of information about other countries around the world. Filled with an amazing depth of information, including both low- and high-resolution reference maps, this site provides current detailed information that is readily available at the click of a mouse. An easy-to-use alphabetical directory enables us to find a given country within a matter of moments. For each country, we are provided with a map and detailed information about the country's geography, people, government, economy, transportation, communications, and defense forces.

Key Feature

The World Factbook is a key repository of geopolitical information. The initial page is extremely easy to navigate. Visitors are provided with a simple graphic and then all other options are provided in text-only. It is a good example of a "no fuss, no muss" site where the primary goal is not for the site to be visually appealing; the primary goal is for the site to be extremely useful (and it is). One is told repeatedly by a blinking note to "Click on the letter to navigate quickly to that section" and then the alphabet is offered. The four hyperlinks (Publication Information, Notes, Definitions, and Abbreviations, Appendices, and Reference Maps) presented on the World Factbook Home Page are easy to understand and use.

Pitfalls and Fixes

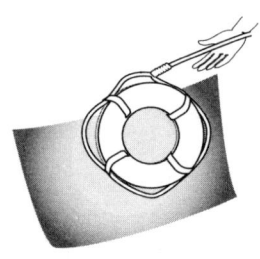

Pitfall: This site uses the blink feature offered by Netscape. While it is fair to say that the "blink" feature does attract one's attention, it is also fair to say that after a while the blinking becomes somewhat annoying. Also note that the site URL changes each year.

Fix: Be careful when you use the blink feature; some would advise not using it at all.

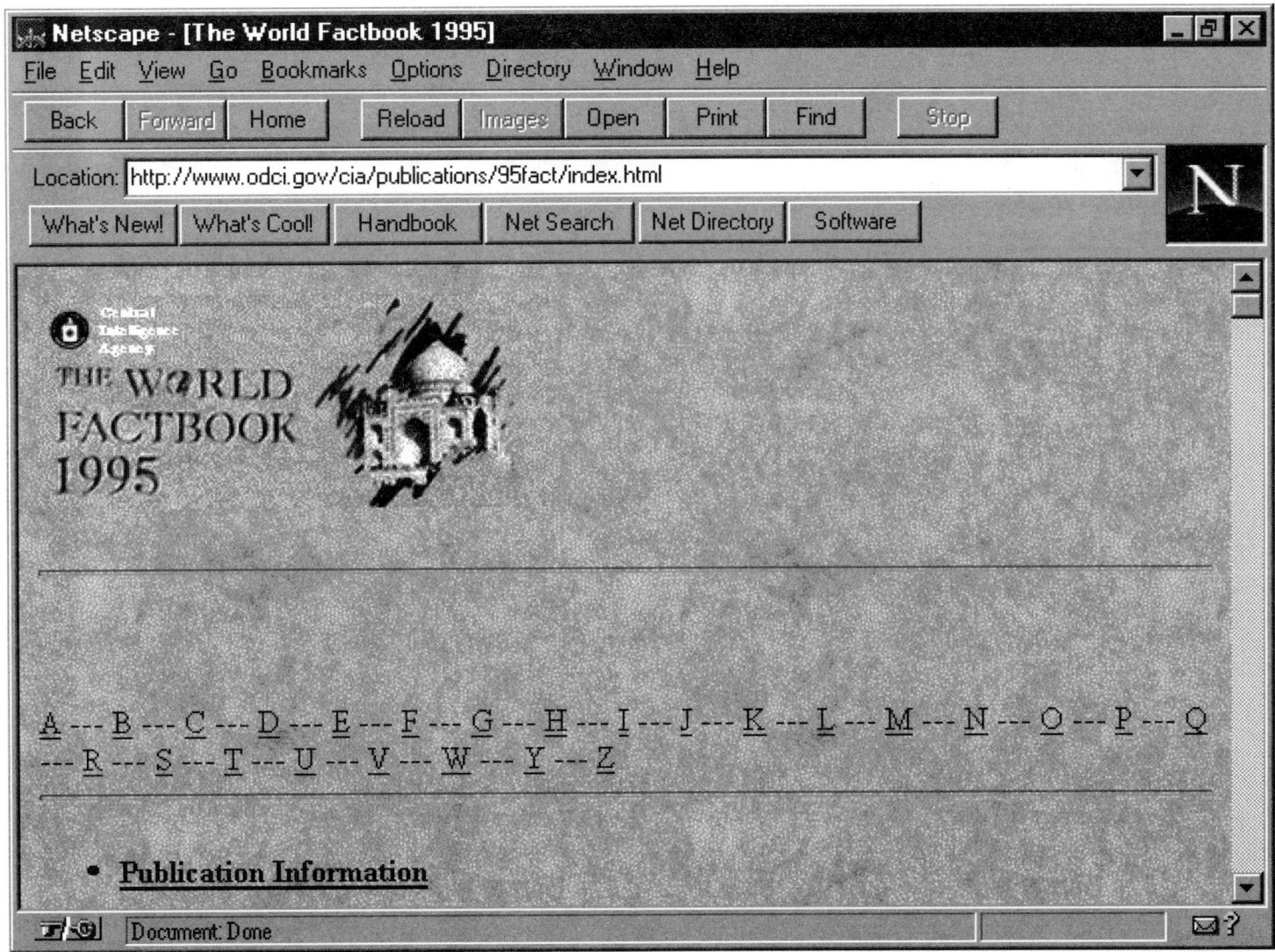

City.Net

URL: http://www.city.net

City.Net "your guide to the world" is a comprehensive international guide to cities around the world. It is updated daily and provides easy access to timely information about travel, entertainment, and local business, as well as government and community services. Navigating through this site is remarkably simple using the six text hyperlinks provided on the home page. Notice also that this site is provided by Architext Software, the same people who provide the World Wide Web search engine known as Excite. The very first hyperlink that is provided takes you to Excite, and two small ads for Excite appear on the City.Net Home Page. The City.Net site is invaluable for anyone who must travel; it is also clearly intended to provide advertising for Architext Software, but it does so in a nonintrusive fashion.

Key Feature

The City.Net site is a wonderful example of a content-driven site that provides extremely useful information for travelers. This content-driven site continues to increase in size at almost breathtaking speed. The screen shot on the opposite page, taken on April 11, 1996, indicates that there were 2,047 cities and 750 other destinations online. Only eight days later, on April 19 when we returned to this site, those numbers had increased to 2,102 cities and 782 destinations. This content-driven site continues to make itself more and more valuable to its visitors. That attention to detail is well worth emulating!

In addition, as was true with the CIA World Fact Book, the initial home page is less focused on its visual appeal, and (far more appropriately) focused on its usefulness. Apart from some simple graphics at the top and bottom, this page is all text, with clear, easy to follow navigational aids (home, contents, index, and search) presented at the top and bottom of the page and throughout the site. There are lots of excellent graphics available at this site; however, they are presented only when a user has made a selection about the information that is desired.

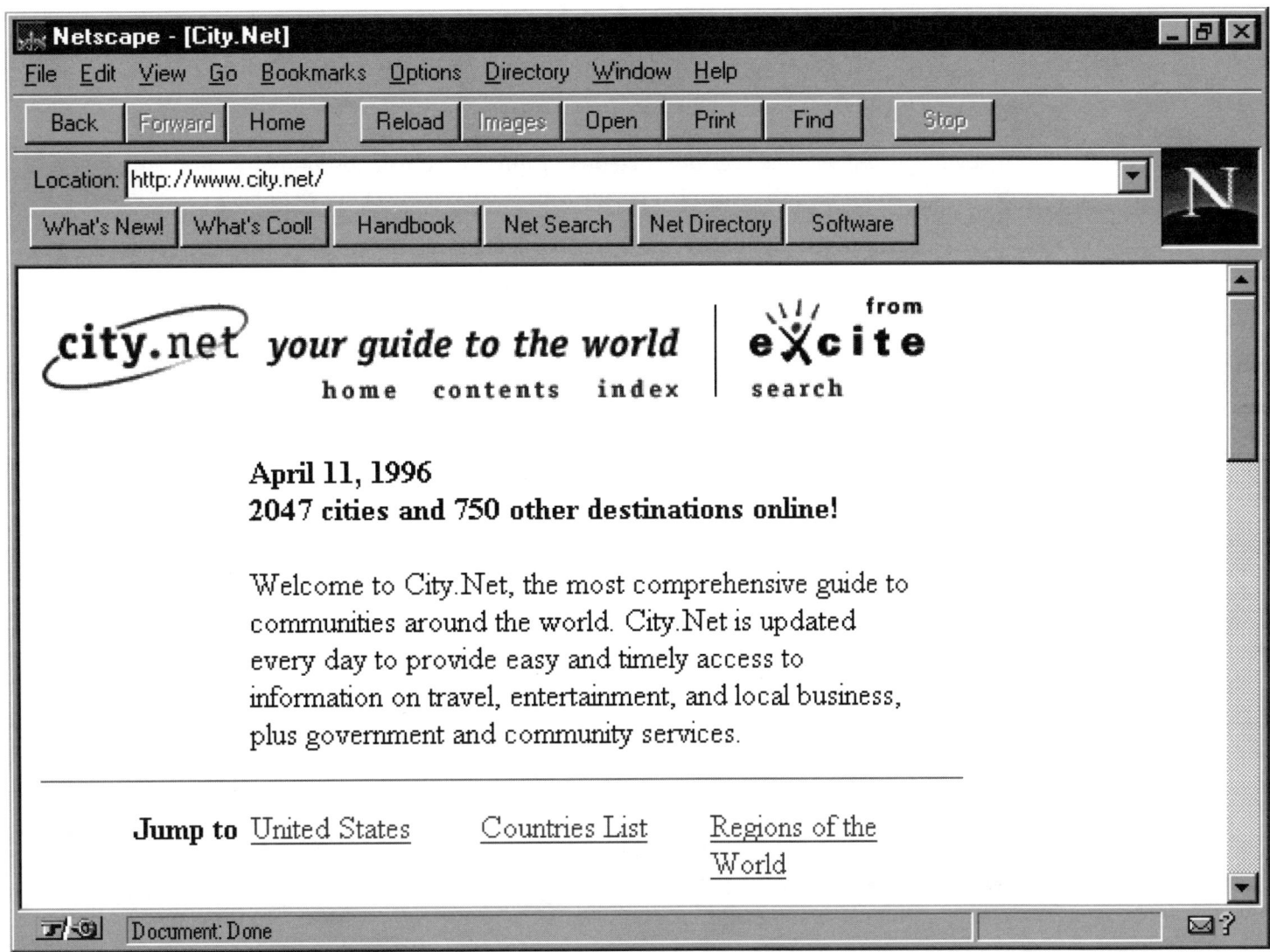

Claritin Allergy Relief

URL: `http://www.allergy-relief.com/`

The Allergy Relief Home Page provided by Claritin is filled with lots of useful information for those who suffer from seasonal nasal allergy symptoms. Claritin has done a good job of assembling quite a bit of information about allergies in general, as well as specific information for those with allergies who wish to garden. The fun aspect of this particular site (which probably depends upon your definition of fun) is provided by The Sneeze Page. There one can listen to a varied array of sneezes, including a Man's Allergy Sneeze, an Explosive Sneeze, a Little Sneeze, and others. Lots of information about allergies and their treatment is provided by Claritin. They also provide a set of hyperlinks to other Internet sites that provide allergy information and make it easy for visitors to search the Internet for allergy information. Obviously, Claritin is using this page as a sales and marketing tool, as evidenced by the ads they have provided, the 800 number that is offered, and the discount coupon.

Key Feature

The Allergy Relief Home Page is a valuable provider of information for those suffering from seasonal nasal allergy symptoms. The information that is provided is timely; for example, there is a Pollen Report which provides complete and up-to-date allergy index information from around the United States. In addition, the Sneeze Page provides some funny sneezes (for those who think such things are funny).

Pitfalls and Fixes

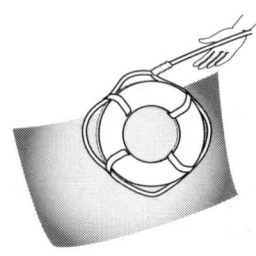

Pitfall: Be warned! The Sneeze page going off in your office could cause your co-workers to jump a bit (some of the sneezes are quite loud). You will need a sound-equipped personal computer if you wish to hear this page. A possible pitfall of this humor is that there are some who might not find it at all funny (especially those with severe allergies)!

Fix: Humor is always a complicated issue. In this particular case, the page seems to be pretty funny (and has elicited a lot of laughs from those first encountering it). One wonders how well this page remains funny for repeat visitors.

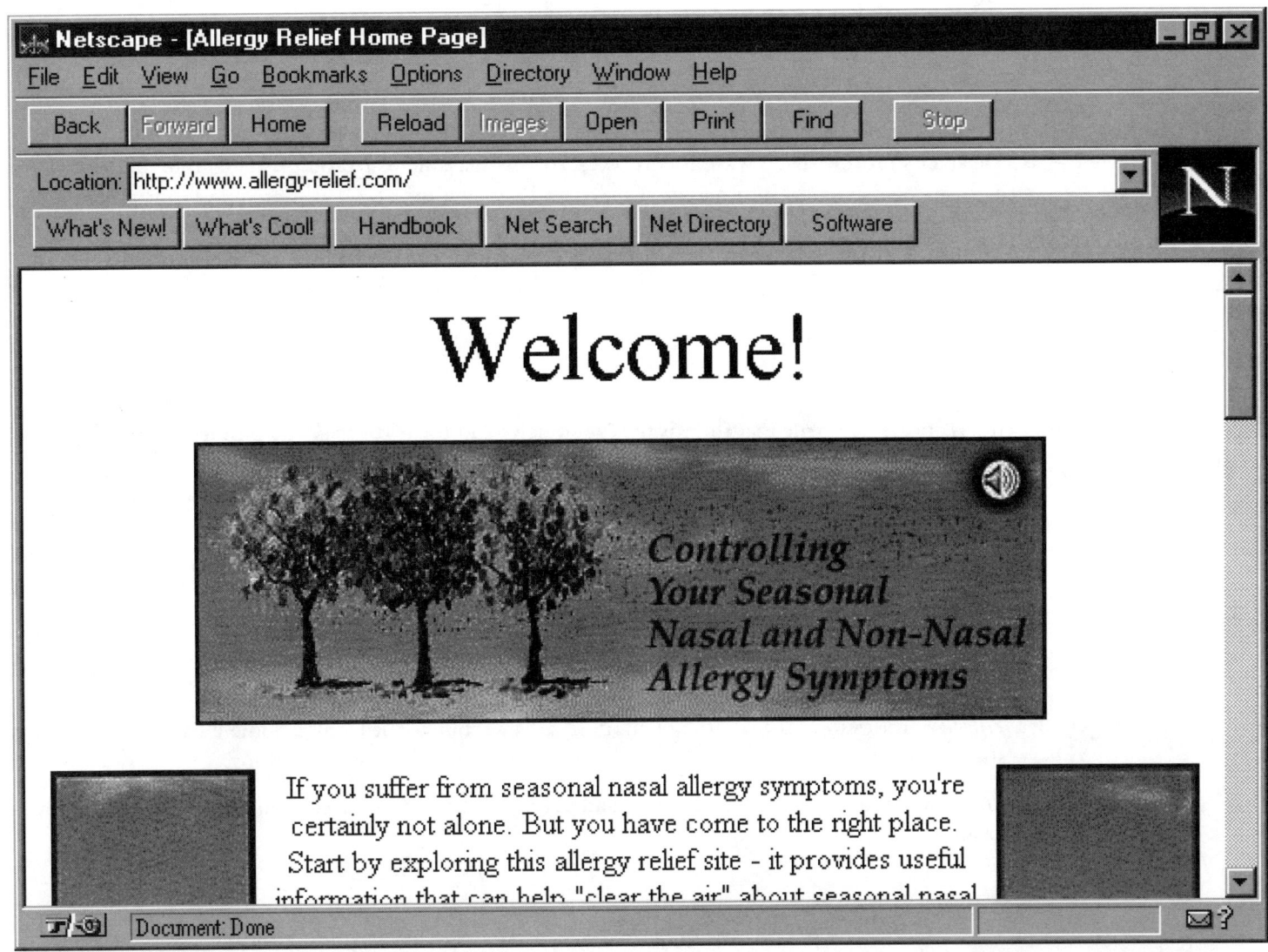

DejaNews Research Service

URL: http://www.dejanews.com

DejaNews provides users with instant access to information located on the many thousands of Usenet archives. Searching for information is quick and easy, with the built-in searching forms providing a simple way to find the information you seek. Ample support for first-time users is provided, and additional help for more detailed searches is provided as well. DejaNews is an important resource for those who wish to have timely access to information that is located on any or all of the many thousands of Usenet Newsgroups.

Key Feature

It has always been true that there is the "good news and the bad news" (no pun intended) about Usenet Newsgroups. We have always known that there is lots of information about many different topics. However, until DejaNews appeared on the scene, it was very difficult to find what you might want, quickly and efficiently. DejaNews has changed all that forever by providing this extremely easy to use and very powerful service. They refer to themselves as "The Premier Usenet Search Utility" and they seem to have done an excellent job of living up to that epithet. DejaNews makes it easy to quickly and efficiently access Usenet archives.

Pitfalls and Fixes

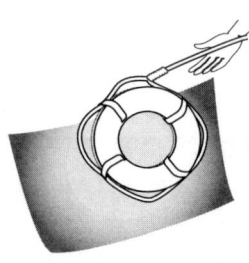

Pitfall: Some caution is advised, not about DejaNews, but about Usenet. Some Usenet groups contain strong and offensive language. You or others may trip over this while searching.

Fix: Supervision is advised for children and young adults due to the content of a relatively few newsgroups.

GE Plastics

URL: `http://www.ge.com/gep/homepage.html`

The GE Plastics Home Page is an excellent example of how a company can provide highly technical information to a very focused and technical audience using the World Wide Web. The user is provided with crisp, clear navigational directions. Each piece of information provides both a hyperlink and a short, descriptive sentence about that hyperlink. In addition, there are two opportunities for visitors to this site to communicate with the people at GE Plastics. The first one, "Tell Us About Yourself," is there because "we want our Web site to provide the highest possible value to our visitors." The second one, "Comments and Questions," is provided because "your comments are important to us and we would like the chance to respond to any questions you may have."

Key Feature

The GE Plastics Home Page is extremely helpful for resin buyers and plastics engineers. This site, which provides an amazing amount of content, is an excellent example of how a company can choose to focus the information they provide to a niche audience. The site is valuable to those who are interested in plastics, because it provides a wide array of content, in great detail, with excellent navigational tools. In addition, those who provide this site keep it current; there is always a "Tech Tip of the Week" (and tips from previous weeks are archived) as well as "GE Plastics News." The site provides lots of educational information and tips about various aspects of the plastics industry in a very accessible fashion.

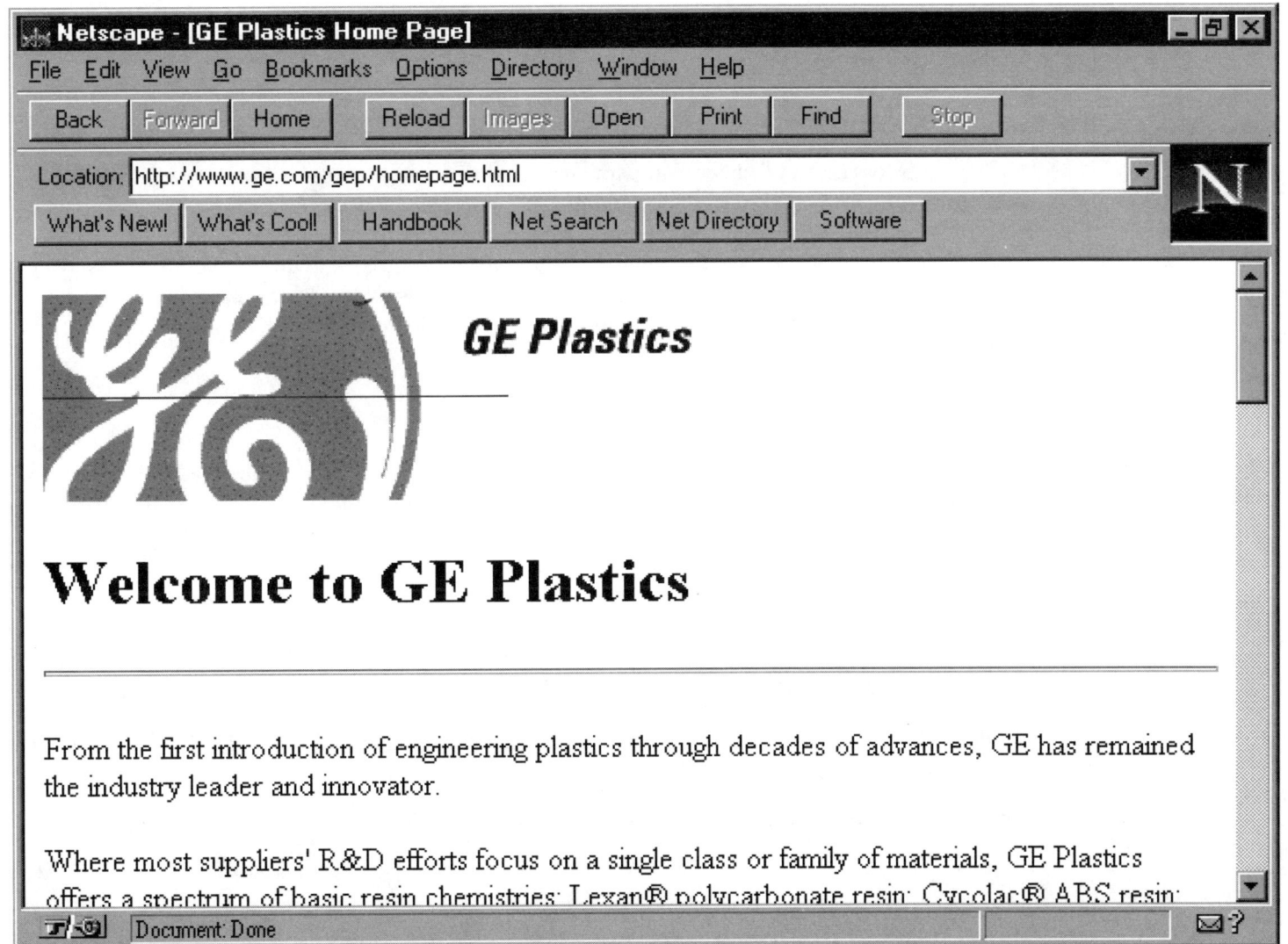

Back | Forward | Home | Reload | Images | Open | Print | Find | Stop

Location: http://www.ge.com/gep/homepage.html

What's New! | What's Cool! | Handbook | Net Search | Net Directory | Software

GE Plastics

Welcome to GE Plastics

From the first introduction of engineering plastics through decades of advances, GE has remained the industry leader and innovator.

Where most suppliers' R&D efforts focus on a single class or family of materials, GE Plastics offers a spectrum of basic resin chemistries: Lexan® polycarbonate resin; Cycolac® ABS resin;

Document: Done

Goodyear Tire and Rubber Company

URL: http://www.goodyear.com

The Goodyear Tire and Rubber Company presents an amazing array of information about tires. One can go to the Tire School to learn everything you might possibly want to learn about tires. There is a wealth of information presented here, about all aspects of tire buying and care, including how to read tires, how to care for tires, a tire wear advisory, and tire assurance. In addition, Goodyear has made it easy for you to select the right tires for your vehicles as well as to find your nearest Goodyear store. Recently they have added a set of hyperlinks that provide visitors with a list of other interesting auto-related sites.

Key Feature

The Goodyear Tire and Rubber Company site is one that is highly content driven. While it is obviously designed to help visitors purchase Goodyear Tires from Goodyear dealers, it is also a very useful site for those who would like to have more information about tires. For those who are interested, it is helpful to have easy access to tire wear information, a buyer's guide, a tire selector, a store selector, and other related information. Navigation throughout the site is well done, and information is presented in a clear, easy-to-follow fashion.

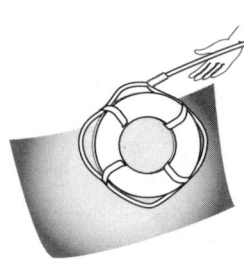

Pitfalls and Fixes

Pitfall: The main graphic is an image map which takes some time to download over a slower speed modem.

Fix: A text option near the top would be easy to include and would be useful.

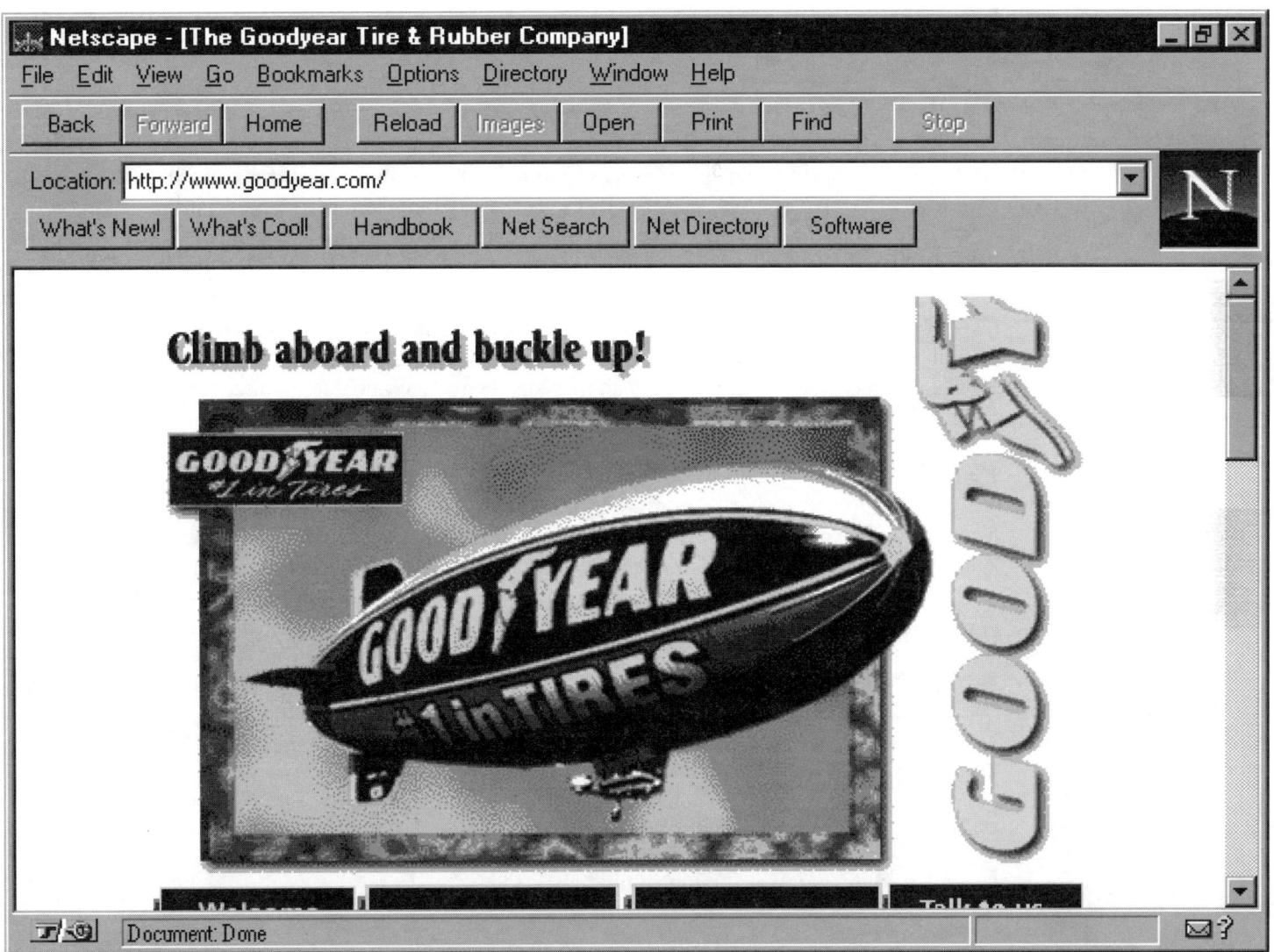

Courtesy of The Goodyear Tire & Rubber Co.

Hoover's Online

URL: http://www.hoovers.com

As they say on their home page, Hoover's Online is "the ultimate source for company information." This Web site provides Hoover's Masterlist Plus that enables viewers to tap into information on over 8,500 companies. The in-depth profiles of over 2,500 companies included in the Hoover's Company Profile Database are available to subscribers only for a small monthly fee, while the information in the Sponsored Databases is available free of charge. In addition, there is the Corporate Web Register that lists over 1,180 sites that have corporate news as well as information on products, investor relations, and job opportunities. Hot Links to stock quotes, SEC documents, and stock charts and hyperlinks to Web search tools are provided. All in all, this is an extremely valuable resource for those who are interested in information about companies.

Key Feature

Hoover's Online offers an enormous amount of information for those who are eager to know more about particular companies. This site represents a good blend of the "for free/for fee" information that is available on the World Wide Web. They do provide a fair amount of free information to those who visit the site; however, there is also strong encouragement for visitors to become members. ("To get the full experience on Hoover's Online it helps to be a member. Members get access to several exclusive databases including the award-winning Hoover's Company Profile Database.") This is a good example of a content-driven site that is providing information about a very specific area in great detail.

Pitfalls and Fixes

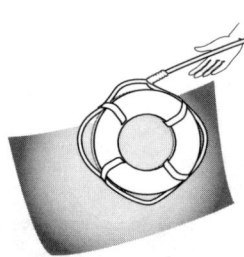

Pitfall: The initial image map graphic is about 40,000 bytes.

Fix: A text-only option at the top would help.

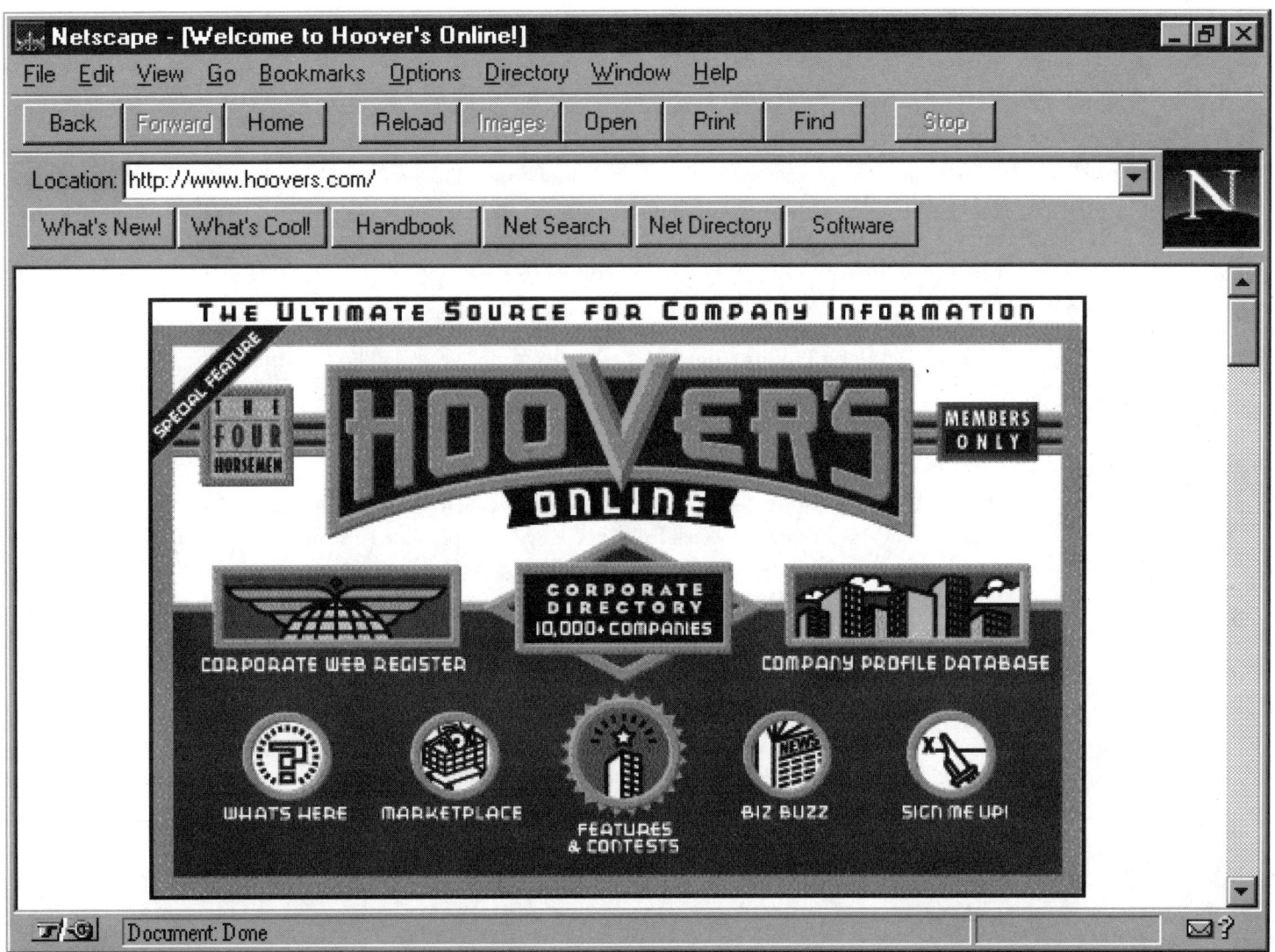

Courtesy of Hoover's, Inc.

Infoseek Guide

URL: `http://www.infoseek.com`

Infoseek is an extremely valuable resource providing quick and efficient ways to search the Internet. Using Infoseek is remarkably simple: Just type in the keywords that are of interest to you, and in a few short seconds Infoseek will provide you with a response. Ten of these responses (all hyperlinks) are provided each time, and each one is accompanied by a short paragraph of descriptive information. Infoseek provides both free and fee services. For those who wish to try their more detailed (and sometimes quicker) fee-based services, there is a one-month complimentary trial period. Infoseek is valuable for all who wish to find information on the World Wide Web quickly and efficiently.

Key Feature

Infoseek is a wonderful example of a function-driven site that has continued to improve its functionality with time. Infoseek was initially an extremely valuable resource for searching the World Wide Web. Today, one can use Infoseek in several ways. It is possible to search the World Wide Web, Infoseek Select Sites, Categories of Sites, Usenet Newsgroups, E-mail Addresses, and Web FAQs. By broadening their database, they have made themselves even more valuable than they were initially. Infoseek was one of the early search engines available for searching the World Wide Web and it continues to be an important component of many bookmark lists.

Pitfalls and Fixes

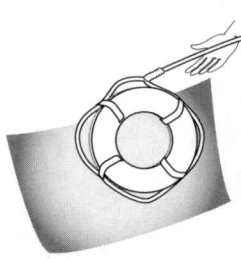

Pitfall: If there is a pitfall to this site, it is that it contains access to Usenet Newsgroups. As we mentioned earlier when we looked at DejaNews, some Usenet Newsgroups contain language that is quite offensive.

Fix: If the concern about Usenet Newsgroups is important to you, you might wish to limit children's and young adults' access to them.

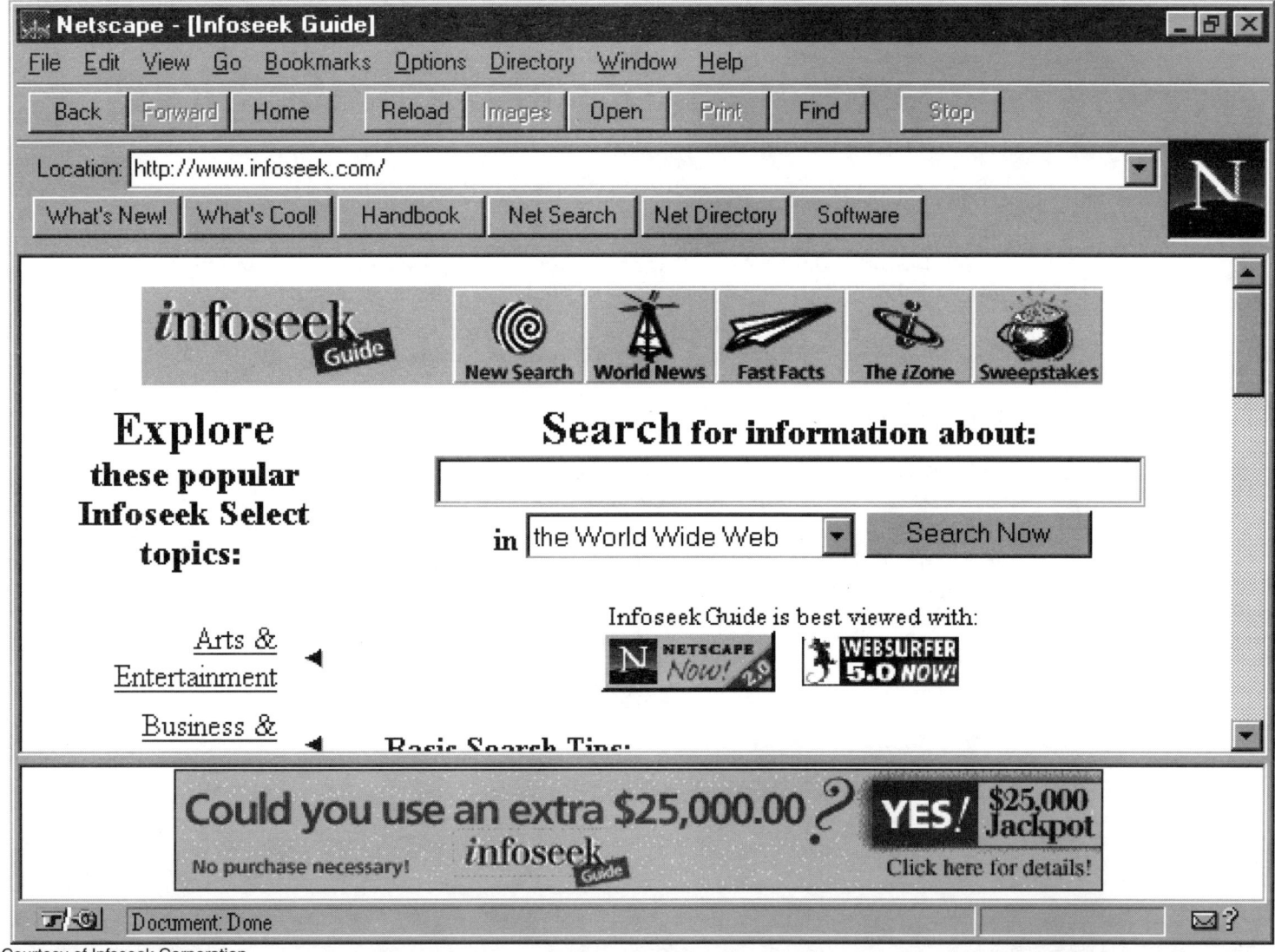

IRnetserv, Inc.
(Investor Relations Network Services)

URL: `http://www.irnetserv.com/index.htm`

IRnetserv, Inc. (Investor Relations Network Services) focuses exclusively on providing investor relations information on the World Wide Web and as such, provides valuable resources to the investor. It is intended to provide corporate investor relations professionals with the ability to communicate effectively to shareholders using the World Wide Web. Accessing the data provided is quite simple: Just click on the letter of the alphabet for the company you are seeking.

Key Feature

This site is clearly one that is content driven. It focuses on public companies and provides quick and easy access to information about them. The IRnetserv, Inc. Home Page is quite simple to use. The first choice for viewers is to select the letter of the alphabet that corresponds to the company in which they are interested. They also provide a listing of companies by industry. Finally, they supply other financial resources on the Web such as EDGAR, PAWWS, the MIT Stock Market Data, and others.

The List

URL: http://www.thelist.com

The List provides the names of Internet Service Providers grouped by state, area code, country, and country code. A convenient search box lets you look for an Internet Service Provider by name or domain name, should you happen to know it. If you do not know the name of the Internet Service Provider, a series of easy-to-use hyperlinks permits you to search for providers who might serve the particular state or area code that is of interest to you. For each provider, you are given E-mail, phone, and fax information, as well as their URL, the services they provide, and the fees for those services. The information appears to be reasonably current and very complete.

Key Feature

The List is a wonderful example of a content-driven site that continues to remain current. The figure shown on the opposite page indicates that there are 1,966 Internet Service Providers; a visit to this site one week later provided a screen indicating that there were 2,101 Internet Service Providers. This site is constantly kept current, as indicated by information at the bottom of the screen (not shown). The fact that it continues to grow means that its value and utility will continue. References to The List abound throughout the Internet, attesting to its value for many.

Pitfalls and Fixes

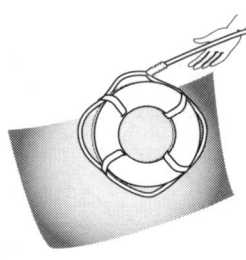

Pitfall: The one obvious problem is that although this site is very useful, it is useful only to those who already have Internet connectivity and a browser.

Fix: The obvious solution is that those who are interested in having access to this information but who do not have it themselves should find someone who already has Internet connectivity and a browser!

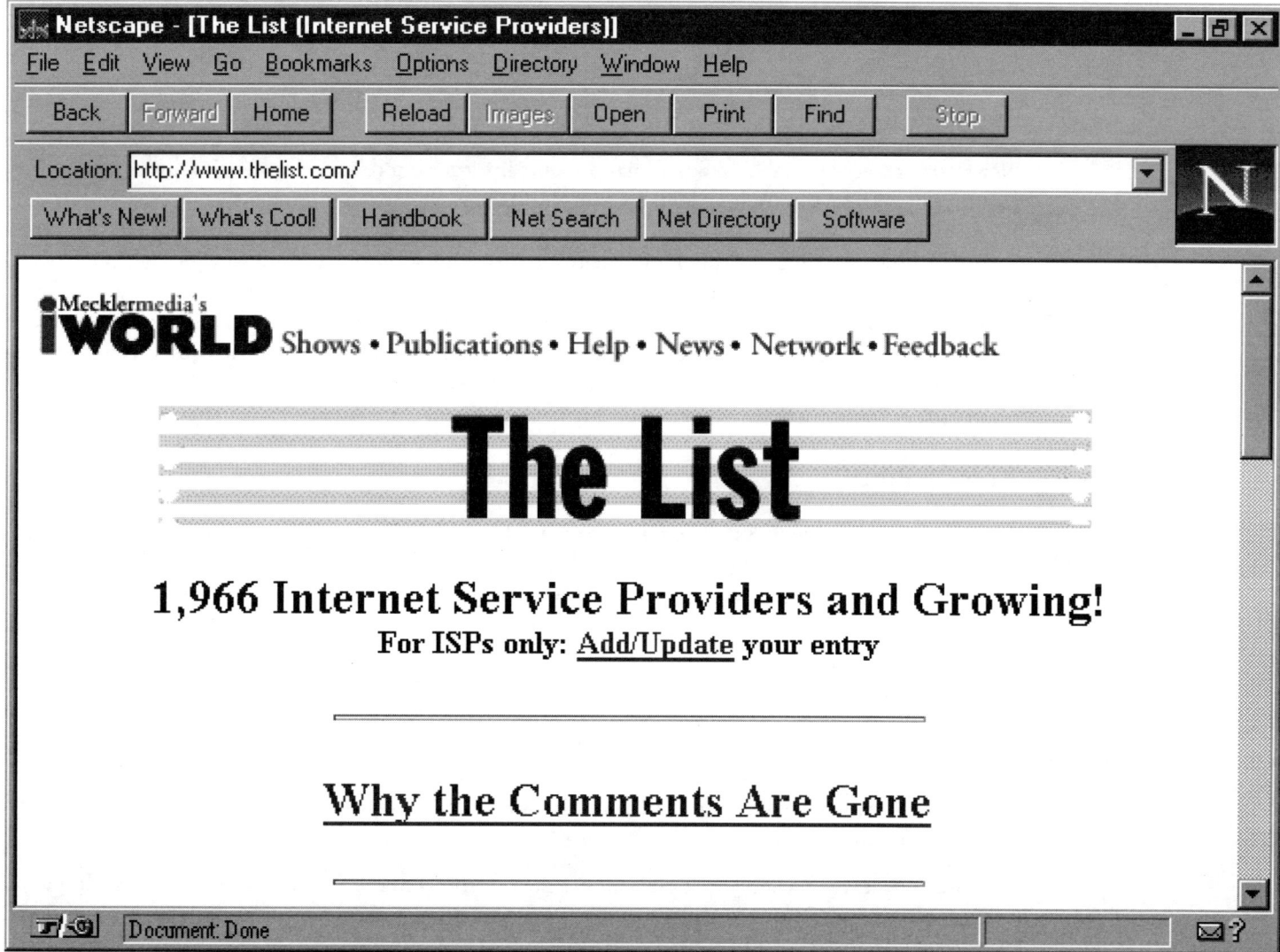

NewsPage

URL: http://www.newspage.com/

NewsPage is a very valuable resource that presents information derived from 600 sources. They claim that 25,000 pages are refreshed daily, making NewsPage the most comprehensive news site on the Web. NewsPage is easy to use and provides free access to today's news headlines and news briefs. Information is provided about 19 different categories, including Computer Hardware and Peripherals, Data Communications, Interactive Media and Multimedia, Telecommunications, Automotive, Business Management, Energy, Healthcare, Aerospace and Defense, Insurance, and Transportation and Distribution. In order to have access to the full-text versions of the NewsPage articles, it is necessary to register with NewsPage. Those who register can have access to Basic Sources free of charge, or to Basic Sources and Premium Sources for a monthly fee.

Key Feature

NewsPage is an extremely valuable repository of information gathered from a wide array of sources. Their content covers both the breadth and depth of many industries, and the data is kept timely and current. There is an enormous amount of information available from this site.

Pitfalls and Fixes

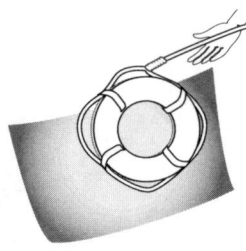

Pitfall: Registration is required for all, and varying access to different amounts of information is available for varying amounts of money. Unlimited access to full-text versions of information from Basic Sources is available free of charge. Other information and services are available only to those willing to pay for Premium Service or NewsPage Direct Service.

Fix: It is not clear yet whether people who use the Internet and the World Wide Web will willingly pay for access to information. Recent reports indicate resistance to this idea. Other sites have determined that it would be best to sell advertising for their sites, rather than to charge individual users.

Southwest Airlines Home Gate

URL: `http://www.iflyswa.com/luvhome.html`

The Southwest Airlines Home Gate is a good example of a useful site that provides information clearly and quickly to potential customers. As you might imagine, they use the site to provide information about flights and fares, as well as special promotions that are underway. The site is clear about its goals and objectives: They are there to provide you with information about the airline and its services quickly and efficiently. With the exception of the large graphic (mentioned below), they do a good job of that.

Key Feature

The Southwest Airlines Home Gate has been designed to be a useful site that provides a wide array of information for present and potential customers. The site is visually attractive, and as soon as you select the General Index hyperlink located below the main graphic, you are taken to an easy-to-use alphabetical listing of the resources Southwest Airlines provides. They have an interesting array of information, a partial list of which includes a collection of their print and video ads, information about Boeing aircraft, airport information, city information, fares, financial reports, and lots of information about Southwest Airlines employees. They are focused on their corporate objective of providing clear information about their airline, and they do so well.

Pitfalls and Fixes

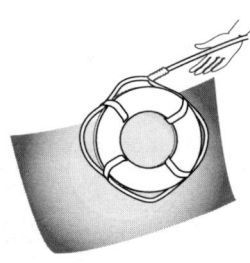

Pitfalls: This site has good information; however, the initial image map of 27,000 bytes downloads slowly (about 30 seconds using a 28.8 modem). In addition, it is not always clear what information is provided by the image map, or where you should click to get there.

Fix: It might be useful to provide viewers with a text-only option early on in the viewing process. And, better labeling of the image map might make it more useful.

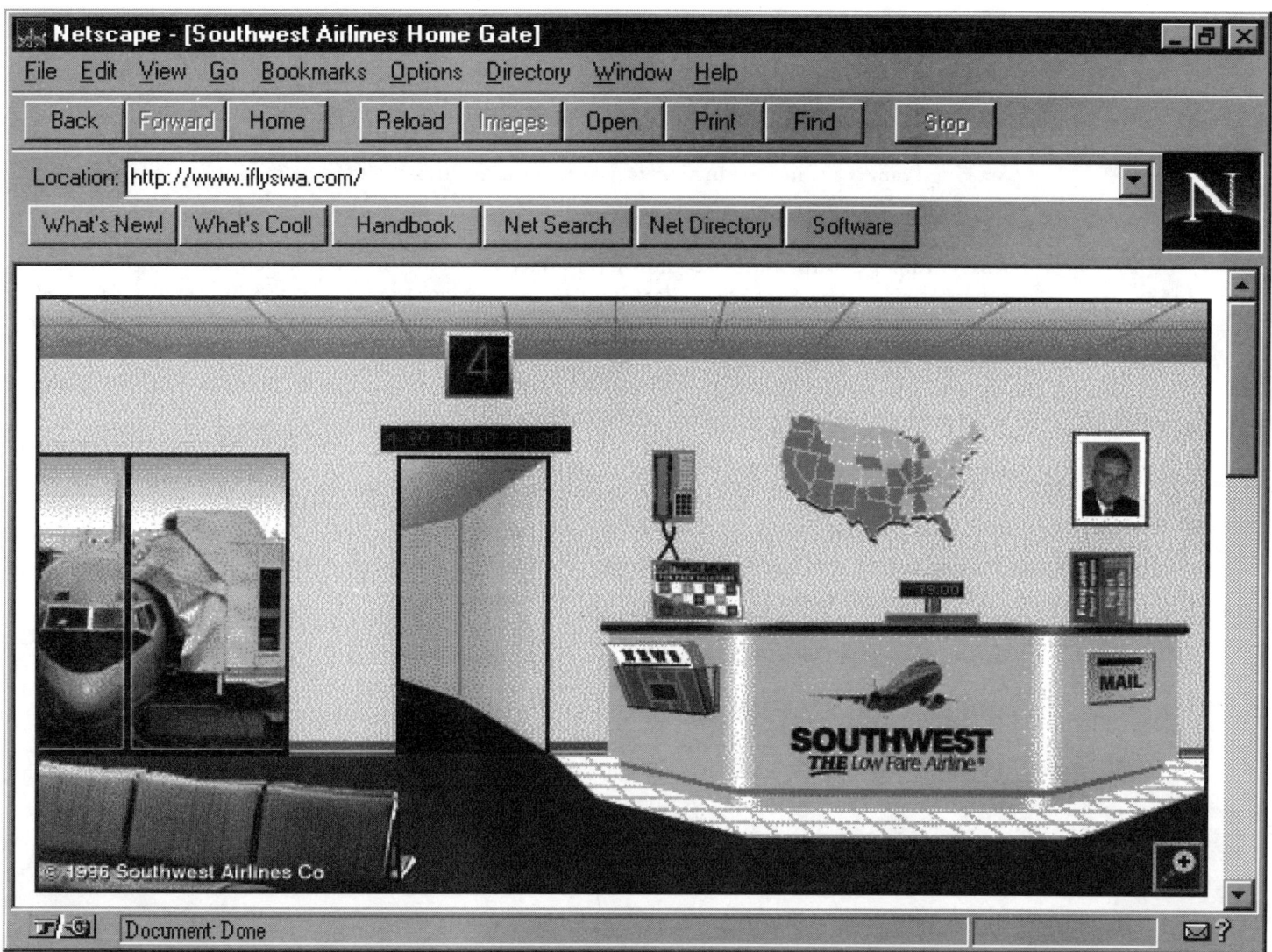

Starting Point

URL: `http://www.stpt.com`

Starting Point is a valuable function-driven resource for those who are searching for information on the World Wide Web. Of particular value is the Starting Point - MetaSearch that enables you to search the Web's most extensive databases using one simple search form. Sixteen databases are accessible as of this writing, including the better known ones such as Excite, InfoSeek, Open Text, Alta Vista, and others. Once you have searched a database, clicking on your browser's BACK button will return you to the Starting Point - MetaSearch page where you can then search additional databases or refine your search. The MetaSearch page is obtained by clicking on the SEARCH button on the Starting Point Home Page. The site is extremely useful due to the function that it provides so well: It makes it so much easier for visitors to search the World Wide Web.

Key Feature

Starting Point provides quick and easy access to a wide array of World Wide Web search engines. Starting Point provides an easy-to-use text box into which to enter your search terms. In addition, the 12 Starting Point Choice Topics include a wealth of additional information and provide a more focused search. Excellent navigational tools are provided throughout the site, making it easy for visitors to always know their location.

Pitfalls and Fixes

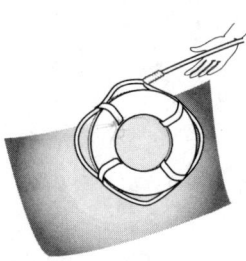

Pitfall: The real pitfall when using the World Wide Web is how to remember the names of all of the search engines and where to find them.

Fix: Use Starting Point. One bookmark takes you to most of the search engines.

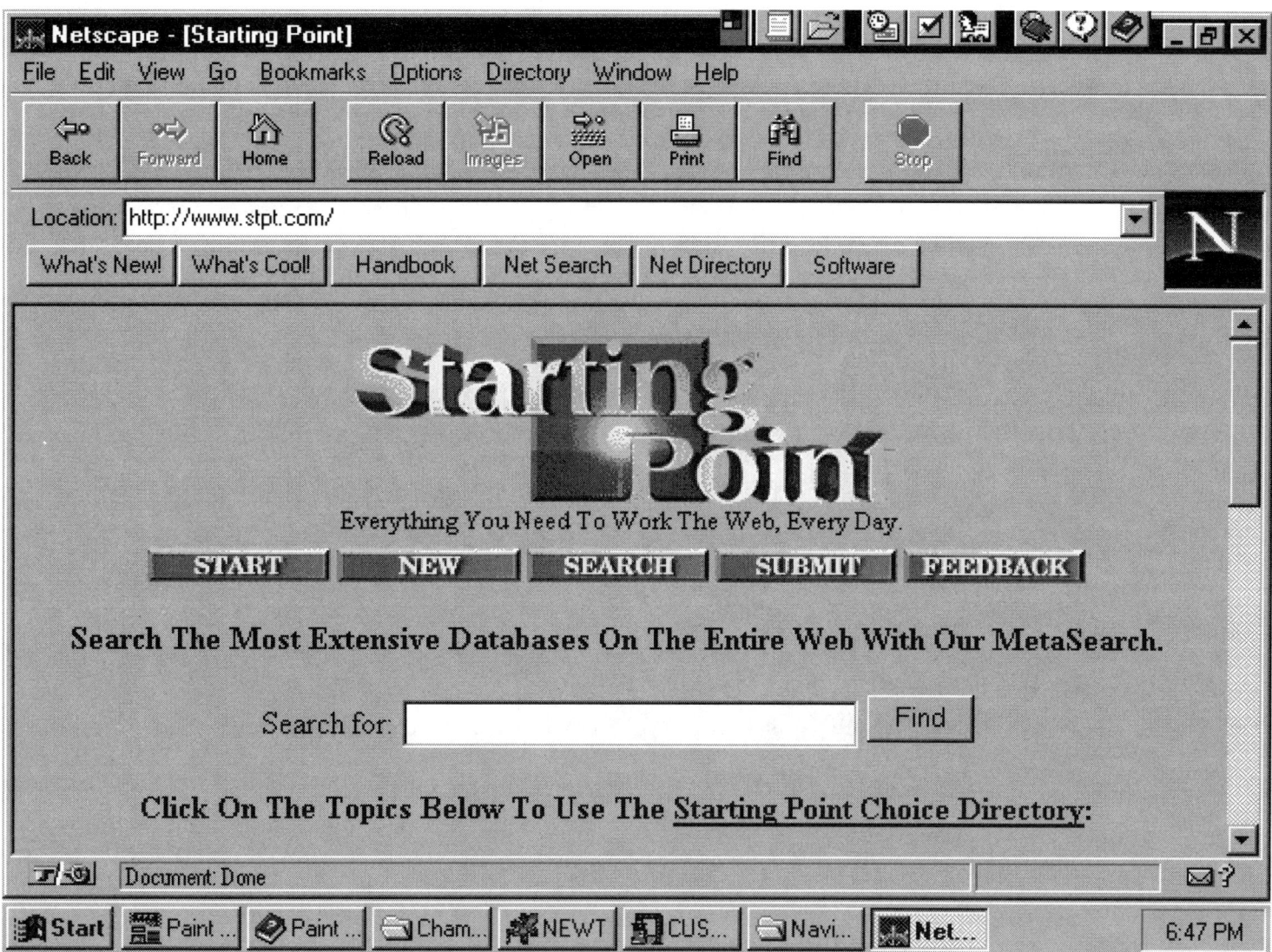

Courtesy of Starting Point L.L.C.

Weblint

URL: `www.khoros.unm.edu/staff/neilb/weblint.html`

Weblint is a syntax and minimal style checker for HTML. It is a perl script which picks fluff off HTML pages, much as traditional lint picks fluff off C programs. If that sentence makes sense, then this program will be extremely valuable to you. (If it doesn't, then just go on to the next page!) Designed to help in the final production of HTML documents, Weblint is a prized possession of those who create HTML documents as an important part of their job description. Be sure to add Weblint to your software toolkit if this applies to you!

Key Feature

Weblint is a wonderful resource for those who are developing HTML pages in a UNIX environment. The software does an excellent job of "proofreading" HTML pages and providing a detailed line-by-line analysis of where the pages do not match up to the HTML standards. It will quickly and efficiently scan an entire document, and the printout is clear and very useful. This site provides a particular function extremely well, and in the process has made itself invaluable.

Pitfalls and Fixes

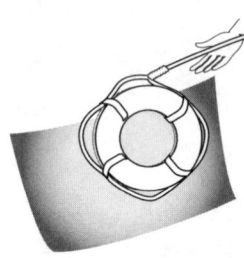

Pitfall: At this writing, Weblint works only in a UNIX environment.

Fix: HTML authors will be happy when other environments are supported.

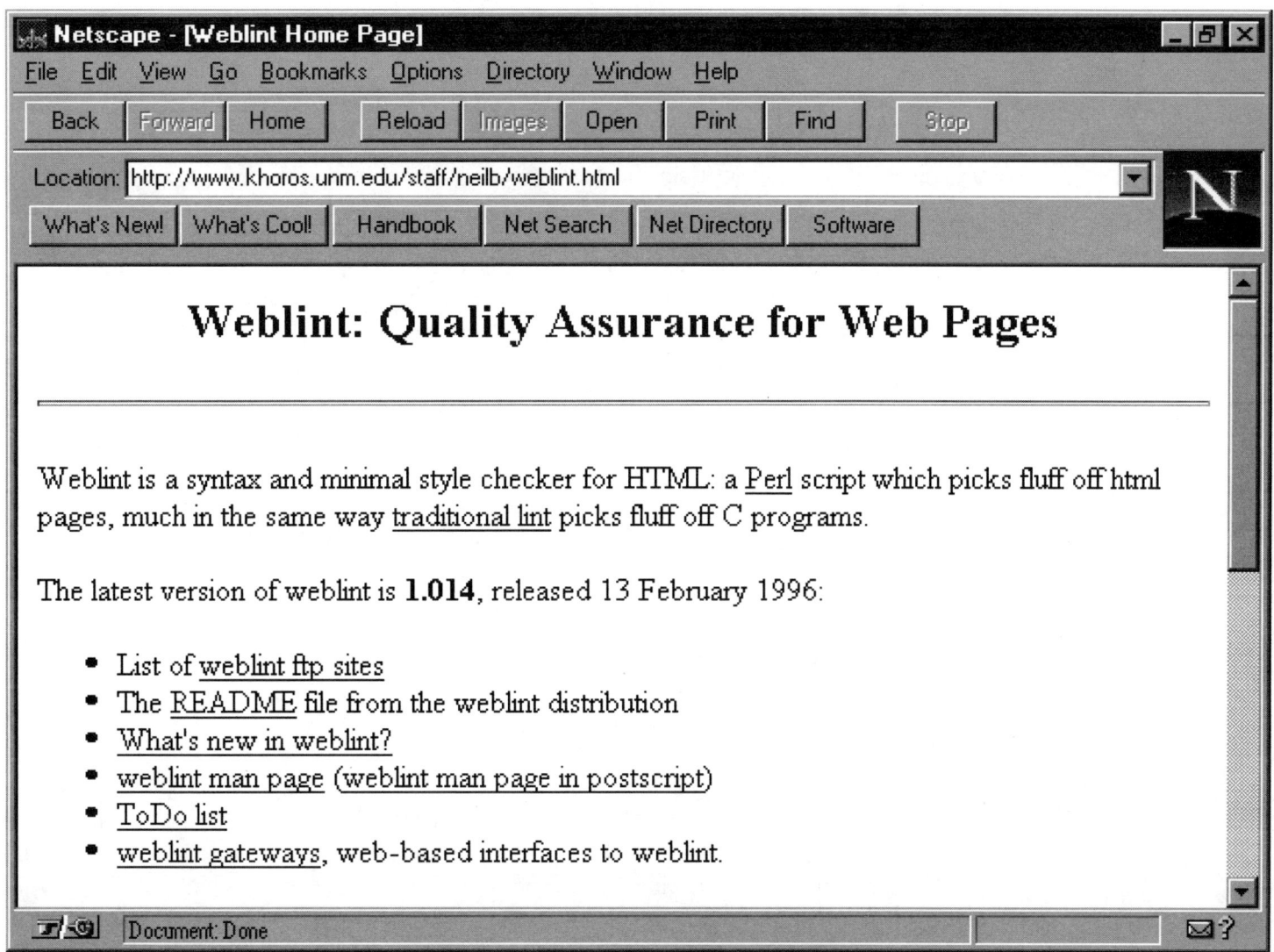

Weblint: Quality Assurance for Web Pages

Weblint is a syntax and minimal style checker for HTML: a <u>Perl</u> script which picks fluff off html pages, much in the same way <u>traditional lint</u> picks fluff off C programs.

The latest version of weblint is **1.014**, released 13 February 1996:

- List of <u>weblint ftp sites</u>
- The <u>README</u> file from the weblint distribution
- <u>What's new in weblint?</u>
- <u>weblint man page</u> (<u>weblint man page in postscript</u>)
- <u>ToDo list</u>
- <u>weblint gateways</u>, web-based interfaces to weblint.

Courtesy of Khoral Research, Inc.

Wild Dunes

URL: `http://www.persimmon.com/WildDunes/welcome.html`

Wild Dunes is another fun Web site that has been designed to provide pleasure to those who choose to visit. In addition, it is clearly a sales and marketing tool developed by Persimmon IT, an information technology company that believes that the Internet and underlying technologies can be a powerful business tool. Those who visit the site can learn lots about Wild Dunes, one of South Carolina's premier ocean front golf resorts, and the facilities available at this Charleston island resort including The Links golf course, some customized golf packages, the tennis center, and the yacht harbor. The fun comes when you click on The Links hyperlink and can play a round of golf. And, the photography is sensational!

Key Feature

Wild Dunes is a fun site; there is lots to do and see and you might learn about a great place for a vacation while playing golf! The site is chock-full of wonderful, beautiful photographs (see more about that below) and an enormous amount of information about South Carolina and Charleston.

Pitfalls and Fixes

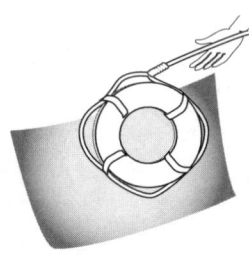

Pitfalls: This site relies heavily upon graphics. For users of slower modems, there might not be a lot of pleasure derived from having to wait a long time while the graphics appear.

Fix: Persimmon IT, Inc., has done a wonderful job of warning their visitors about the size of the photographs. They declare that "we use thumbnail pictures for the in-line images because the full-size versions are each about 100 Kilobytes." The thumbnails are large enough to provide a sense of what the full-size pictures are all about. Should viewers choose to download the full-size pictures, they will know in advance that the full-size pictures are large and will take some time to download.

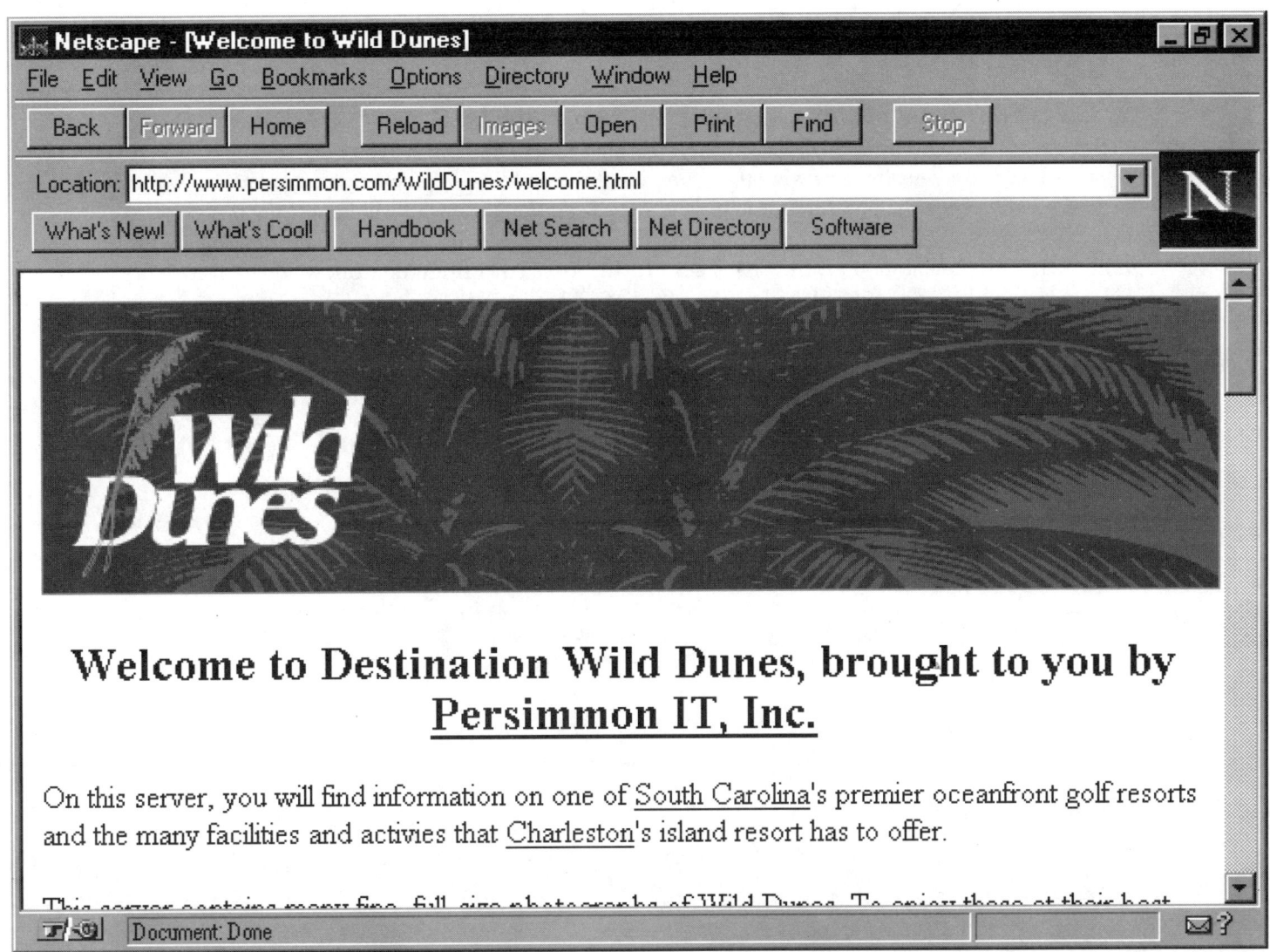

Netscape - [Welcome to Wild Dunes]

File   Edit   View   Go   Bookmarks   Options   Directory   Window   Help

| Back | Forward | Home | | Reload | Images | Open | Print | Find | | Stop |

Location: http://www.persimmon.com/WildDunes/welcome.html

| What's New! | What's Cool! | Handbook | Net Search | Net Directory | Software |

Welcome to Destination Wild Dunes, brought to you by Persimmon IT, Inc.

On this server, you will find information on one of South Carolina's premier oceanfront golf resorts and the many facilities and activies that Charleston's island resort has to offer.

This server contains many fine, full-size photographs of Wild Dunes. To enjoy these at their best

Document: Done

Summary

You have seen a number of valuable, useful, or fun sites in this chapter. Those that are most valuable or useful pay close attention to the function they provide or their content. As you have seen, the successful sites are continually improving their functionality or adding significantly more content. With luck, that will enable them to stay ahead of new arrivals on the scene who will be seeking to usurp them. The fun sites are often silly, such as the Claritin page of sneezes, or perhaps wonderfully beautiful, such as the Persimmon IT, Inc. site. They provide some relief from the work we do each day and give us some indication of the playful nature of the World Wide Web.

Chapter 5

KEY 3:

Current and Timely

Introduction to Key 3 — Current and Timely

The Web does many things well, but perhaps its most stellar features are speed and currency. Speed is limited only by the transport medium and currency is limited by the ingenuity of Webmasters. In this chapter, we will look at a number of sites that are **current and timely**.

At a recent Internet conference, a speaker noted that "the world is now 1 1/2 seconds in diameter." We can deliver almost any kind of information or entertainment around the world in seconds! As transmission media speeds continue to increase, delivery will become even faster and our dependence on the Web will continue to grow.

How current is current?

In this chapter we will look at Web sites where currency is defined by the information that is carried. For example, the currency of a magazine is usually measured by the month; a newspaper, by the day; radio news, by the hour; and so on. Within the Web, we now have sites that are automatically updated by the second or each time we ask them for information.

Currency, then, is relative to what the site does. A magazine three months out of date is as bad as yesterday's news broadcast. Some very current sites are enhancing their value to users by maintaining a library of previous issues or archived information.

The Importance of Being Honest

However currency is defined, effective Web sites tell us right up front how current they are. This may be implicit, as in a date on a newspaper masthead, or it may be explicit by time and date stamping on the page. Many automatic tools exist to show the current time and date from the server's clock. Automatic time stamping is risky as other information on the page may tell the visitor that the page lies! Be honest when putting in dates and times. If the page changes hourly, put the time (and country and time zone) in as the change is made.

We will see several sites in our examples which use timeliness as a way to draw in visitors as a public service. These will be frequently visited sites. Consequently, some of these sites have begun to earn revenue for themselves by charging others who wish to place their advertisements on these sites. All Web sites should be current and timely, but the sites you are about to see illustrate some of the best.

Technical Points

Significant and Continuing Resource Commitment

Web pages striving to be current and timely have made a major commitment of their people, content, and software resources. As you will see in our examples, many are already major content providers in other media. This allows them to use that content online.

The editorial and people resources are not, however, small. Each one of these sites, and sites like them, makes the commitment to do this every day and to keep it up indefinitely. If you are planning a "current and timely" type site, size, measure and re-size this commitment regularly.

If you use software to update your site automatically as is done in the LA Freeway Speeds site, be sure that you check the site very frequently with both automatic tools and with people. These marvelous sites have a reputation which could easily be damaged by outages or software freezes.

Access and Offering of Helper Applications

If your current and timely site requires visitors to have helper applications or plug-ins, such as RealAudio or QuickTime for Windows, be sure to place an easily seen link on your page so your visitors can quickly and easily acquire them. Also, be sure that you offer information about both current and earlier helpers. (See the NPR site.) Generally, you will want to use only "free viewer" applications such as RealAudio or Adobe Acrobat.

Information Availability to Text Browsers

It may be hard to believe, but many people still use text browsers such as Lynx. Others choose to turn off graphics to speed their response over modem lines. For these people, always use the ALT part of the IMG tag. And use it to tell them what they are missing.

For example, [Photo] may work if it is after a person's name, but [Photo of 777 Landing in Singapore] tells your visitor more.

A recent Web survey found that over 20 percent of Web users have access to browsers that are text-only or they choose to turn off graphics. Don't lose these visitors if you can help it!

Tight Linkage to Other Regular Information Channels

If you provide a Web edition of material from another medium, be sure that the content is the same. This may seem obvious, but it is an easy place to stumble and to create credibility problems for your site. If you are current and timely, you must also be correct.

Use of Backup Power, Lines, Equipment, and Servers

If you are encouraging visitors to depend on you, more than your content and code must be reliable. Your site must be there when people call. Plan on backup power, secondary access lines, backup server hardware, and, of course, regular code and content backup procedures. You may be in the critical information services business.

Now let's look at a number of sites that do an excellent job of being current and timely. These sites are shown as of 1996 and are being viewed with Netscape 2.0 and Windows 95.

ABC News Reports

URL: http://www.realaudio.com/contentp/abc.html

The ABC Radio Network offers timely news, sports, and commentary broadcasts—on the Internet. Why not just use a radio? Many reasons make this a compelling site. The hourly news is yours when you want it, not just on the hour. And it's available anywhere on the globe! Want to keep in touch while traveling? Here's news from the United States wherever you may be, and *you* control when you view it. Users can also get sports news and commentary. You will need the RealAudio helper application for your browser, but easy instructions help you get it.

Key Feature

The Welcome to ABC site provides viewers with hourly radio news, sports, and commentary, anywhere, any time. Internet hourly news is updated at 15 minutes past the hour, and archives are available. Access to all the audio programming is free to all registered visitors. RealAudio files arrive quite quickly, and while the sound is not quite perfect, it is getting better all the time!

Pitfalls and Fixes

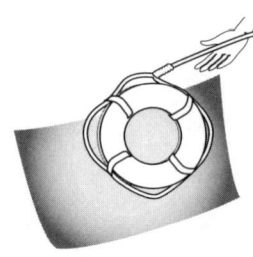

Pitfall: As we write this, ABC requires a free registration. Visitors need to provide their E-mail address and their user name. This helps ABC keep track of their users. However, some people find it annoying to have to register to have access to free information. Another possible pitfall is that those who wish to have access to these files must have a copy of the RealAudio software and must have installed it correctly on their computers.

Fix: There are many interesting ways (other than registration) being used to capture information about visitors to Web sites. A number of them will be discussed in greater detail in Chapter 8. The RealAudio site is readily accessible and provides both current and older versions of the RealAudio software, as well as directions telling how to install it with various browsers.

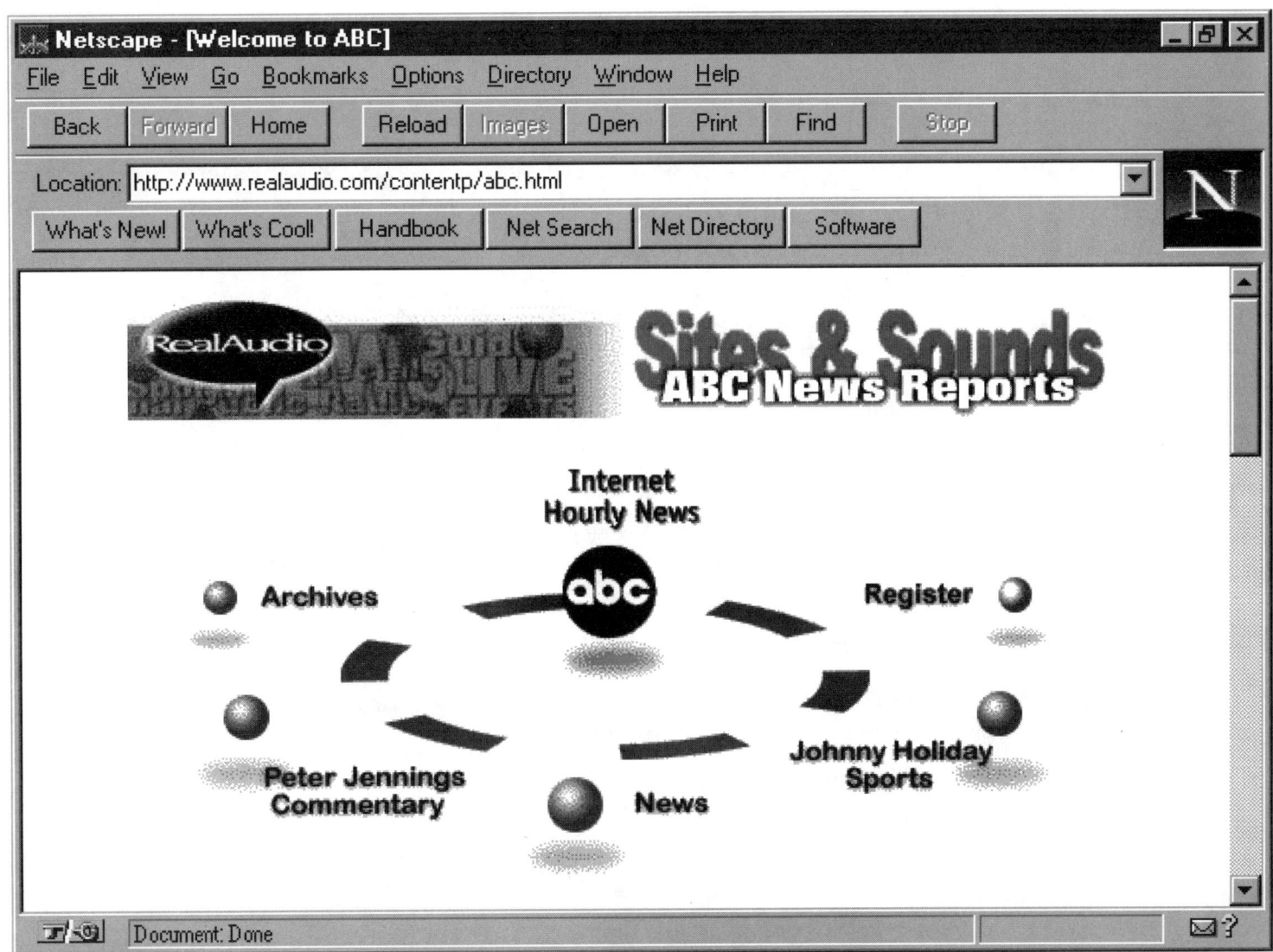

Courtesy of ABC News

Electronic Newsstand

URL: `http://enews.com/`

The Electronic Newsstand is exactly what it says: a newsstand right on your computer. Not only will they provide you with an entire magazine, but they will also give you access to selections from the *New Yorker, Business Week, Internet World,* and many, many more magazines, newsletters, and catalogs. The Electronic Newsstand includes hyperlinks to the sites of many newspapers and magazines. This allows you to use the Electronic Newsstand as a master reference for papers and magazines without book-marking them all. Another feature is called "The Monster Magazine List" that claims to be the largest list of magazines in the world.

Key Feature

The Electronic Newsstand has done an excellent job of making themselves into a one-stop shop for over 2,000 current magazines and newspapers. Their "Monster Magazine List" is well organized with a built-in search engine, and they do seem to have included almost every magazine and newspaper one has ever heard of. In addition, they have a wonderful new feature that enables visitors to create their own Custom Newsstand, which is a personalized list of a visitor's own favorite magazine sites.

Pitfalls and Fixes

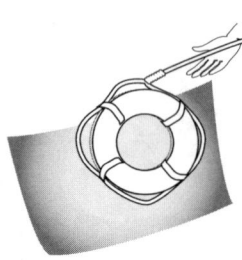

Pitfall: The initial image map for the Electronic Newsstand is large (42,000 bytes) and downloads slowly (about 45 seconds) over a high-speed (28.8) modem.

Fix: The use of smaller images and fewer colors would shorten the download time.

Courtesy of The Electronic Newsstand

ESPNET SportsZone

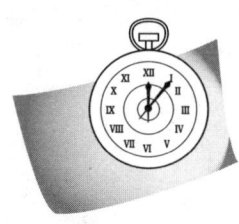

URL: `http://espnet.sportszone.com/`

Sports enthusiasts for almost any sport can find a home at ESPN's SportsZone. This is an example of currency and timeliness down to the hour. It is also a treasure-trove of game previews, current scores, past scores, and late-breaking stories about sports.

This site also handles the subscriber issue very well. While offering many free features to all visitors, there is also an enticing offer to become a subscriber. Subscribers can pay a few dollars a month for extra features of multimedia and dynamic graphics, in-depth analyses, and a wealth of statistics. Video highlights of major sports events are also offered to subscribers.

Key Feature

Timely and current sports news about baseball, hockey, basketball, football, soccer, and other sports makes this an extremely interesting site to visit. The site is valued highly by those who like their sports information to be current, and the ESPNET SportsZone has earned a well-deserved reputation for its complete and timely information. In addition, they have done an excellent job of instantly providing viewers with text-only and Java options. There is a hyperlink that offers a "Mostly Text Front Page" for those who would like their information without any graphics. And, for those who have access to newer browsers that can properly display Java, there is a hyperlink for a "Java Front Page." Instructions to access both these options are prominently displayed on the home page.

Pitfalls and Fixes

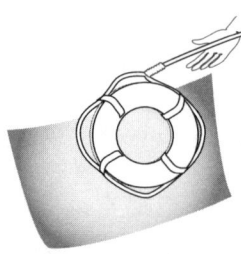

It's hard to find any faults with this sports lovers' Web treasure!

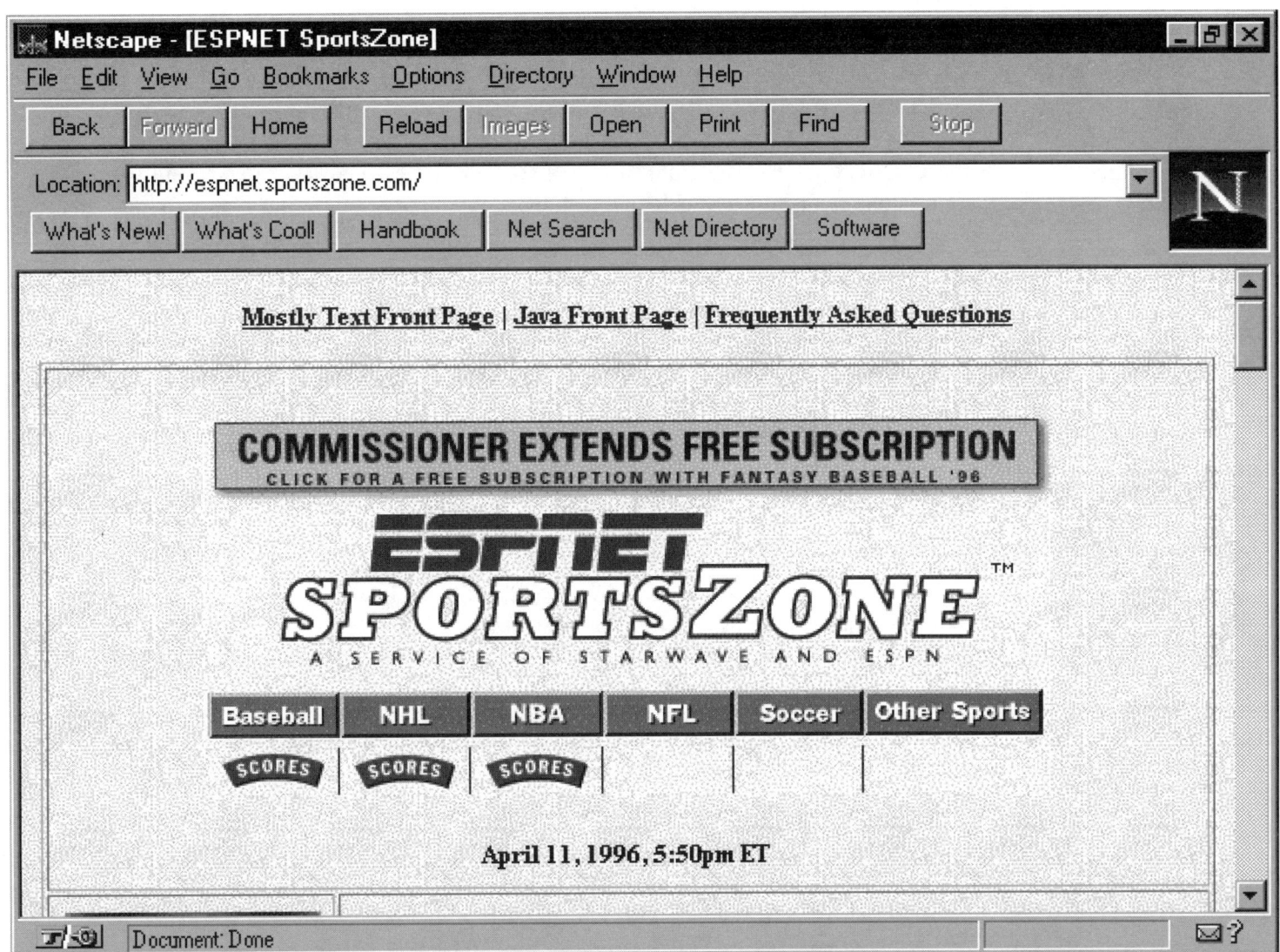

Intellicast

URL: http://www.intellicast.com/

The NBC News Intellicast site is one of several weather information sites, but it is one with a twist. Not only is this among the best U.S. and worldwide weather references, but it also presents ski conditions. And the information about ski conditions is becoming more worldwide with each passing month.

Weather is the main focus and currency is king. Weather conditions and forecasts are given in summary, in detail, and in image form. The site offers the latest satellite maps, images, and weather radar for the United States. The site is careful not only to show "last updated" time stamps for each page but also to tell visitors when each image was captured.

We all need to know the weather and the NBC Intellicast keeps us very current.

Key Feature

NBC Intellicast provides up-to-the-minute and useful U.S. and worldwide weather conditions and forecasts. The initial image map is attractive, downloads quickly, and is also very well designed. It is easy to determine the options that are available and where one must click to access them. Six choices are provided on the image map, and five of them (not NBC News) are repeated immediately below with text hyperlinks. Visitors to this site immediately know what their choices are, and how to access them. This careful attention to navigational detail is provided throughout the site. One always knows where one is, and how to get to the other options that are available. The information is presented in a timely fashion, and a new feature includes RealAudio or more traditional audio sound clips.

Courtesy of WSI Corporation

Interactive Weather Browser

URL: `http://wxweb.msu.edu/weather/interactive.html`

What Michigan State University's Interactive Weather Browser lacks in global coverage is compensated for by its ease of use. By pointing on the map of the United States to an area of interest, we are given the actual conditions at the closest weather reporting station. For those familiar with weather station codes, an option allows a direct jump to that station. Frequent travelers will welcome this, as airport codes work well here. (Airports, of course, are also weather stations.) The page not only tells you the current time and date automatically but also gives the reporting time from each station queried.

Key Feature

The Interactive Weather Browser is a fast and easy-to-use U.S. weather reference.

Pitfalls and Fixes

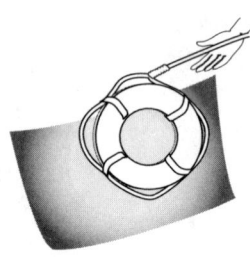

Pitfall: The page layout causes the report to come in just below the visible screen.

Fix: If the report area were placed higher on the screen, then no up/down movement of the screen would be needed to see the requested conditions.

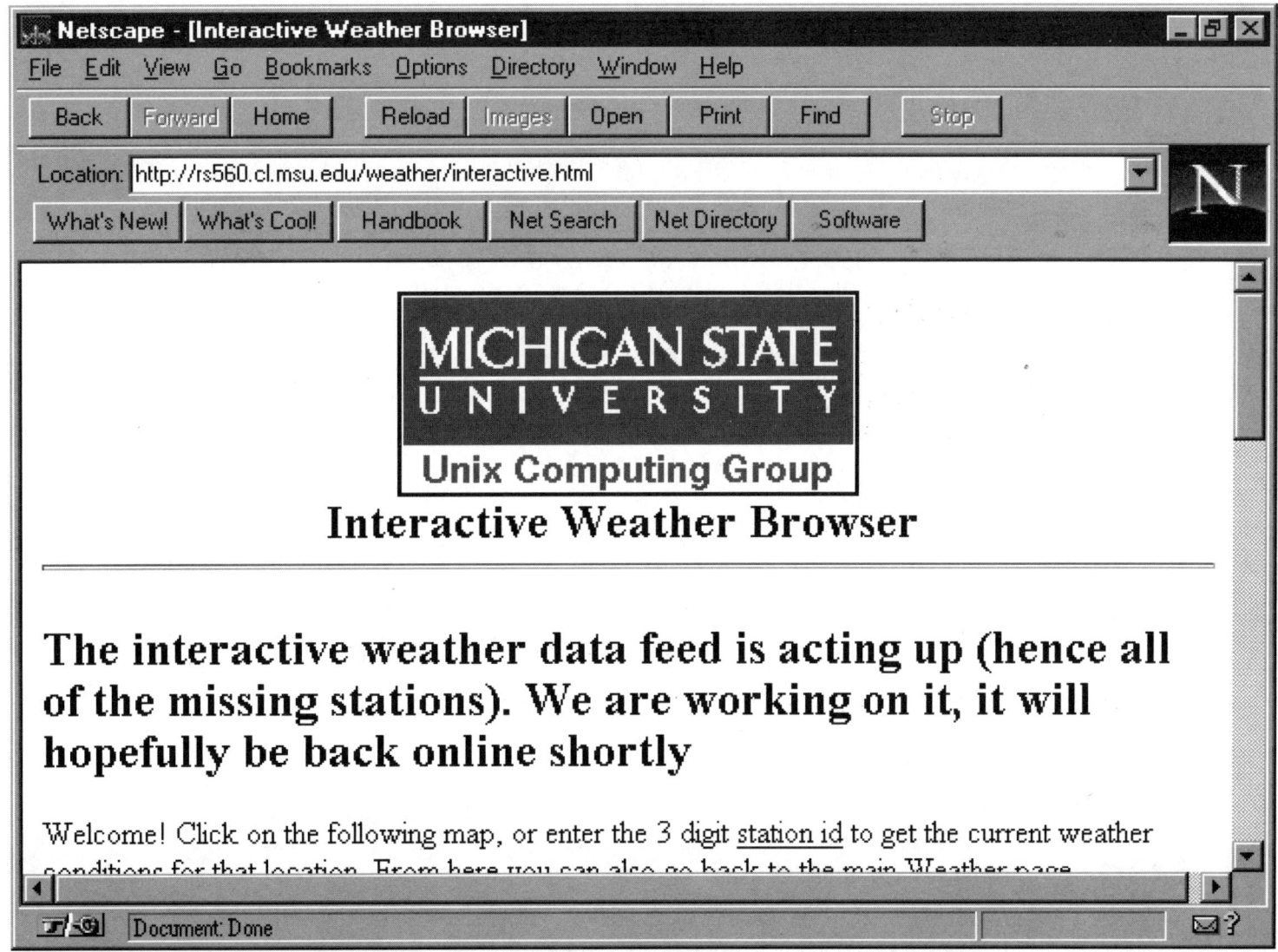

IRS - The Digital Daily

URL: `http://www.irs.ustreas.gov/prod/cover.html`

The Internal Revenue Service? Are you kidding? No, we're not. The IRS Web site may be the first crack of a grin in this formerly humorless and dreaded agency. Not only is it a lighthearted site, but it also offers current and timely tax news, as well as forms and publications available in many popular formats. Imagine the convenience when you discover you suddenly need an IRS form and find you can have it with the click of a mouse! They have a newsstand of current tax information, tax regulations (in plain English), and a very attractive site.

While many people only think of the IRS near April 15th, many of us need the odd form or publication at other times of the year. Here is a timely service in that it's *our* time they are saving. The IRS—who would have thought it?

Key Feature

The IRS Digital Daily provides current U.S. tax information with a light touch. They have done a wonderful job of providing an enormous amount of information in an easy-to-use, friendly fashion. The site includes tax information for individuals and businesses, electronic services, and a wealth of other information. All of it is presented clearly with both colorful graphics and text hyperlinks. In addition, the IRS has a scrolling message on the status line—watch for it. This is a very good early example of JavaScript being used effectively.

Pitfalls and Fixes

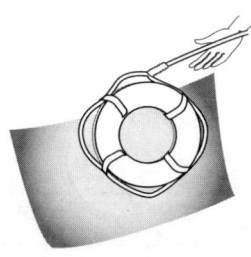

Pitfall: When this site downloads over a modem, it takes quite some time until anything other than the title bar appears on the viewer's computer. Lots of activity is taking place, but the screen remains blank until the whole file has been downloaded.

Fix: It would be better if some of the graphics appeared more quickly on the visitor's screen. Waiting for it all to appear at once is a bit disconcerting.

LA Freeway Speeds

URL: `http://www.scubed.com/caltrans/la/la_big_map.shtml`

Our best example of timeliness comes from Los Angeles, although other cities are now bringing up similar systems. Here, timely is measured in seconds. What you see on this site is the current (usually to the minute) status of traffic speeds on all major freeways in Los Angeles County. Both directions of traffic are shown and the speeds are indicated by colored dots along each freeway. The map is time and date stamped and is rarely more than a minute out of date. Red dots means speeds below 20 mph; green dots mean speeds above 35 mph; and yellow dots mean speeds from 20–35 mph. Blue dots indicate suspected traffic incidents.

Viewing this map of the current traffic before traveling in Los Angeles can save you from ending up in a jam that's already started. Of course, you may find your own jam after you leave.

Key Feature

The LA Freeway Speeds provided by Maxwell Laboratories presents immediate traffic-flow reports. The site is extremely well organized and informative. They have done an excellent job of giving instructions on how to use the LA traffic report and also provide a good "heads-up" about the size of the maps to be downloaded and what features are offered. For example, they note that the REALTIME Big Map is "Clickable, but slow links beware! ~32Kb"—this is priceless information, and it is presented in a clear and useful fashion. For those with slower links, they do offer the REALTIME Small Map and explain that it is "About 20 Kb, not clickable."

Pitfalls and Fixes

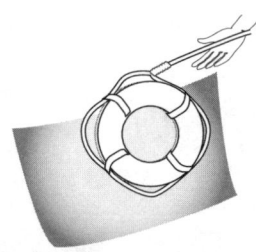

Pitfall: Many browsers cache or store images. The map can be stored if you have visited here before. This means that your computer will show you the previously stored image, not the current one.

Fix: This fix is up to the person who is using the browser. Check the date and time of the page that is visible and reload if it is not current.

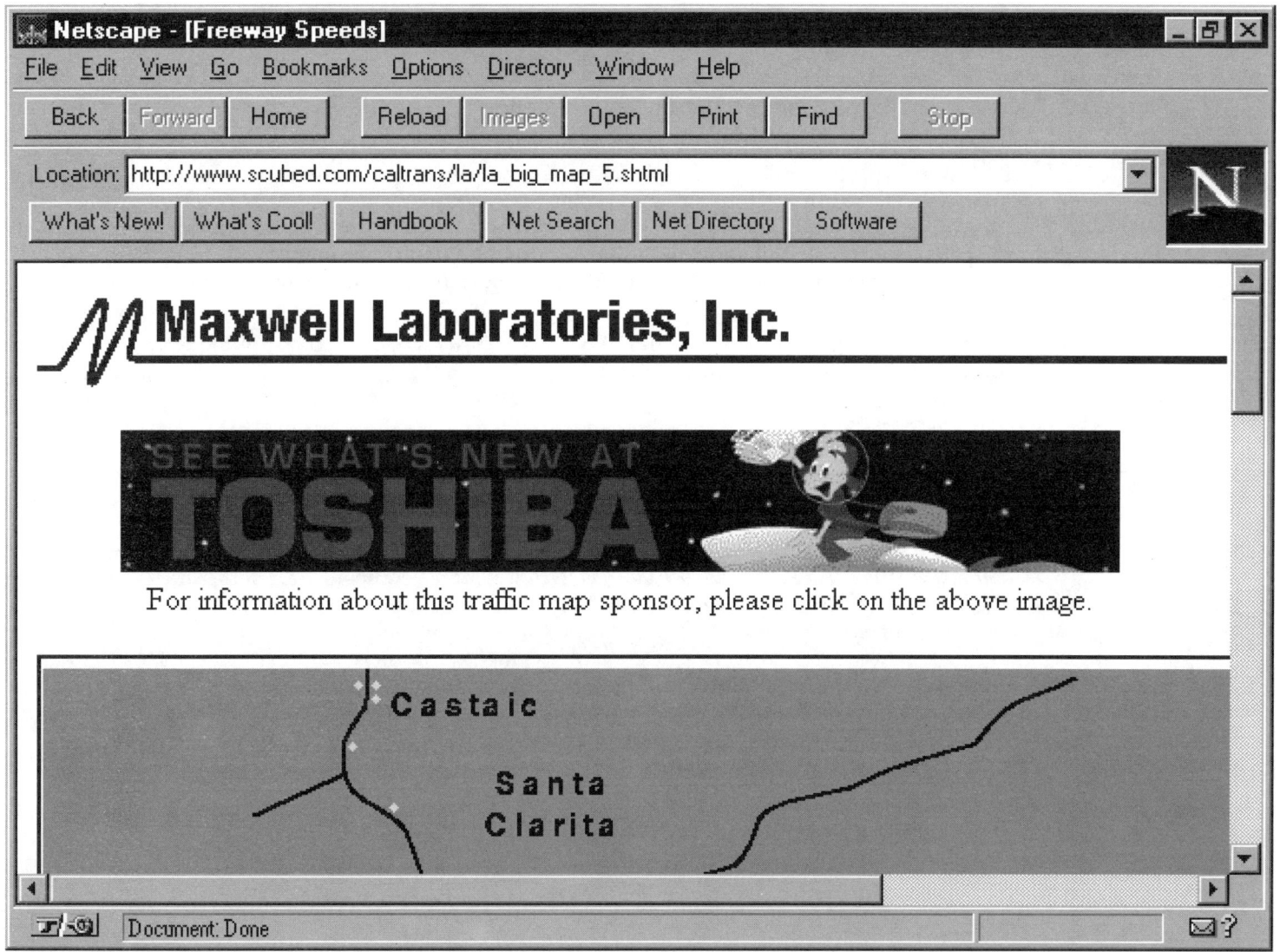

Mercury Center

URL: `http://www.sjmercury.com/`

The first of our daily newspaper examples is the San Jose, California, *Mercury News*. The *Mercury News* is, of course, the prime daily in Silicon Valley. As you would expect, the page allows easy access to the local news and weather, and also provides many special features such as a local "mall" of services. Mercury Center is more than just a Web version of a newspaper, but it retains many of the key features of the parent paper. Generally, after the features, breaking news can be found further down the page. This site also designs their home page to move you quickly to the news area of your interest.

Mercury Center not only does current very well, but it also handles the login issue neatly. While most services on this site are free, a small monthly charge allows access to full text of the paper, comics, and some columns that are not provided in the free section.

Key Feature

Mercury Center is a full-service newspaper site. Clicking once on the down arrow in the Sections Spin box enables the visitor to choose from among the Index, Breaking News, Business, Comics, Entertainment, Home Page, Living, News, Opinion, or Sports. Clicking once on the down arrow in the Services Spin box enables the visitor to choose from among the Mercury Mall, Classified, Family, Cyberspace, Mortgage Watch, NewsHound, NewsLibrary, Newsstand, Search the site, Talent Scout, and Weather offerings. They have managed to pack a lot of choices into very little space and provide a wide array of services that go above and beyond what one would normally expect to find in a local newspaper. In addition, they do a great job of keeping the information timely. They also provide good, clear navigation throughout the site. The three primary choices (Sections, Services, and Subscribe) are presented at the top of each new page, and it is always possible to click on the Mercury Center Home and Index text hyperlinks at the bottom of each page.

Pitfalls and Fixes

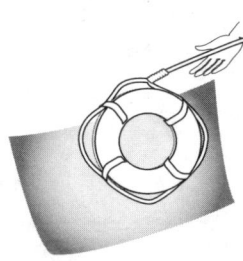

This well-designed and informative site is a good example of how to avoid pitfalls.

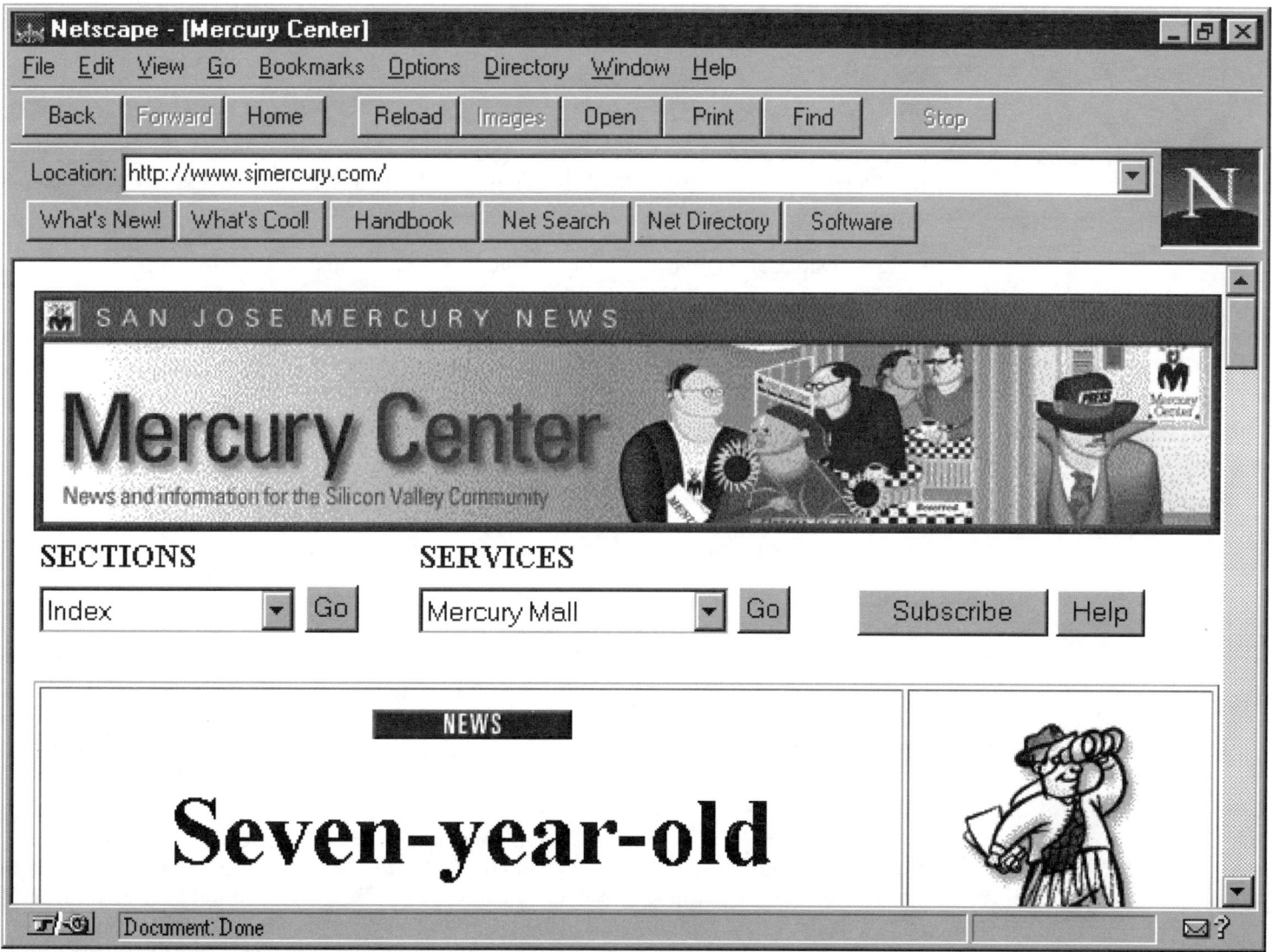

Courtesy of Mercury Center

National Public Radio

URL: `http://www.npr.org`

Unlike ABC Radio News, National Public Radio (NPR) is both an audio and text site. Some of the NPR special interest programs, such as science shows for children, can be viewed as text with rich references and resource lists. But like ABC, NPR offers audio broadcasts of breaking and current news. In addition, NPR offers special programs and features from its on-air shows. For their loyal listener set, NPR provides advance program overviews and rundowns of previous shows, some back to 1994.

Unlike ABC, there is no login requirement and the audio is available seconds after you make your selection from the day's offerings. The date, time, and time zone of the Breaking News are shown, so there is no doubt about the currency of the information.

Key Feature

NPR Online is a noncommercial radio site that provides quite an array of news and features. They do a good job of providing both sound files and transcripts of their news. In addition, they provide a text hyperlink that makes it easy for visitors to download and install the RealAudio player. The site features news and audio clips that would appeal to young and old alike.

Pitfalls and Fixes

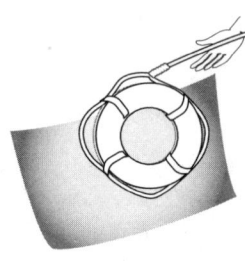

Pitfalls: There are three possible pitfalls with this otherwise quite wonderful site. First, RealAudio is used and a player is needed. RealAudio with a 28,800-bps modem is an improvement over the slower 1.0 release, but sound quality is still a little like shortwave radio. Second, the size of the initial bit-mapped image is quite large. It is 42,000 bytes and takes quite some time to download over a high-speed modem. Third, although the initial image map does provide access to a number of sound files, this is not at all obvious from the graphic.

Fix: There are several suggestions. First, NPR Online makes it easy to get access to the RealAudio player. With higher connection speeds, the quality of the RealAudio sound files improves. Second, as smaller images download more quickly, smaller graphics might be appreciated by those with modem connectivity. Finally, if the goal of the image map is to provide a set of sound files, it might be advisable to make this fact more obvious and to indicate more clearly what files are available.

NETworth by GALT Technologies

URL: `http://networth.galt.com/www/home/networth.html`

NETworth, now owned by Quicken, offers 15-minute delayed Standard & Poors stock index information and many other financial services such as stock quotes and recent activity graphs. The site offers much additional information on mutual funds as well as investment advice. As we write, all services are free, although the site requests registration to access some of their online information, such as prospectuses and net asset values. As with most other sites requesting registration, you have the option of whether or not you wish to receive mailings.

This is an excellent Web site for those interested in financial markets to access current market data.

Key Feature

NETworth by Galt Technologies, Inc., provides near real-time stock market information as well as a wide array of information on mutual funds and financial planning.

Pitfalls and Fixes

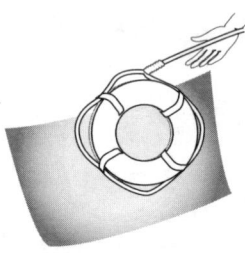

Pitfall: One pitfall with this site is the amount of time it takes for the initial home page to download. The graphics are gorgeous, but the top image map is 40,000 bytes, and right below it is one that is 15,000 bytes. Over a high-speed (28.8) modem, the files take quite some time to download. A second possible pitfall is that this site requests registration, although much of their content does not require it.

Fix: Smaller images, with fewer colors, would result in a site that would download more quickly. Providing a text-only option to viewers at the top of the initial page would be helpful. However, it should be noted that all the options on the image map are offered with text hyperlinks below the graphics at the top of the page.

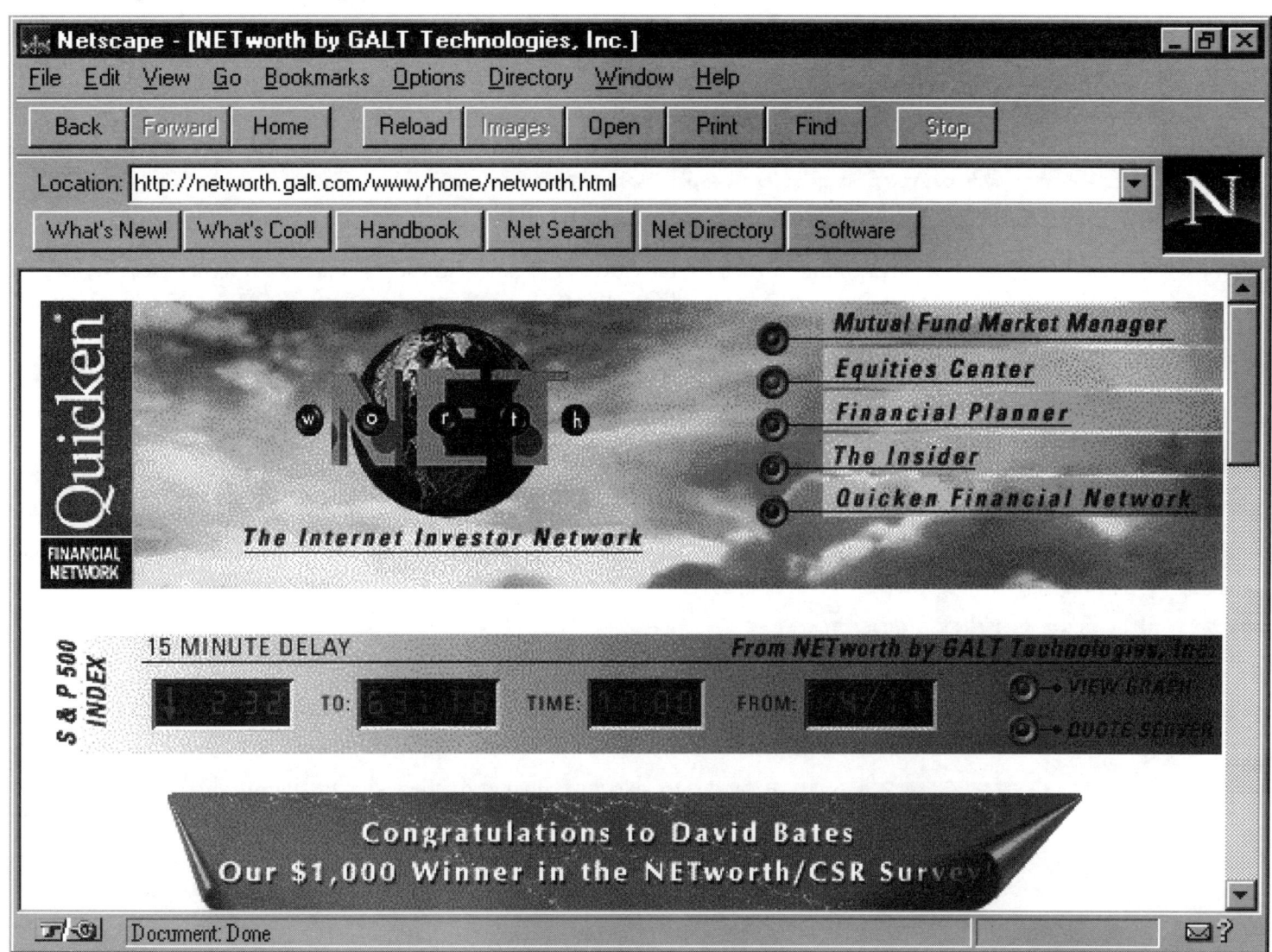

The New York Times

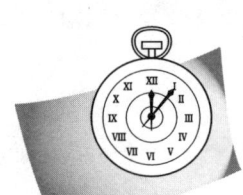

URL: `http://www.nytimes.com`

One of America's premier newspapers, the *New York Times*, has finally come to the Web with a true Web edition. The new Web version, the successor of a so-called fax edition, is stunning in appearance and very current. Unlike its parent paper, the Web edition is updated several times daily. In addition to news, weather, and features from the daily paper, a new feature is offered to Internet users. Called CyberTimes, it focuses on news of the information industries and contains features that don't appear in the parent paper.

Key Feature

The New York Times On The Web is a world-class newspaper on the World Wide Web. Information is presented in a timely fashion, and navigation is clear and easy to follow. They do a good job of providing lots of graphic and text options throughout this site which makes it possible to always know one's location. In addition, they provide a choice for a "Low Graphics Version" right on the home page, which is a nice touch.

Pitfalls and Fixes

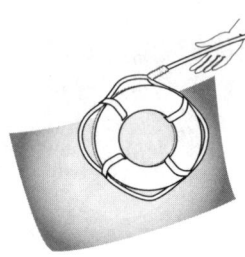

Pitfall: The New York Times requires that you register which, as we write, is available for no cost. This "free" login also needs to be confirmed, as they send a confirmation code to your E-mail address. Registration requires only a name and E-mail address, but some visitors may find this to be an annoyance.

Fix: As we will discuss in far greater detail in Chapter 8, other sites are finding alternate ways to capture information from their visitors without requiring that they register.

Playbill

URL: `http://www.playbill.com`

Playbill should be familiar to anyone who attends the theater. On the Web, it has become a wonderful resource with timely theater news and features. It's also a place to see video clips of current theatrical productions. Perhaps the most valuable and timely feature is the Theater Listings. Anyone interested in attending a play or musical will want to refer to these pages. Playbill currently offers listings not only for New York (Broadway and Off-Broadway) and London, but also for regional theaters and touring companies. In addition, they have a special feature—a listing of theaters with shows suitable for children. Regional theaters range from Abingdon, Virginia, to Worchester, Massachusetts. About 400 regional theaters are included. Hotels and restaurants are also listed to complete the theater experience. As we write, the site is piloting online ticket sales.

Key Feature

Playbill On-line is a very complete repository of current national theatrical listings. The site has a full array of services for theatergoers and continues to add new ones. They have a built-in search engine that facilitates finding desired information quickly. This site has a central focus and does an outstanding job of providing almost anything associated with theater.

Pitfalls and Fixes

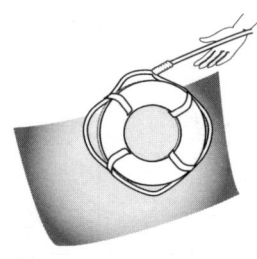

Pitfall: The only possible pitfall might be the fact that the initial bit-mapped image is 68,000 bytes, which obviously means that it downloads slowly (over one minute) over high-speed (28.8) modem connections. There also does not appear to be a text-only version of this page.

Fix: Providing a text-only option might be a good idea, and some visitors to this site might appreciate an initial page with low- or high-graphics options that other sites like Classroom Connect offer.

Purdue Weather Processor

URL: `http://thunder.atms.purdue.edu`

Our third weather site is certainly the most colorful of the three. The Purdue Weather Processor shows an annotated full-color satellite rendering of the current U.S. weather situation. In addition, further down the page are many small images (larger than thumbnails) of weather satellite pictures, surface and upper air data, and weather radar maps. Each image can be viewed fully by clicking on it. Some of the actual data is also available in text form.

Like the Interactive Weather Browser seen earlier, this site focuses on the United States.

Key Feature

The Purdue Weather Processor provides complete U.S. Weather information in a colorful format. The information is timely and quite useful for those who need access to it. This site is also filled with a wide array of GIF files and MPEG (Motion Picture Experts Group) movies.

Pitfalls and Fixes

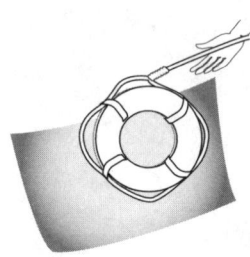

Pitfall: One concern has to do with the fact that the main weather map is large (about 60,000 bytes), although it does seem to download fairly quickly on a fast modem. A second concern has to do with all of the GIF and MPEG files that are included. The files are wonderful, but there is no indication of their size or the time it might take to download them. One only finds out by actually downloading the files.

Fix: The text-only option, "Goto Main Index (no tables/images)," is near the top of the page allowing users with slow lines to stop and switch to text. A quick way to address the second concern would be to provide some indication of the size of each of the GIF and MPEG files that are available. The GIF files are relatively large (79,000 bytes is not unusual) and the MPEG files are *huge*! Some indication of this to visitors would greatly enhance the value and utility of this site.

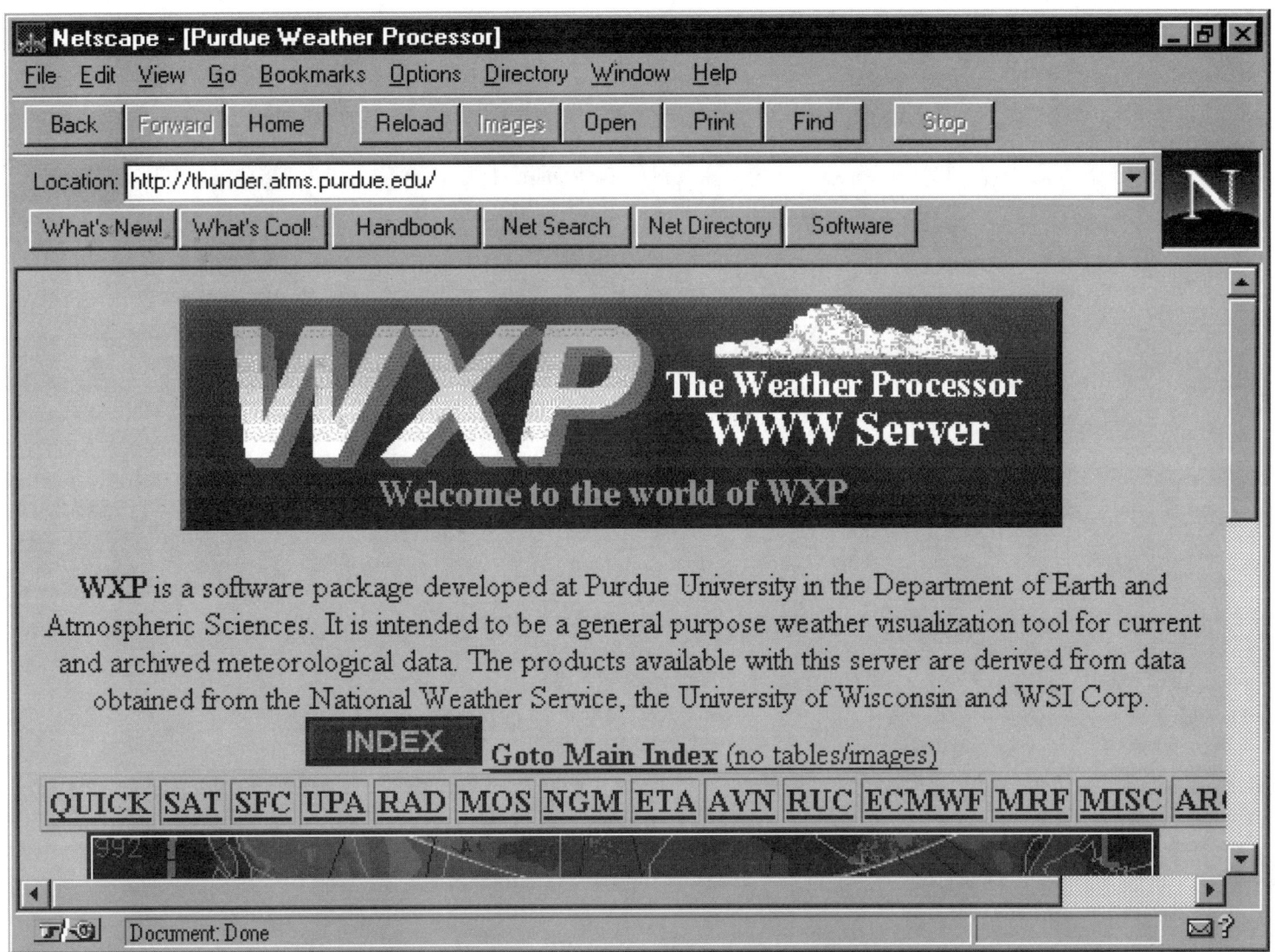

THOMAS: Legislative Information

URL: `http://thomas.loc.gov/`

The THOMAS site, as most people know, is named for Thomas Jefferson and is sponsored by the Library of Congress. It has rapidly become a wealthy repository of information of and about United States legislation. This site offers not only current information about the activities of the United States Congress, but also very interesting background on the legislative process. In addition, full-text files of legislation and the *Congressional Record* are available. You can also search this immense fund of information. This is a clean, well-organized site. All legislation submitted to the Executive branch, either passed or vetoed, can also be viewed.

Key Feature

THOMAS: Legislative Information on the Internet provides full and searchable text of U.S. legislation in a timely fashion. The site is well organized with clear navigational aids throughout. One can easily choose Bills, the Congressional Record, Congressional Advisory Board Reports, The Legislative Process, Legislative Branch Internet Sites, and U.S. Government Internet Resources.

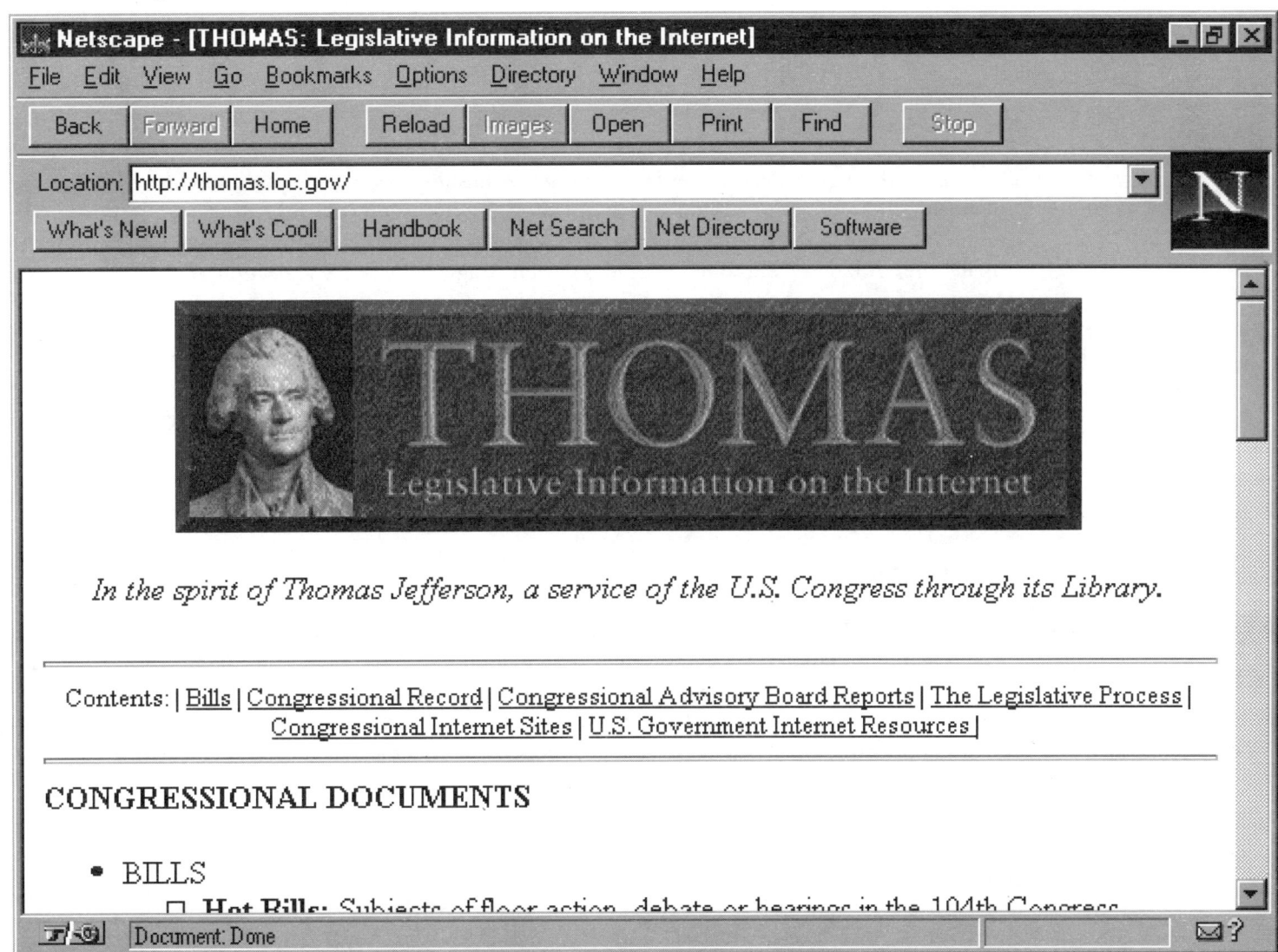

USA Today

URL: http://www.usatoday.com

USA Today, the national newspaper from Gannett Publishing, offers a daily edition on the Web. All of the features from the print edition are presented on this lively and colorful set of pages, but there is more. This is one of the few places on the Web where lottery players can find winning lottery numbers for all states. Another "Web-only" feature is Cyberlistings, USA Today's selection of interesting places to be found today on the Internet.

Not only are online sites described, but there is also a listing of who will appear on the major online services' chat rooms. This includes America Online, Microsoft Network, and Prodigy.

The regular format of the print edition is followed: News, Sports, Life, Money, and Weather. This gives the site an easy familiarity for those who read the print edition. The graphics, while colorful and appealing, are small enough to load quickly. In a recent edition, the masthead was a GIF under 30,000 bytes and the lead photo was a JPEG under 10,000 bytes.

Key Feature

USA Today has done an excellent job of putting a national U.S. newspaper right on the World Wide Web. Their information is kept exceedingly current and timely, and they even advise visitors to the site to "click reload often for latest version." The colorful graphics are interesting to view and change frequently. In addition, they make it easy for visitors to have access to Top News and also to Search for news or stories that are of interest to them. Good navigational tools make it easy to move through this site quickly and efficiently.

The Wall Street Journal Interactive Edition

URL: `http://interactive3.wsj.com/home.html`

The Wall Street Journal provides the Wall Street Journal Interactive Edition. There is a free registration requirement. Once registered, visitors are shown the familiar "What's News" column from the print edition of the *Wall Street Journal*. Additionally, highlights of business and market news are available.

In keeping with the worldwide nature of the Web, this edition of the *Wall Street Journal* offers news not only from the large and small markets in the United States, but also from markets in the Americas, Europe, and Asia. This feature gives investors a unique spot on the Web to track the rest of the financial world outside the United States.

The "Heard on the Street" column, commodities, foreign exchange, credit markets, and mutual funds are also highlighted.

Key Feature

The Wall Street Journal Interactive Edition provides up-to-date global market and investment information. The information is timely, informative, and quite detailed.

Pitfalls and Fixes

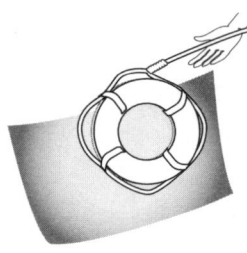

Pitfall: The visitor registration issue, requiring visitors to remember account names and passwords, reappears here.

Fix: As we will see in Chapter 8, there are other ways to elicit information from visitors to a site. Some of them are less cumbersome than the registration process.

Summary

We have seen a number of excellent sites in this chapter that do an outstanding job of presenting current and timely information. Clearly, many of them have made a strong commitment of time, energy, and financial resources toward making this happen. The sites we have visited are among the best in being current and timely. Viewers are showing an increasing interest in companies and organizations that provide all of us, no matter where on the globe we might be, with current, timely, and accurate information, about the weather, news, theater listings, sports, or traffic. One can only imagine what the future will bring!

Chapter

6

KEY 4:

Easy to Find and Use

Introduction to Key 4—Easy to Find and Use

This chapter focuses on those Web sites that are both **easy to find and easy to use.** In a World Wide Web that is increasing rapidly in size with every passing day, it is imperative that sites be found quickly and easily and that they can be used by viewers with little or no additional information. It is important that domain names (if at all possible) be obvious and easy—ones such as `www.ibm.com` or `www.fedex.com` or `www.compaq.com` are so obvious that you almost can guess them without being told. Netscape browsers will now be able to convert simple names in the .com domain to full URLs. If your easy-to-find name is Wimbat Corp., typing wimbat will translate to `http://www.wimbat.com` in Netscape.

In addition, it is imperative that your Web site address be integrated into all of your existing documentation as well as your publicity and advertising channels. Including your Web site address on all your business cards, brochures, fax forms, mailings, letterhead, and business cards will help your regular customers learn about your new mode of communication. In addition, there may be opportunities for you and some of your business partners to do referrals to each other's Web sites.

Having a Web site is a good beginning, but it is not nearly enough. As you will see later in this chapter, there are sites whose sole mission in life is to provide you with quick and easy ways to register your Web site with a whole array of locations on the World Wide Web. You want information about your site to be *everywhere*; in particular, it must be where your potential customers are likely to look. And most importantly, it must be where they are likely to look when they don't already know who you are and what your line of business is really all about.

For example, when the wife of one of the authors recently wanted to purchase a particular type of hair brush (a Mason Pearson hair brush), we were able to use a search engine (`www.excite.com`) to quickly find that Arnette's in Charlottesville, Virginia, sells these brushes. (It is interesting to note that this site is *not* particularly high tech in its use of the Internet; we were not able to order the brush online, nor were we able to fill in any sort of form. However, we were provided with the phone number, and two days after calling, the order arrived at our home in New York, many miles from Charlottesville, Virginia.)

Technical Points

The Internet's Domain Name System

With the explosion of commercial interest in the Web, domain names are becoming the jewels of the Web business. If your company or enterprise already has a commercial domain name, such as ibm.com or compaq.com, you are in luck. If not, you may want to register one as soon as possible.

Names are registered with a Network Information Center. For North America, this is known as internic.net.

The global Internet's domain-name system is called a "flat" name space which means that there can be only one "best.com" even though there are Best Cleaners, Best Pizzas, Best Car Repair, and so on. The example used earlier in the chapter of wimbat.com is still, at this writing, available.

How to Find If a Name Is Registered

The quickest way is to use a browser and point it at `http://www.internic.net`

When you arrive, click on Registration Services. This is a searchable form. We suggest that you enter a well-known name like `ibm.com` or `purdue.edu` to see the type of results you get. You might try entering `wimbat.com` to see if it is registered yet.

Then try some of the names you would like to use. You may find that many of the simpler forms of the name are already taken. By the way, the InterNIC now charges a fee ($100 per year at this writing) for a domain name. You should have some legal rights to the name such as a registered trade or service mark. Although it is not required, if your name should be challenged by someone else, this protection will prevent the InterNIC from "escrowing" the name while the parties sort it out.

Suggestions for Domain Names

Most commercial enterprises want to get a .com name, but there are many alternatives. Clearly `wimbat.com` is the easiest if you are Wimbat. You might consider, however, a geographic form:

`wimbat.sf.ca.us` if you are in San Francisco or

`wimbat.ch.il.us` if you are in Chicago

Another alternative is to lengthen the name a bit. For instance;

`wimbatcorp.com` or `wimbatsown.com` or `wimbatstuff.com`

If you are an educational institution you might try

`wimbat.edu or wimbat.k12`

If you are a not-for-profit organization you might try

`wimbat.org`

Outside of the United States, the geographic option is usually best. Then you could become

`wimbat.com.ca` in Canada or `wimbat.co.jp` in Japan.

Tricks to Think About

If the name is not that important, you might also just be an "account" at someone else's domain. For instance, if Wimbat just used an account at the Internet service provider `whosis.com`, it could become

`whosis.com/~wimbat`

where the tilde character (~) points to an account on `whosis.com`'s system.

How to Register a Domain Name

There are two basic ways to register a domain name after you are certain it has not previously been registered. The easiest is through an Internet service or presence provider. The second is to do it yourself.

1. Through an Internet Service Provider

With this option, the provider does all the work for you. There will be a charge, of course, but it is usually not more than a few hundred dollars. You will have to pay an annual fee in addition to the InterNIC charge, but the registration process is done for you.

2. Directly through the InterNIC

If you choose to do it yourself, go to the InterNIC Web page and find the "templates" section. Follow the instructions there and prepare the templates. You will need to know the Internet Protocol (IP) addresses of two (2) nameserver machines that will recognize your new domain name when it is registered. If providing this information is too complex for your site, use method 1.

Now, let's look now at a number of sites that are both easy to find and easy to use.

3M Innovation Network

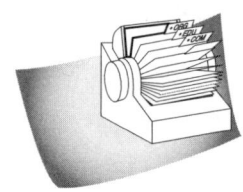

URL: `http://www.mmm.com/`

The 3M site is certainly easy to find and their home page is a model of clarity. Their address is intuitively obvious and the buttons across the top of the page are clear and easy to use. Their use of graphics is good and not overwhelming, and those visiting this site in text-only mode are able to access the same information that the buttons provide. Hyperlinks repeating all the information provided by the buttons are located further down on the page. In addition, lots of hyperlinks to other information are on this first page, all in a neat, clear format.

Key Feature

This site is easy to find as the name is intuitively obvious. There is lots of information about 3M and 3M products located only one click away from the home page.

Pitfalls and Fixes

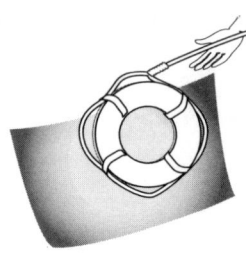

Pitfall: There is no text-only option provided on this screen.

Fix: The graphics are not overwhelming, but some viewers might prefer the text-only option.

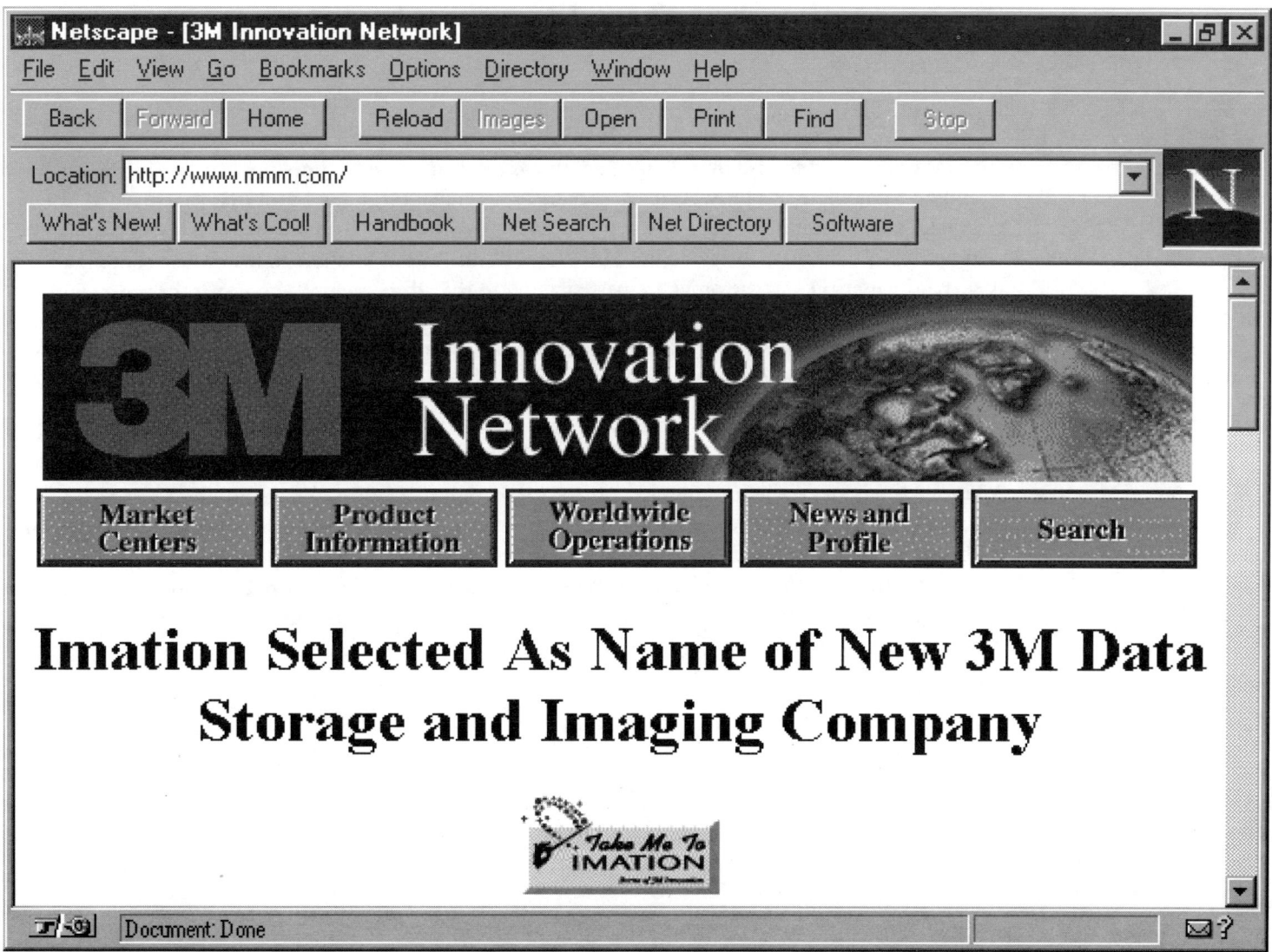

Courtesy of 3M

Amazon.com Books

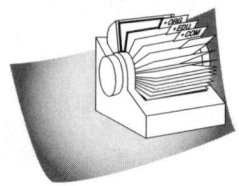

URL: `http://www.amazon.com`

This location is easy to find by anyone who knows the name of the company. A reasonably good guess would take you there instantly. And, once there, you will be intrigued by all that they have to offer— especially the one million book titles that are readily available. Each user is provided with a unique ID number when they enter the site. Should the user decide to put books into his or her "shopping basket," the user ID and the order are passed along to the amazon.com Web server for processing. Visitors to this site have a wonderfully easy time browsing for books, searching for the ones they desire, and ordering them. In addition, Amazon.com provides some useful services such as their personal notification service to its visitors.

Key Feature

Amazon.com is an excellent resource for those interested in acquiring books online. The site is extremely easy to find and remarkably simple to use. One can use their powerful search engine to look for books by author, title, subject, or keyword. In addition, they provide a personal notification service that alerts visitors to the particular book they have been awaiting is in stock. They also provide easy-to-use navigation throughout the site, enabling visitors to review their accounts, send E-mail to Amazon.com, or ask for help.

The American Stock Exchange

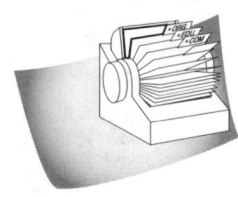

URL: http://www.amex.com/

The URL of this site is particularly easy to find by anyone who is aware that the American Stock exchange is often referred to as AMEX. Lots of information is packed into this home page through the skillful use of small graphics that download quickly. Viewers can quickly and easily obtain market summary information, news, a listing of AMEX companies, information about options and derivatives, as well as other information. Each of the choices is accessible by clicking on either the icons at the top of the page, or the text descriptions at the bottom.

Key Feature

The American Stock Exchange provides useful information about its member companies. The site is easy to locate and well organized.

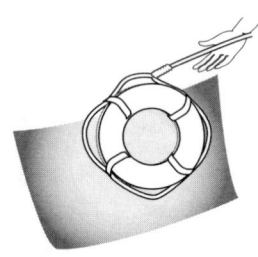

Pitfalls and Fixes

Pitfall: Although visitors might expect to get some current information on the day's market, this site is current only to the preceding day. Information is updated every business day at approximately 6 P.M. Eastern Standard Time.

Fix: Some current-day market information would be useful. We have already seen other sites on the Internet that provide stock market information as current as 15 minutes behind stock market activity. (The stock markets will not permit them to provide information that is more current than that.)

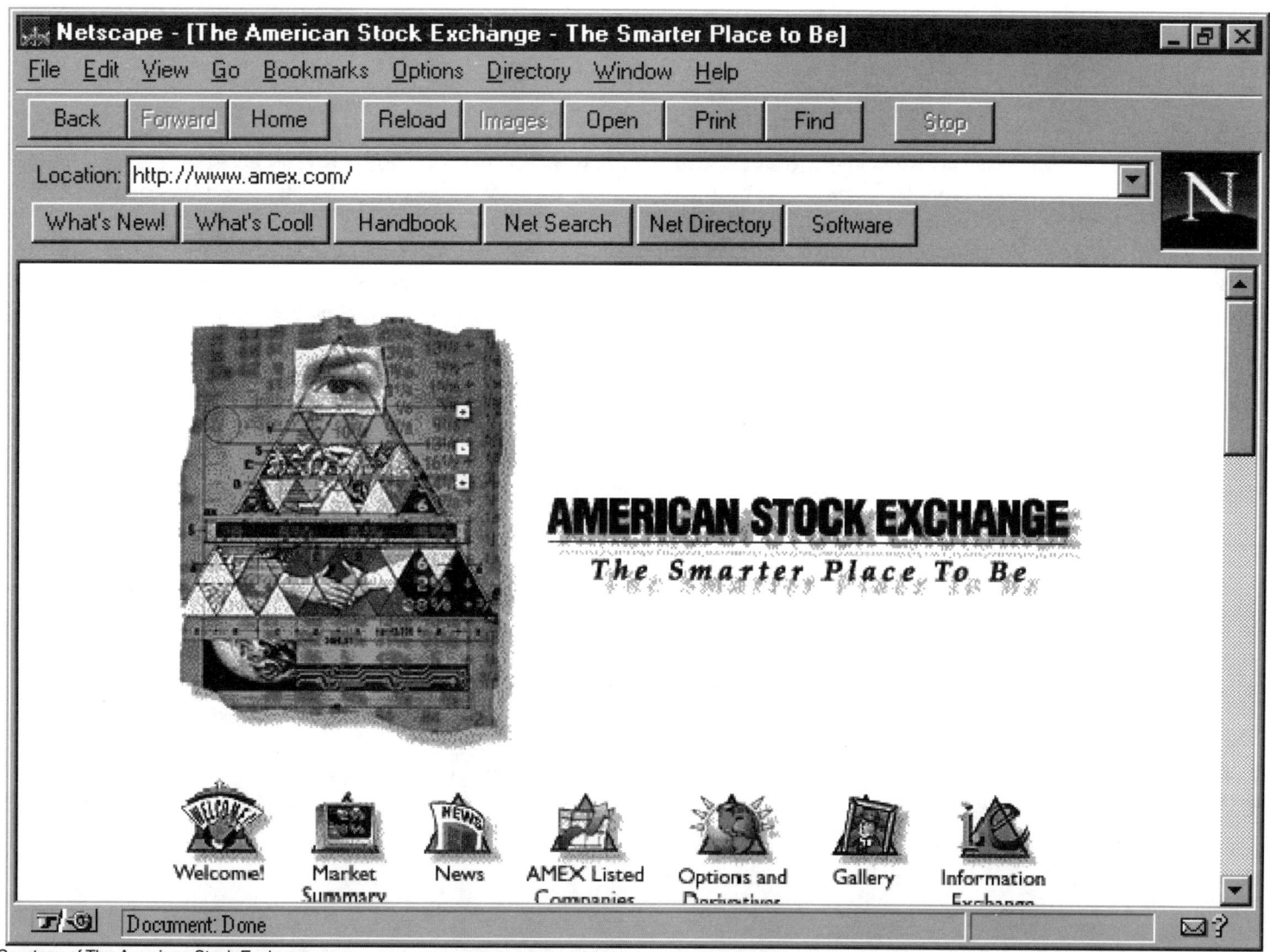

CareerPath.com

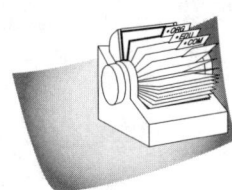

URL: `http://www.careerpath.com`

CareerPath.com is a great concept, executed well. CareerPath.com provides newspaper employment ads from six major cities (Boston, Chicago, Los Angeles, New York, San Jose, and Washington, D.C.) in one easy-to-find and easy-to-use location. Visitors to this site must register once in order to view all the ads that are included. The registration process is quick, simple, and efficient, and viewers are told clearly that CareerPath.com has no interest in selling any products and will not sell registrants' names. Those who have registered can quickly and easily search the employment database by newspaper, job category, and keyword. In addition, visitors can choose to learn more information about the six participating newspapers and can also go directly to their Web sites.

Key Feature

CareerPath.com provides an outstanding example of the power of the Internet and the World Wide Web. Easily located, filled with information, and amazingly simple to use, this site is a great example for others to emulate.

Pitfalls and Fixes

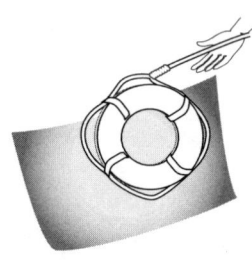

Pitfall: This is a free registration site, which again means that visitors may have to remember yet another user ID and password.

Fix: CareerPath.com does offer examples prior to registration and, their registration process is easy and immediate.

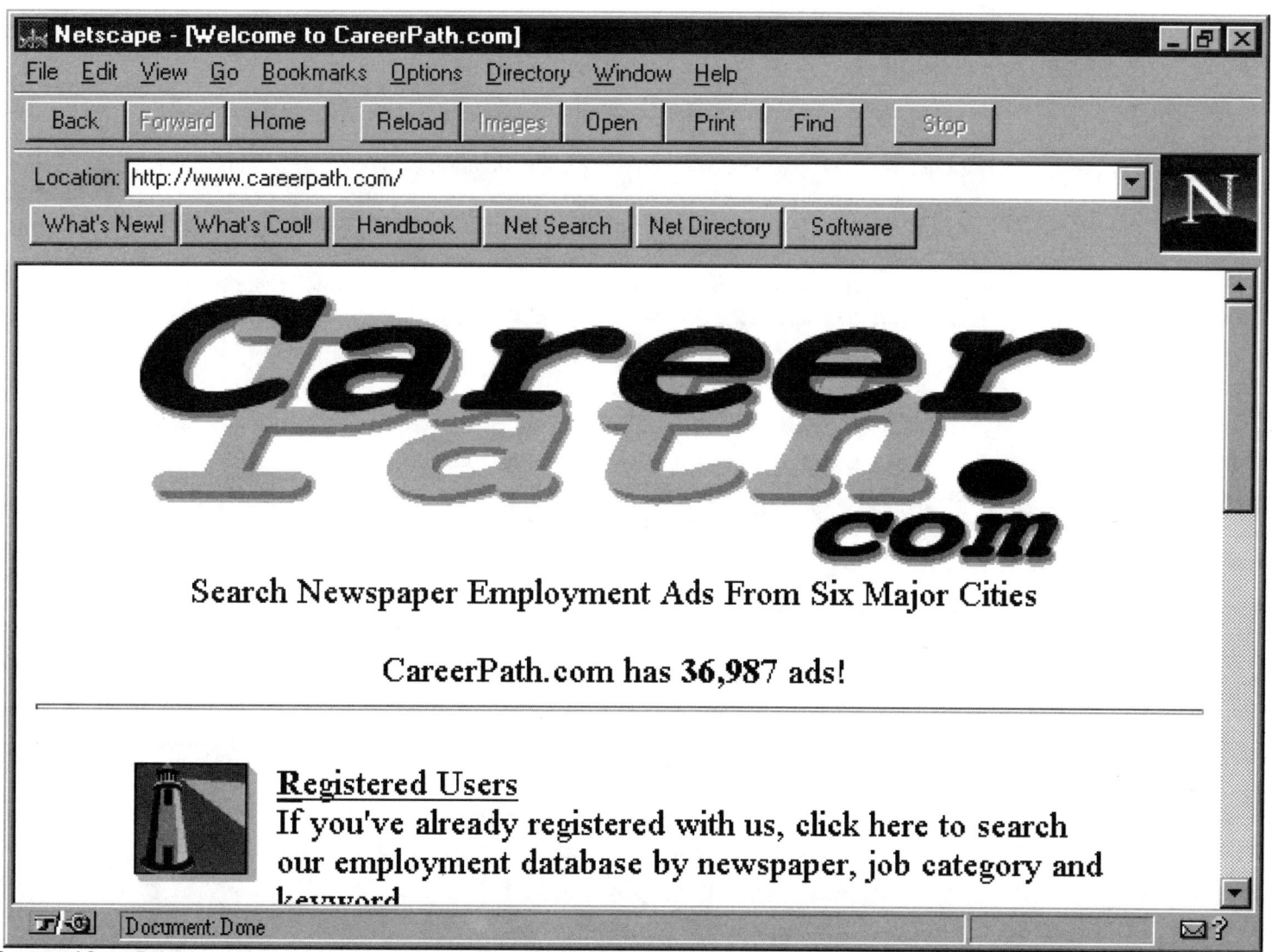

Compaq Computer Corporation

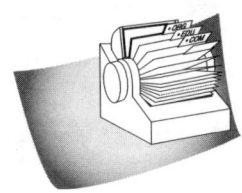

URL: `http://www.compaq.com`

The URL for the Compaq Computer Corporation could not be simpler to find or use. Once you arrive at the Compaq Home Page, you are presented with a colorful array of choices, each of which is reasonably obvious. And, for those who choose not to download graphics, it is quick and simple to make the same selections without using the bit-mapped graphic image. Below the initial image, six options are presented with text hyperlinks; the information is the same as that provided by the graphics, but the graphics are gone. And, should these initial selections not be sufficient, there are also the Search, Contents, and Help buttons located at the bottom of the Compaq Online Home Page.

Key Feature

The Compaq site is easy to find and quite simple to use. The graphics are quite well done but may be ignored by those who have neither the time nor the patience to wait while they arrive. Navigation throughout the site is well organized, and easy to use.

Pitfalls and Fixes

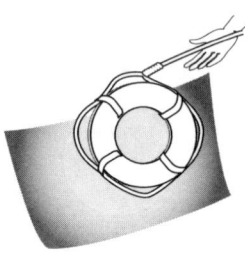

Pitfall: The initial Compaq Home Page (`www.compaq.com`) does have a large image map graphics file on it. Once there, viewers can choose if they want to continue with or without the graphics;

Fix: As we saw earlier with sites such as Classroom Connect, it might be useful to offer visitors that choice before a large graphics file had been downloaded.

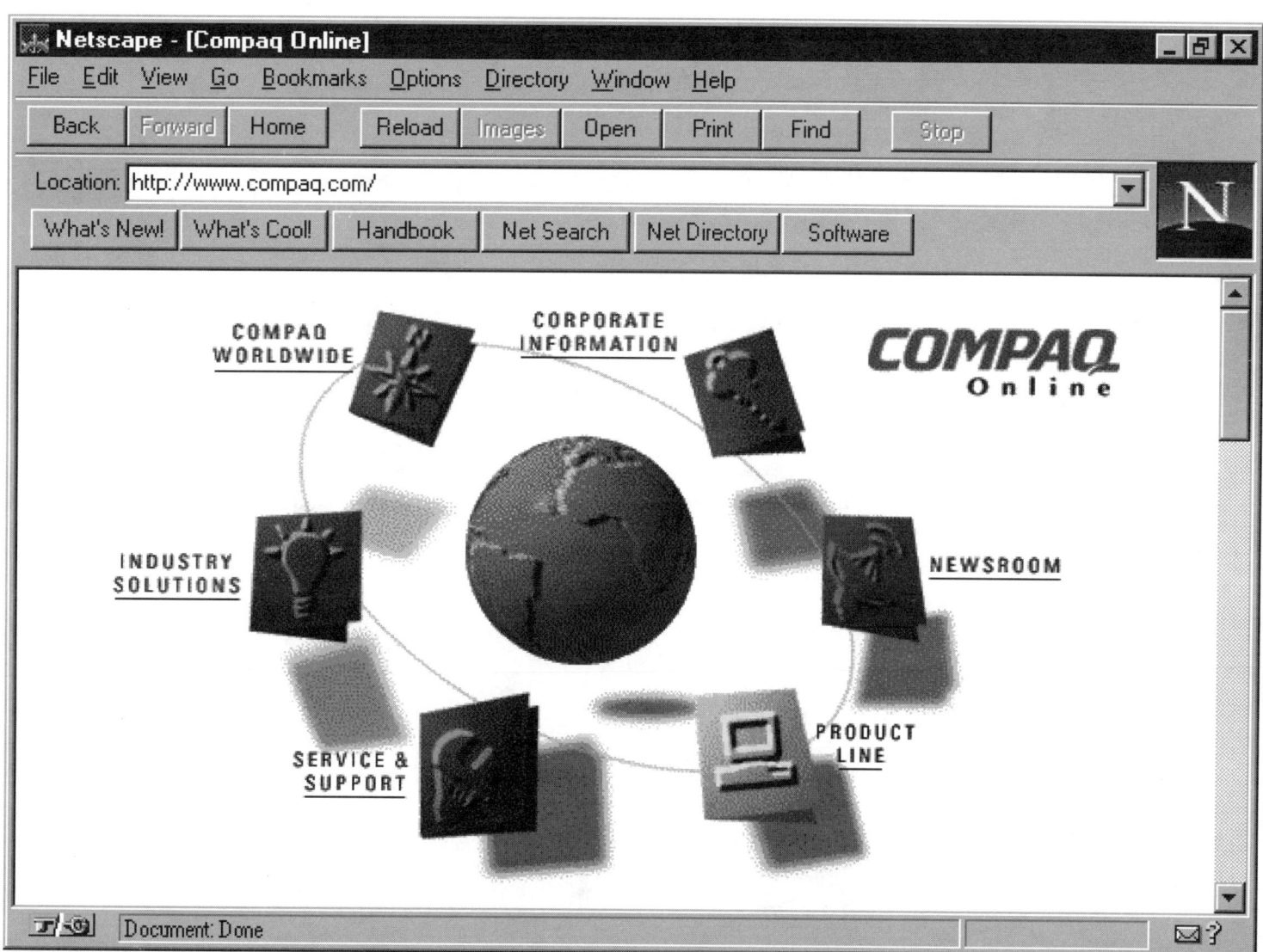

Courtesy of Compaq Computer Corporation

Eastman Kodak Company

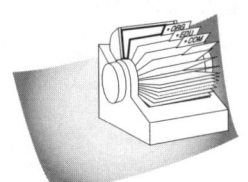

URL: `http://www.kodak.com`

The Eastman Kodak Company site is a good example of a site that is easy to find and to use. The name (`www.kodak.com`) is obvious; the graphic, although large at 49,000 bytes, is attractive; and the information for all the buttons on the graphic is repeated immediately below with text hyperlinks in the same order and with the same keywords as the graphic buttons (other sites, take note!) In addition, there is an ever-changing Kodak Link Of The Week providing new and interesting information to viewers. One is immediately made aware of the fact that the Kodak site is being kept up-to-date; the Last Update information is always current, and the Kodak Link Of The Week changes each week.

Key Feature

The Kodak Web site is easy to find, easy to use, and potentially useful to those who visit. Of particular note is the fact that their graphics are interesting to view, yet download quickly and do not overwhelm their viewers.

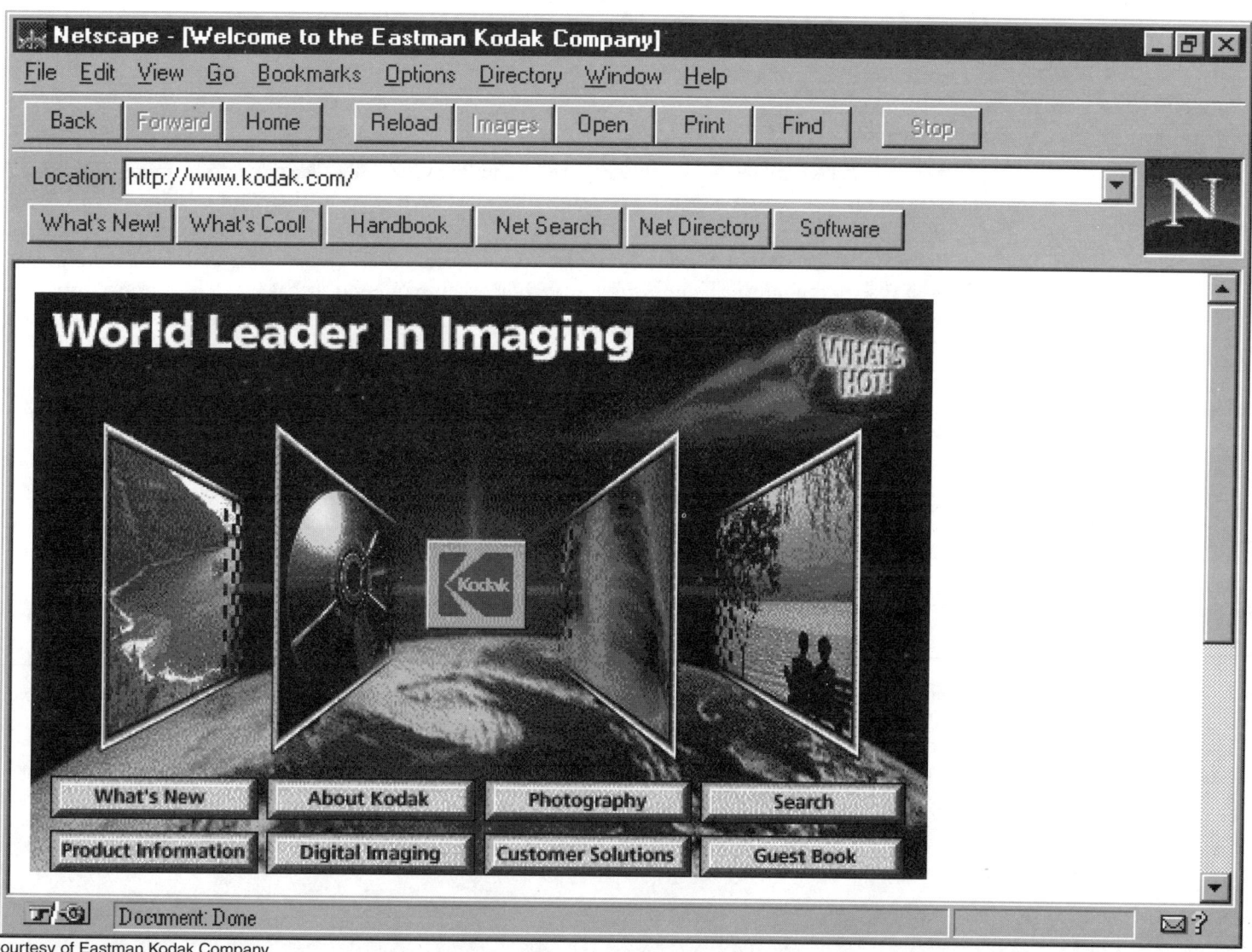

Excite Netsearch

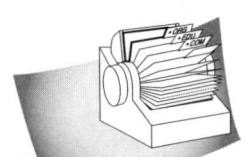

URL: http://www.excite.com

The Excite search engine is remarkably easy to find and wonderfully easy to use. The folks at Architext Software claim they have the largest full-text database of Web pages with an index that contains more than 11.5 million pages which is refreshed weekly. Whether this is true would be hard for a viewer to determine. What is more important, however, is how quickly this search engine does its searching, and how well it seems to return the information that has been requested. It has been the authors' experience that Excite does its searches in record time, and more often than not, finds exactly what has been requested.

Key Feature

The Excite search engine is extremely easy to find and very easy to use. Architext Software has provided us with a very powerful and useful Internet tool. In addition, Excite provides reviews of over 50,000 Web sites, as well as access to more than one million articles from 10,000 Usenet newsgroups. Most recently, they have added an Advanced Query Language that enables visitors to fine-tune their Web searches.

Pitfalls and Fixes

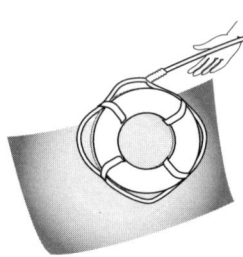

Pitfall: It is important to use caution when searching Usenet newsgroups. There is lots of potentially offensive information to be found there.

Fix: Parents should be careful when children and others who might be easily offended use this particular resource for Usenet searches.

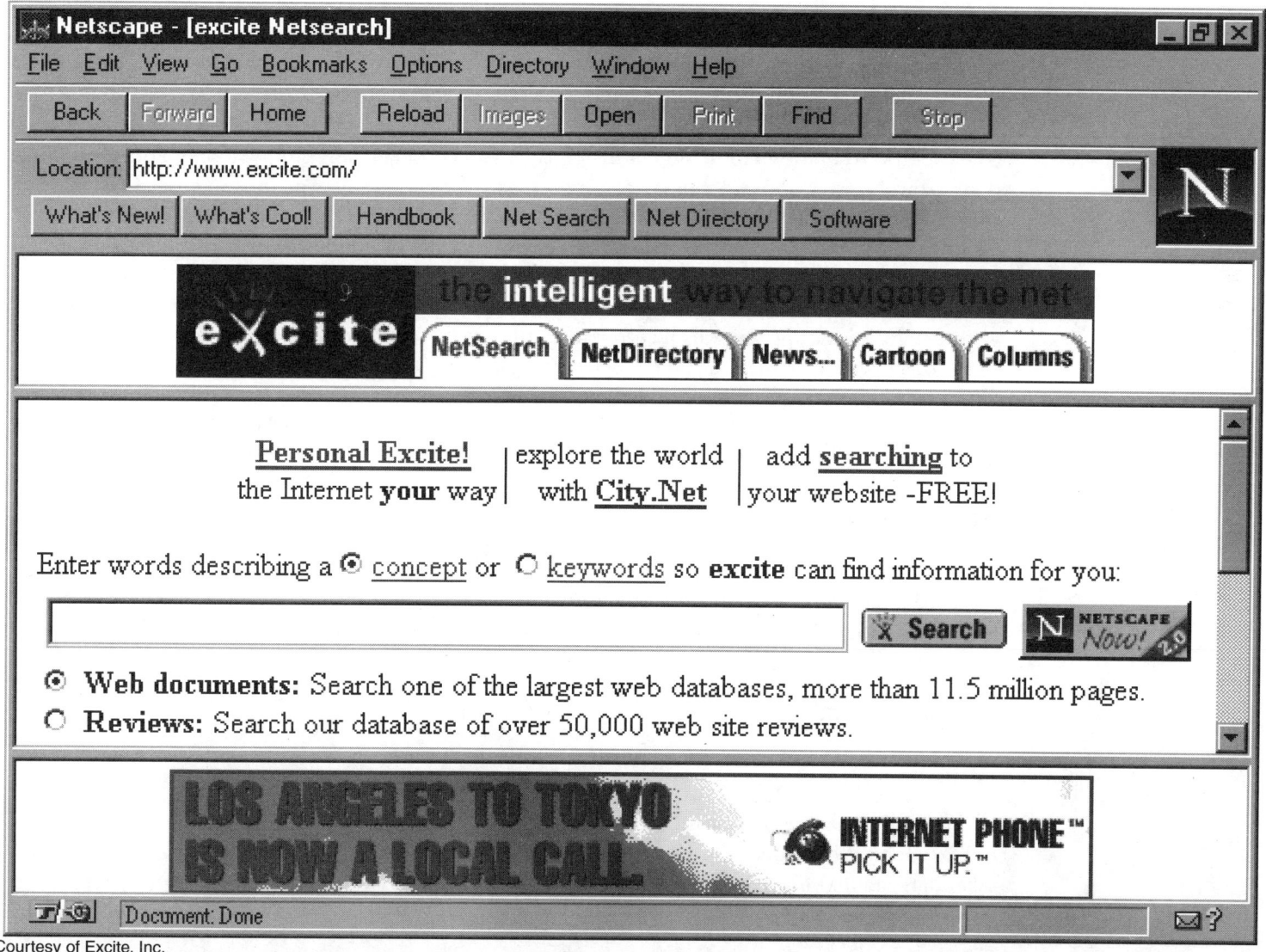

Mobil Corporation Home Page

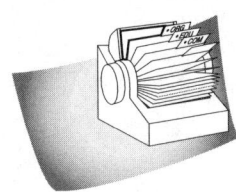

URL: http://www.mobil.com

The Mobil Corporation Home Page is extremely easy to find and very simple to use. Four hyperlinks (Company, News & Views, Products & Services, and Special) are all explained in great detail so viewers know exactly what they are about to choose. In addition to the opportunity to apply for a Mobil credit card, viewers are provided with two interesting selections—the Shareholder Service Center and "Dear U.S. Congress...." The Shareholder Service Center is a clever idea that is not typically provided on corporate home pages, yet once you see it, it seems like such a good idea that you wonder why it is not present on all corporate home pages. What a terrific way to provide stockholders (and others) with information about stock earnings, forecasts, stock price history, and dividends. "Dear U.S. Congress...." provides viewers with pertinent information that will let them quickly convey their thoughts about impending legislation affecting racing, petrochemicals, or other issues to their congressional representatives.

Key Feature

The Mobil Corporation Home Page does a particularly good job of explaining the four icons that fill the screen. Short sentences in close proximity to the icons make it easy for viewers to know exactly what choice they are about to select.

Pitfalls and Fixes

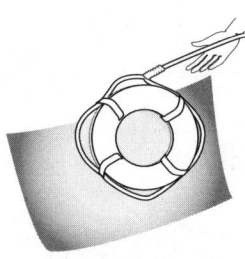

Pitfall: The explanatory sentences that explain each icon appear on the screen in a random order.

Fix: It would be better if the sentences appeared in the order (left to right and top to bottom) in which our eyes look at the icons (Company, News & Views, Products & Services, Special) rather than in the seemingly random order they presently have. This is clearly not a big deal and is obviously easy to remedy. And, most importantly, this does not detract much from an otherwise extremely well-done page.

Mountain Travel*Sobek

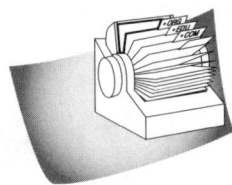

URL: `http://www.mtsobek.com`

Mountain Travel*Sobek is very easy to find, very easy to use, and very interesting. One might expect to find an adventure company using the Internet and the World Wide Web in some interesting and unexpected ways, and they do. One can learn a lot about the various trips offered by Mountain Travel*Sobek, including particular itineraries and their costs. Even more interesting is TerraQuest, the series of Virtual Expeditions being provided by Mountain Travel*Sobek. Virtual Expeditions are designed to allow anyone in the world to log in and follow the expedition in progress, using video, QuickTime VR, digital stills, and live chats. The first one, Virtual Antarctica, took place in December, 1995.

Key Feature

The Mountain Travel*Sobek site is somewhat easy to locate if you can remember the abbreviation. More importantly, it is an engrossing experience for the viewer. The image map contains a wealth of information, all presented in a clear and readable fashion. We know where to click for the information we might want, and are told enough to be able to anticipate what we will find. In addition, text hyper-links at the bottom of the page enable visitors to go quickly to many of the same locations that are listed on the bit-mapped graphic. However, it is hard to imagine anyone enjoying much about this site if they don't have graphics capabilities! Navigation throughout this site is particularly well done. Each page contains consistent links to Adventures, Hot News, The Palace, About Us, Reservations, Site Map, and Home, and the particular location where one presently is located is highlighted.

Pitfalls and Fixes

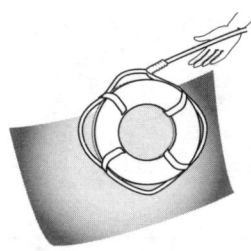

Pitfall: The initial graphic for the Mountain Travel*Sobek Home Page is 89,000 bytes. Although it is interesting to look at and very beautiful, it does take a long time to download, even over a high-speed modem. This might be somewhat of a deterrent to those who are interested in the (primarily text) information that is provided by this site.

Fix: Offer a text option near the top of the page.

Courtesy of Mountain Travel*Sobek and Green Room Productions

Pointers To Pointers

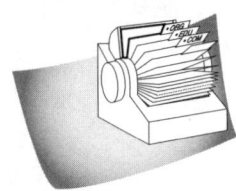

URL: `http://www.homecom.com/global/pointers.html`

This is one of the two sites featured in this chapter that will help you make *your* site easy to find and use. It is fair to say that the URL of Pointers to Pointers is not intuitively (or even remotely) obvious. However, the importance of this site cannot be overstated. Pointers To Pointers is a service provided by HomeCom Communications to help users learn where to go on the Internet to advertise their sites. Once you fill in the form that is provided, you can then submit information about your page or pages to the many Web sites, newsgroups, and mailing lists that are listed.

Key Feature

Pointers To Pointers is a very important and very useful resource for those wishing to make their sites better known to others on the Internet. The service is easy to use, powerful, and free.

Pitfalls and Fixes

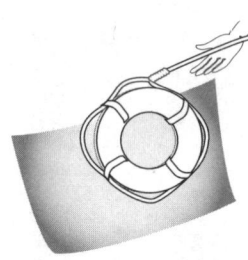

Pitfall: The URL for this location is not intuitively obvious.

Fix: It would be more useful if the site and its address were easier to locate.

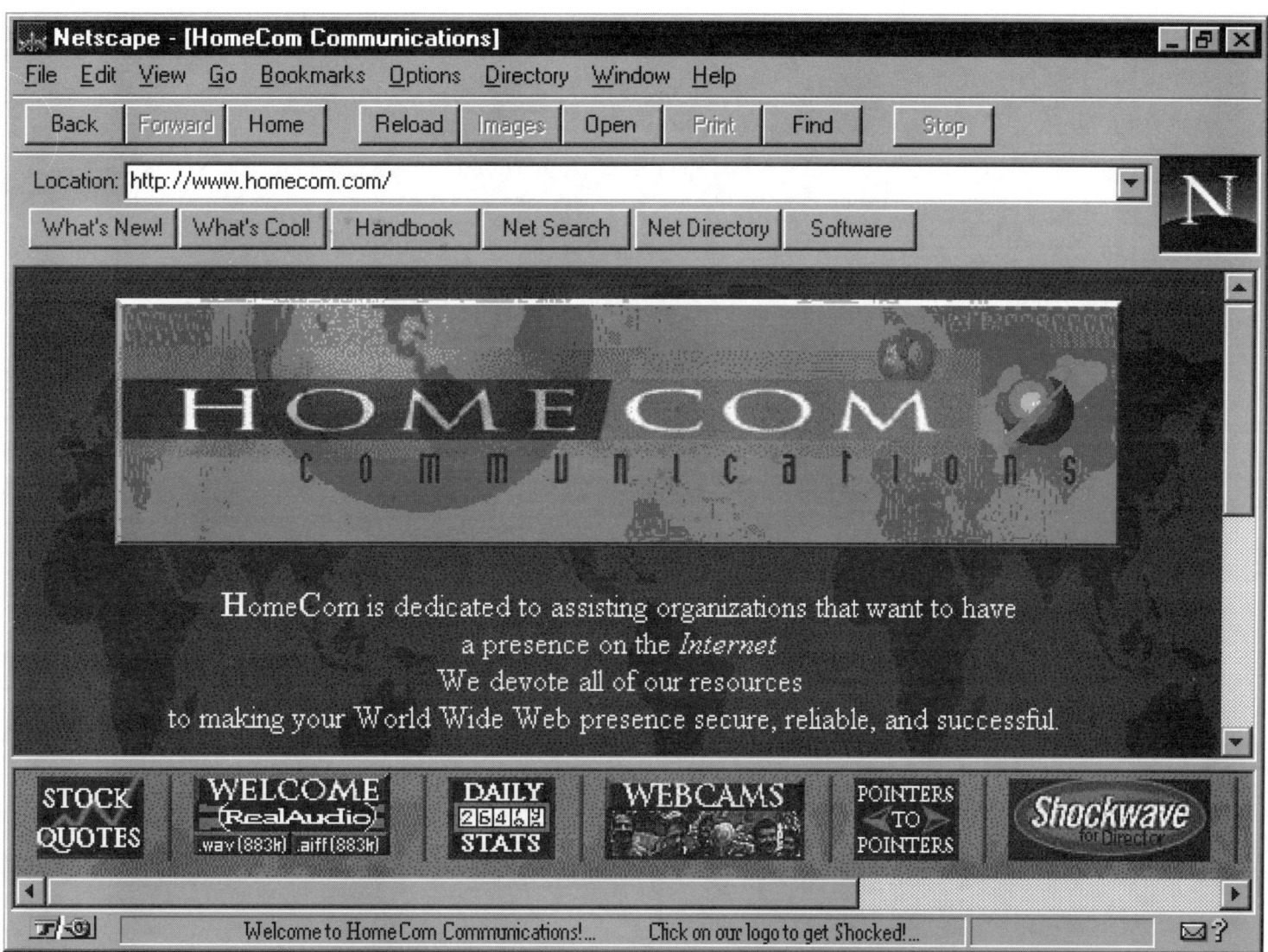

Courtesy of HomeCom Communications

Schwab Online

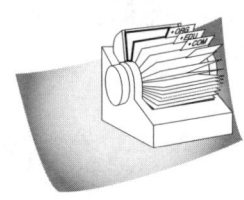

URL: `http://www.schwab.com`

Schwab Online is easy to find and presents information in a quick and easy fashion. Viewers can choose from among the six buttons that are offered with the initial graphic (What's New, Software Center, Mutual Funds, Investor Tools, Accounts & Services, and Contacting Schwab) or from the same six choices plus Fixed Income and Help that are offered as text hyperlinks below. The Schwab Online Home Page loads quickly (although it is a large image map) and the information is presented clearly.

Key Feature

Schwab Online has done a good job of focusing on their primary objective: helping investors help themselves. They provide an excellent array of "Investor Tools" and other resources that should be of use to those wishing to invest in the stock market more profitably.

Pitfalls and Fixes

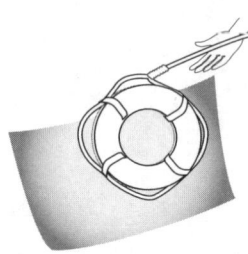

Pitfall: Another large (49,000 bytes) main graphic without a text option.

Fix: As with many other sites, a text-only or a reduced-graphics option would be useful.

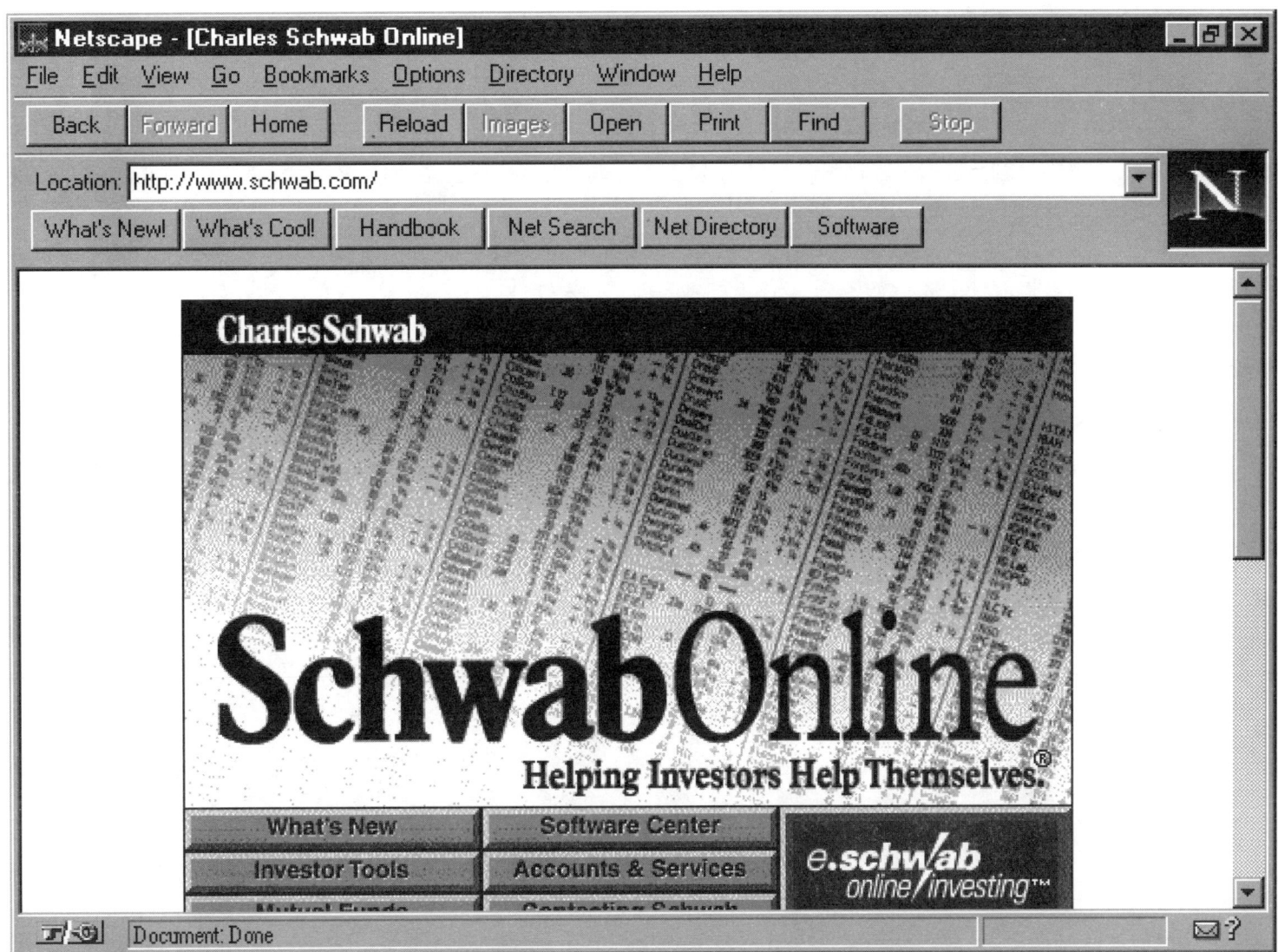

Courtesy of Charles Schwab & Co.

Shareware.com

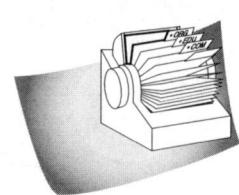

URL: http://www.shareware.com

Shareware.com, provided by c|net, is a very valuable resource that is easy to find and quite easy to use. With its database of over 210,000 (!) software files, it is also a very important resource for computer users. The home page loads quickly, and the descriptions of their services are presently crisply and clearly. This is a searchable archive of freeware and shareware, including fixes, patches, and upgrades.

Key Feature

Shareware.com is an extremely valuable resource of freeware and shareware software. It is very easy to find and very easy (and powerful) to use. They use good clear navigational aids throughout the site. Six choices (About, Subscribe, Search, Browse, Registry, and Help) are repeated at the top of each location, making navigation a snap. In addition, the search engine enables viewers to quickly find the software for which they are searching.

Pitfalls and Fixes

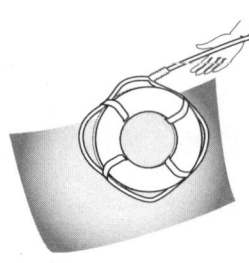

Pitfall: This site makes extensive use of "frames" which are not yet widely accepted by older browsers.

Fix: Fortunately, they offer several options for those using current browsers and older browser software that might not be able to use of frames.

Siemens in the USA

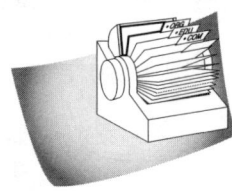

URL: http://www.siemens.com

The Siemens site is easy to find and quite simple to use. The URL is obvious, the graphics load quickly, and the four buttons provided in the bit-mapped image (Siemens USA, Press Gallery, Milestones, and Training) are explained in greater detail and mirrored with text hyperlinks in the first paragraph. Notice also that a reduced graphics version is offered immediately in an obvious location. An interactive quiz is provided, as well as an array of information about "What's New @ Siemens." This site succeeds in providing information about Siemens quickly and efficiently.

Key Feature

The Siemens site is intuitive, presents information clearly, and immediately offers viewers a reduced graphics version. It is extremely easy to find and to use this site.

Pitfalls and Fixes

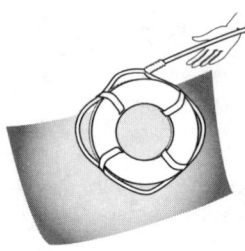

Pitfall: The main graphic is well over 100,000 bytes and presents some changing views. Once it has been downloaded, the viewer is offered the reduced graphics version option.

Fix: One option might be to send the reduced graphic first and offer the larger graphic for faster connections. Or, one could do as Classroom Connect has done with their initial screen: offer a quickly loading file and then provide viewers with two choices.

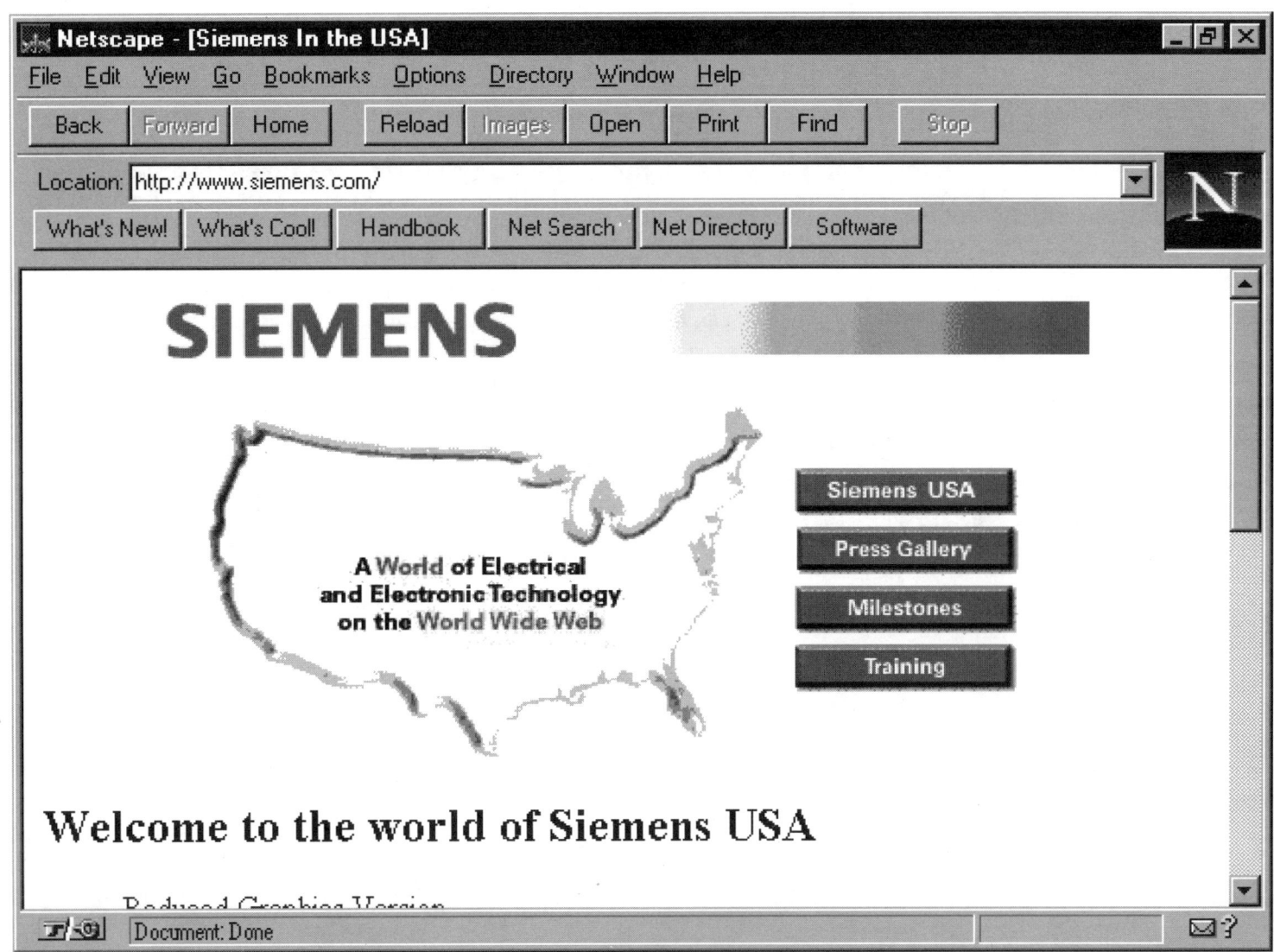

Submit It!

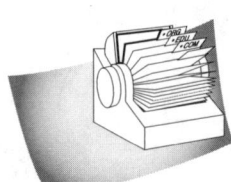

URL: http://www.submit-it.com/

Submit It! is a fabulous resource, particularly for those who want their Web sites to be easily found. Like Pointers to Pointers, this is a service that has been designed to make the process of submitting your URLs to a variety of World Wide Web search engines and directories faster and easier (and free!). You can register with 15 different search engines and directories, including Yahoo!, WebCrawler, Starting Point, Lycos, InfoSeek, Galaxy, Harvest, and others. The submission form is easy to fill out, and the whole process is simple. In addition, Submit It! now includes Metasearch, which enables visitors to quickly and easily enter one set of keywords and then use the search engines provided by Yahoo!, WebCrawler, InfoSeek, Lycos, Open Text, TradeWave, and Alta Vista.

Pitfalls and Fixes

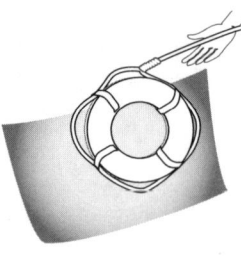

Pitfall: Submit It! is wonderfully easy to use and (almost) wonderfully easy to find. One tiny quibble would be with the hyphen in the URL. It is not intuitively obvious that a hyphen should be included.

Fix: If people were to hear about a great resource such as Submit It! they might have more luck finding it (in other words, guessing its URL) if the URL did not contain the hyphen. Not a big deal, but removing the hyphen from the URL would make this site easier to find.

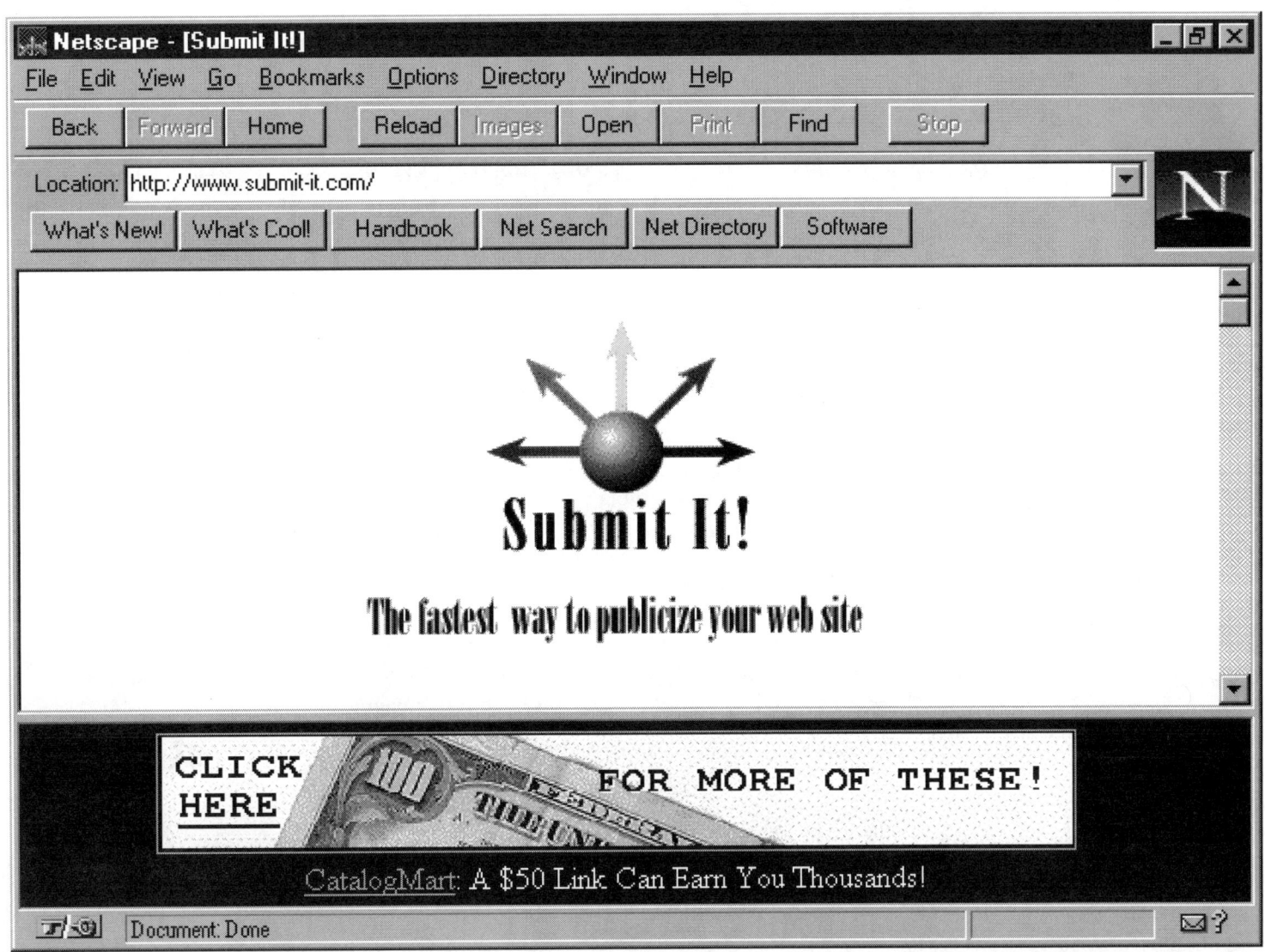

The Virtual Reference Desk

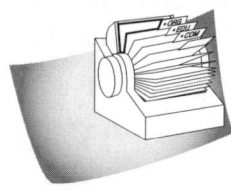

URL: `http://thorplus.lib.purdue.edu/reference/`

Although not intuitively easy to find, the Virtual Reference Desk is an amazing resource that is extremely easy to use and filled with an incredible set of resources. Provided by the Purdue University Libraries, this site should definitely be added to your set of hotlists or bookmarks. The Virtual Reference Desk is remarkably easy to use and does a wonderful job of demonstrating both the power of the Internet and the World Wide Web and its collaborative nature (notice where the many resources are located).

Key Feature

The Virtual Reference Desk is an extremely valuable resource providing an incredible set of information to all those using the Internet and the World Wide Web. This site contains pointers to Government Documents, Information Technology, Dictionaries, Phone Books, Maps, Science Data, as well as many, many, many other reference sources.

Pitfalls and Fixes

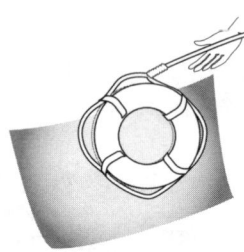

Pitfall: The URL for this location does include the word reference in it, although, unfortunately, there is nothing intuitively obvious or helpful about the URL in its entirety. However, once found, this is an invaluable resource. To find it would clearly require a search engine or a very clear set of directions!

Fix: This site is an example of an excellent resource that can be very hard to find. Changing the URL would make it far more accessible to many more people.

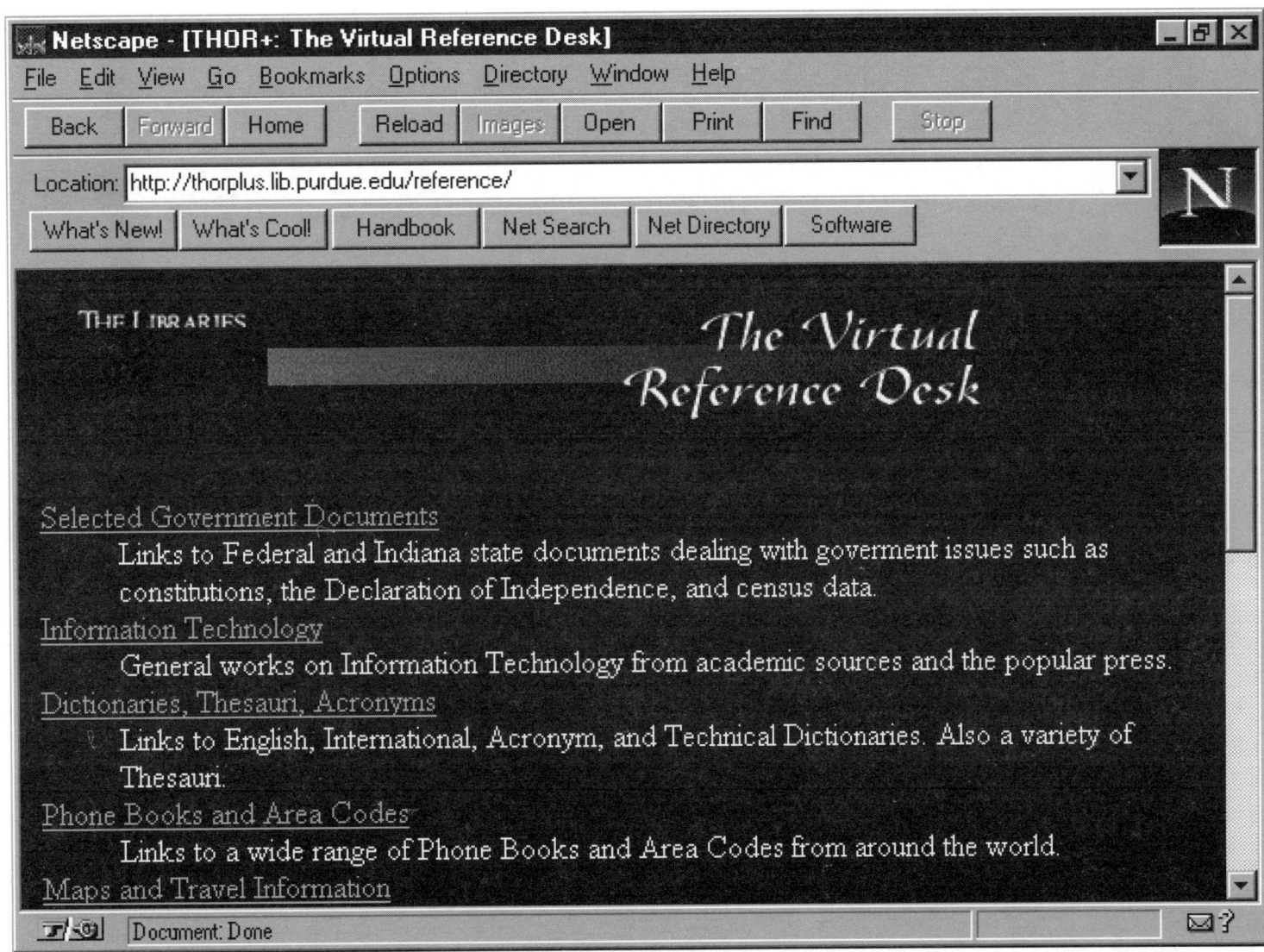

What's New?

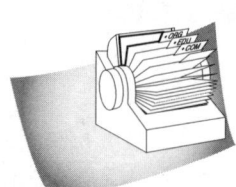

URL: `http://home.netscape.com/home/whats-new.html`

The Netscape What's New? site is extremely easy to find (just click the What's New! directory button on Netscape) and also easy to use. The list is updated frequently and presented in alphabetical order. The folks at Netscape do make it clear that they are not going to include all the new sites that are submitted to them; rather, they are going to present sites that are not only new to the Net but also ones that use or advance the technology of the Net in new ways. A more detailed What's New? listing can be found at What's New on Yahoo! (`http://www.yahoo.com/new/`) or on What's New With NCSA Mosaic (`http://www.ncsa.uiuc.edu/SDG/Software/Mosaic/Docs/whats-new.html`).

Key Feature

Netscape's What's New? page provides a quick and easy way to stay current with the Internet and the World Wide Web. It is accessible to all who use Netscape, and to others who wish to type in the URL.

Pitfalls and Fixes

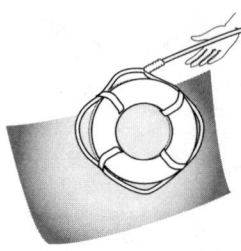

Pitfall: One possible pitfall has to do with the selection process that is used here. Clearly, not all new sites are going to appear here, and it may be that the choices of sites that are new to the Net and that use or advance the technology of the Net may exclude sites you would prefer to see.

Fix: An easy remedy for this is to look at the What's New sites that are provided by Yahoo! or NCSA Mosaic.

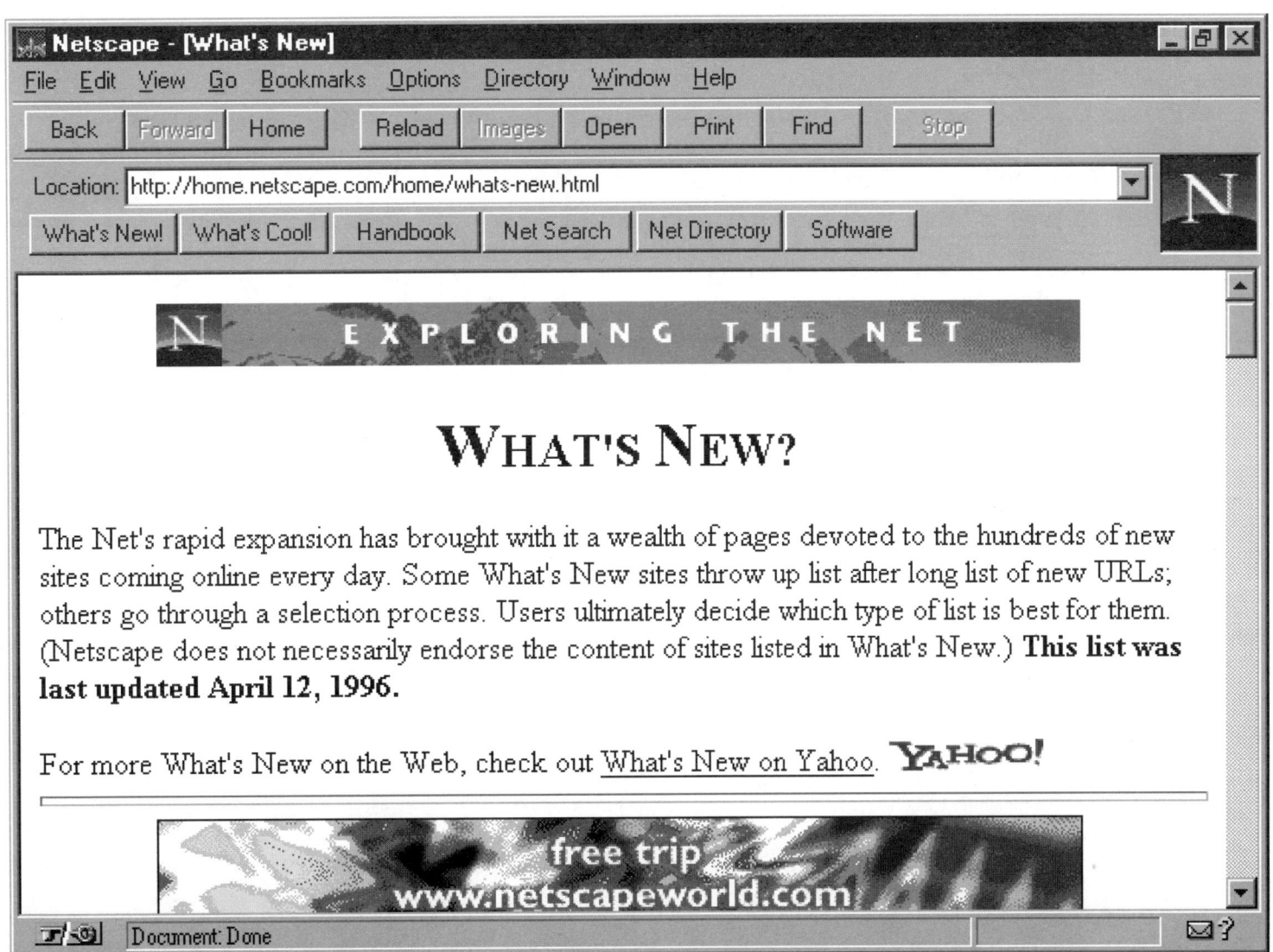

EXPLORING THE NET

WHAT'S NEW?

The Net's rapid expansion has brought with it a wealth of pages devoted to the hundreds of new sites coming online every day. Some What's New sites throw up list after long list of new URLs; others go through a selection process. Users ultimately decide which type of list is best for them. (Netscape does not necessarily endorse the content of sites listed in What's New.) **This list was last updated April 12, 1996.**

For more What's New on the Web, check out What's New on Yahoo. **YAHOO!**

free trip
www.netscapeworld.com

Summary

We have looked at a number of sites in this chapter that are good examples of being easy to find and easy to use. (although a few of them could be a little bit easier to find!). The sites focus on their primary mission, they provide good navigational cues throughout, and many of them remember to offer viewers a text-only or more minimal graphics option. The power of these sites is impressive and their areas of expertise are quite broad. In addition, two of the sites (Pointers To Pointers and Submit It!) are working hard to make *your* site easier for others to find.

Chapter 7

KEY 5:
Intuitive
On-Page
Navigation

Introduction to Key 5—Intuitive On-Page Navigation

Key 5 provides us with an opportunity to think about intuitive on-page navigation on a Web site. We will look at a number of sites that have made it easy for their viewers to quickly and efficiently navigate through their Web site. Visitors can derive lots of information from a site visit as long as they always know where they are, where they might go next, and how to get back to where they began.

As you will see, different sites have adopted different models of navigation for their visitors. While there is no "right" answer, it is clear that each one of these, manages in a nonintrusive way to make it easy for a visitor to find the information they want, or the item they wish to order, quickly. Remember, your viewer is only "one mouse click away from leaving!"

Technical Points

Use of Navigational Icons

In a moment you will have a chance to see many differing methods of navigation used by the sites in this chapter. Almost all of them have clear navigational icons and the icons are nearly always self-describing. However, be cautious not to assume that your icons are self-evident. There is a site we know that has a lovely graphic at the top of its home page. Almost all visitors miss the fact that the graphic represents a series of navigational icons. The icons are so pretty that the entire point of having them there has been missed! If it's navigational, make it very clear.

Use of Image Maps

Image maps are wonderful and colorful tools for navigation. Be sure, if you use image maps, that you have a default URL specified. Also, be sure your images have defined borders rather than fuzzy general areas. While having a default URL is wise, you don't want people ending up there too often. As more browsers support "client-side" image maps, consider using these as an alternative to traditional "server-side" image maps. More information about client-side images maps can be found in most HTML manuals. It is wise to always provide the folks with slow lines an alternative to image maps.

Alternatives for Navigation

Generally, you should always have text hyperlinks located near any image or icon links. While many people will use your colorful icons and maps, many will just admire them and go on to the more familiar text hyperlinks. Remember to use the same words or phrases for both images and text hyperlinks.

If the text hyperlinks are too far away from the maps or icons, visitors may not associate them with the same links that are presented on the image maps or icons. If it looks like a hyperlink, make it a hyperlink.

Remember to always use the IMG ALT parameter. The HTML IMG tag has an ALT parameter. Use it. And put meaningful text in the ALT tag. Don't leave someone guessing what [Photo] means.

Check Your HTML Source Files

All HTML editors now include syntax and style-checking facilities. We strongly recommend you use these frequently. All browsers interpret HTML differently; some are forgiving of errors, some are not. Another alternative is to use an HTML syntax and style program such as the Weblint site we showed in Chapter 4.

Test, Test, Test

Unless you have total control over the browsers your visitors will use, as may be the case of an in-company Intranet, test your site often. All Web sites should be tested regularly using at least the following browsers:

America Online's current browser

CompuServe's current Spry Mosaic

Lynx (the text-only browser)

Microsoft's Internet Explorer (earlier and current versions)

Mosaic (earlier and current versions)

Netscape (earlier and current versions)

Prodigy's current browser

You may also wish to test with some of the browsers that are used less frequently. You may get very interesting results with older versions of Mosaic, Netscape, and the other browsers.

As information service browsers from America Online and Prodigy are continuously updated for their users, it is usually safe to test with just the current browser.

By testing, we mean that you should try visiting your own site with as many of these browsers as possible. Do this personally if at all possible, so that you can get a first-hand impression of how your own handiwork appears to others. If not, be sure to get others whom you know and trust to do this testing for you. You will want to make sure that the colors, screen sizes, and download times all work well under a variety of conditions. Reviewing your site with a number of different browsers and a number of different access speeds may cause you to rethink some of your decisions about the size of graphics, the colors that you use, or the actual size of your initial screen.

Now, let's go look at some sites that do a particularly good job of handling the issue of intuitive on-page navigation.

Alta Vista

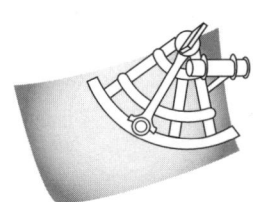

URL: `http://altavista.digital.com/`

The Alta Vista search engine site does a good job of providing navigational clues for its visitors. The graphics are pretty to look at, informative, and appear at the top of every page. The Alta Vista graphic always takes you back to the search engine's home page. The Help graphic provides good, clear help for simple queries. A good array of examples is provided, along with answers to frequently asked questions. Advanced Query provides assistance, as you might imagine, with more advanced search possibilities. And the Surprise graphic takes you to a selection of random locations on the World Wide Web. Doing a search with Alta Vista is remarkably simple and the two defaults, "Search the Web" and "Display the Results in Standard Form," are what most visitors will select most of the time. Searching could not be easier; just enter the word or phrase or terms that interest you and click on the Submit button!

Key Feature

The Alta Vista site exemplifies well how to provide a powerful searching capability quickly and effectively. The graphics are pretty to look at as well as functional and provide an easy way to acquire help. In addition, the graphics are small, so they load quickly from page to page. And, for those who would want to do so, there is a text-only option at the bottom of the Alta Vista: Main Page as well as all other pages. The number of options is kept small (you can choose to Search the Web or to Search Usenet; you can Display the Results in Standard Form, in Compact Form, or in Detailed Form) and context-sensitive help is provided about Simple Queries and Advanced Queries. The help screens are filled with lots of good examples, as well as some good advice about how Alta Vista indexes Web pages.

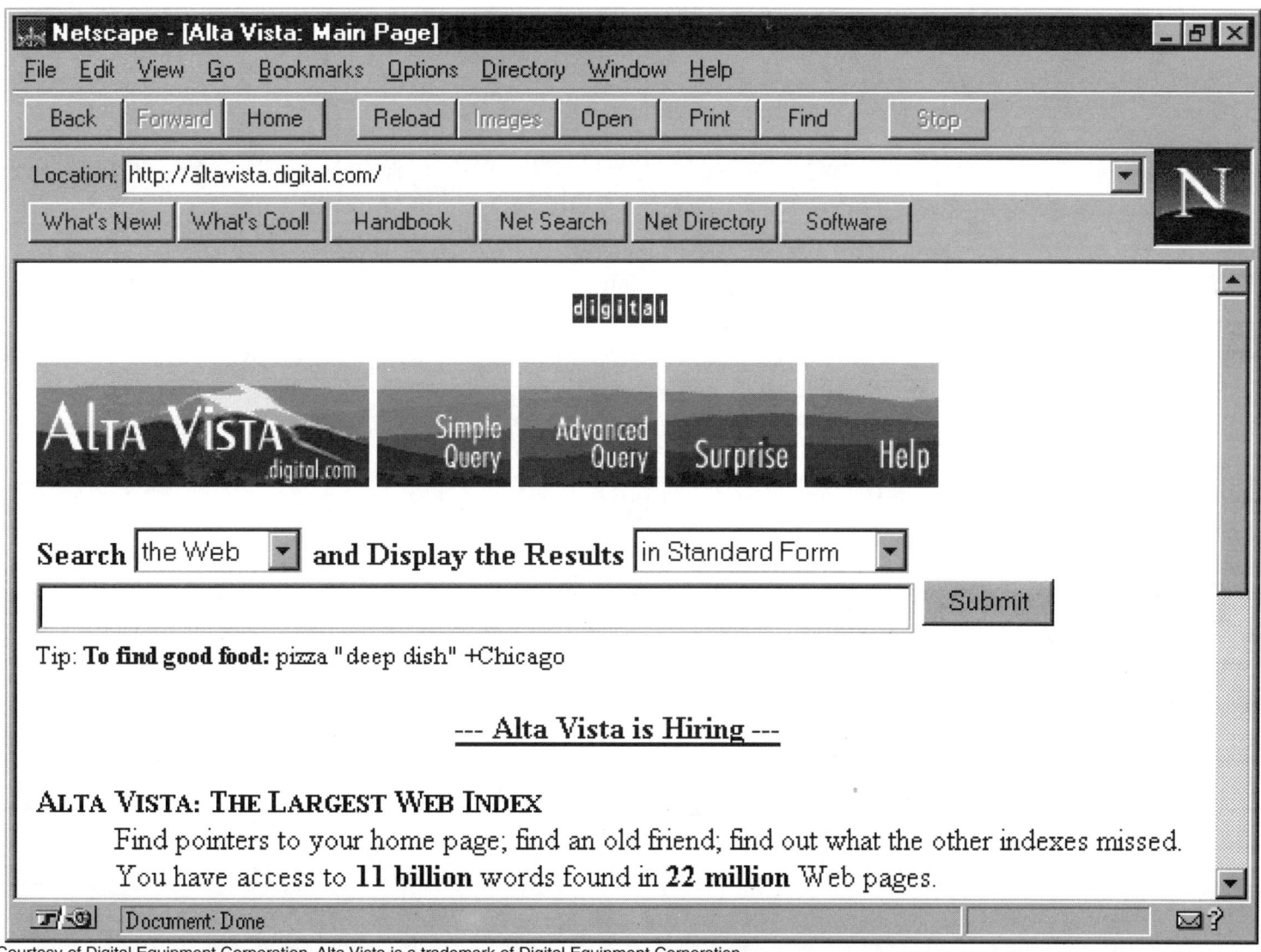

Better Business Bureau

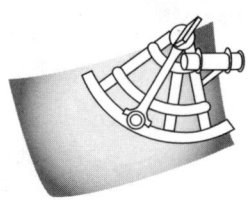

URL: `http://www.bbb.org/bbb`

This site is an excellent example of how to provide clear navigational clues to a visitor. Using the traditional metaphor of a rolodex card, the Better Business Bureau provides 12 possible directions for us to pursue, all in a neat, straightforward, easy-to-read format. The image map loads quickly, and the same 12 selections are reprinted below in the same order as text hyperlinks for those who might want to choose a text-only format. We know intuitively to click on one of the topics listed to proceed to one of the following pages.

When we make a selection, such as Index, the same set of original choices appears as an image map at the top of the Index page. This means that we can use not only the navigational tools of our browser (the back button, for example) but also the image map at the top of any of the pages on this site for navigation. In addition, when we arrive at a subsequent page, we are given a clear, alphabetized listing and a search box into which we can enter the keywords that are of interest to us.

Key Feature

The Better Business Bureau site is an outstanding example of how to make it possible for a visitor to quickly navigate to the information or resources that are desired. A simple color palette (red, blue, and black) and well-designed image map that is carried throughout the site make navigation a snap. In addition, the words on the image map are always divided by lines or bullets, so there is no question about where we should place our cursor before clicking. Nor is there any doubt about which selection we are about to make. If only other sites would be so attentive to such details!

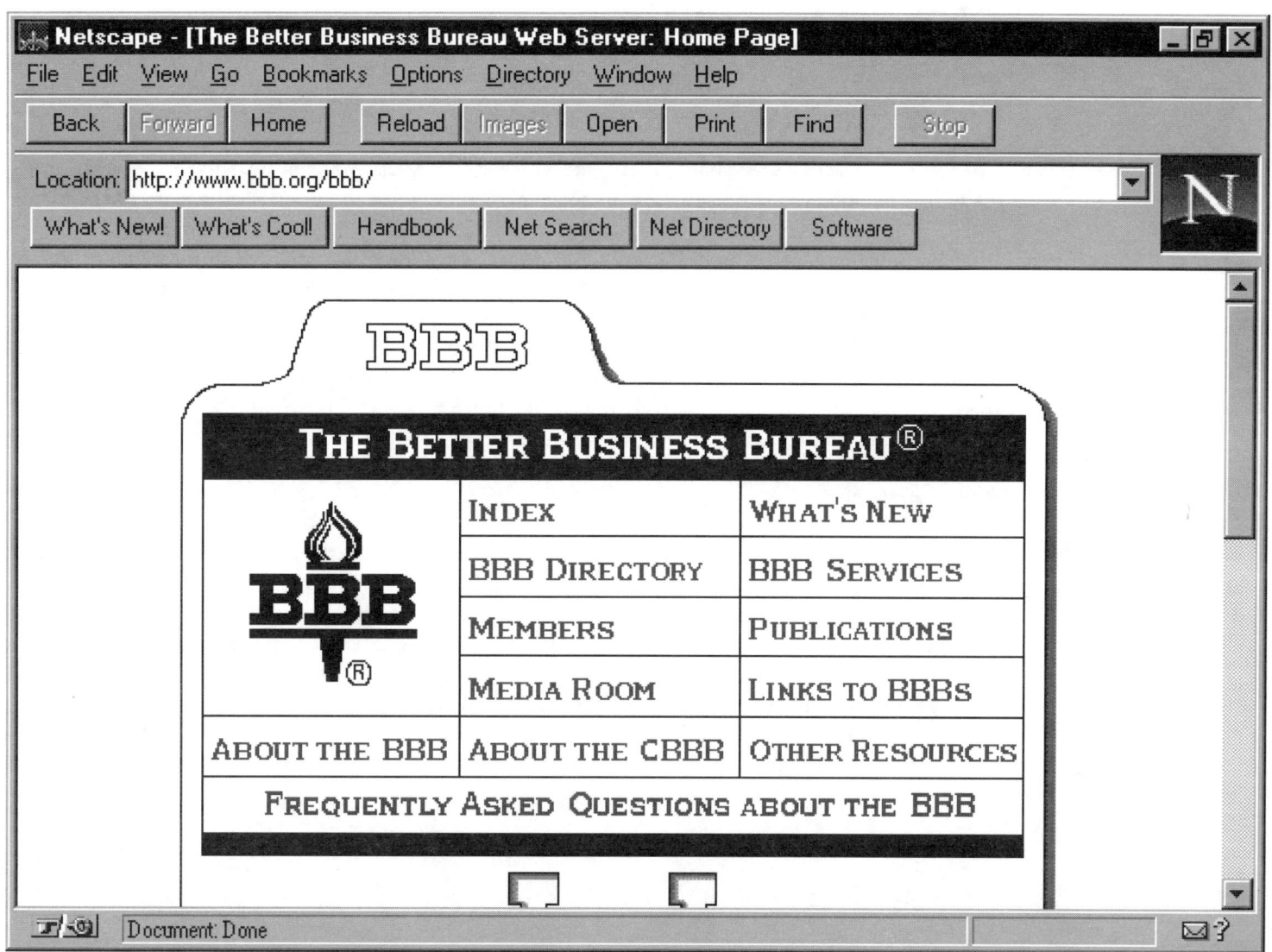

Courtesy of Council of Better Business Bureaus.

CNN Interactive

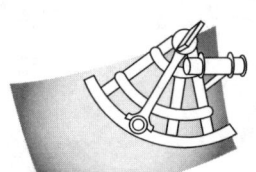

URL: `http://www.cnn.com`

The CNN Interactive site is both visually attractive and very easy to navigate. One can quickly and easily select among the ten major content areas that are provided. In addition, the main image map and the four buttons (Contents, Search, Welcome Page, and Help) are repeated with minor variations (they become Contents, Search, Back to CNN Home Page, Feedback, and Help) throughout the site. And, these five hyperlinks appear at both the top and bottom of each page. They are present, and useful, without being intrusive. It is also important to note that the viewer is quickly and clearly provided with a "Text-only version" option at the top of the initial CNN Interactive Home Page. Small graphics are included where appropriate, and there is an indication of the site's sponsors and links to them, but they appear rather discreetly toward the bottom of the home page. The site is updated frequently and that information is provided as well.

Key Feature

The CNN Interactive site is a good, quick way to stay current with the news. One can comfortably navigate through this site using its many helpful graphic and text options. The image maps are always divided into clear segments, leaving no doubt about where one should click for a desired option. The reader is provided with enough information about a given topic before making a choice to read the "Full Story." Convenient hyperlinks make that choice an easy one. This is an excellent example of a site that is both rich in content and extremely easy to navigate.

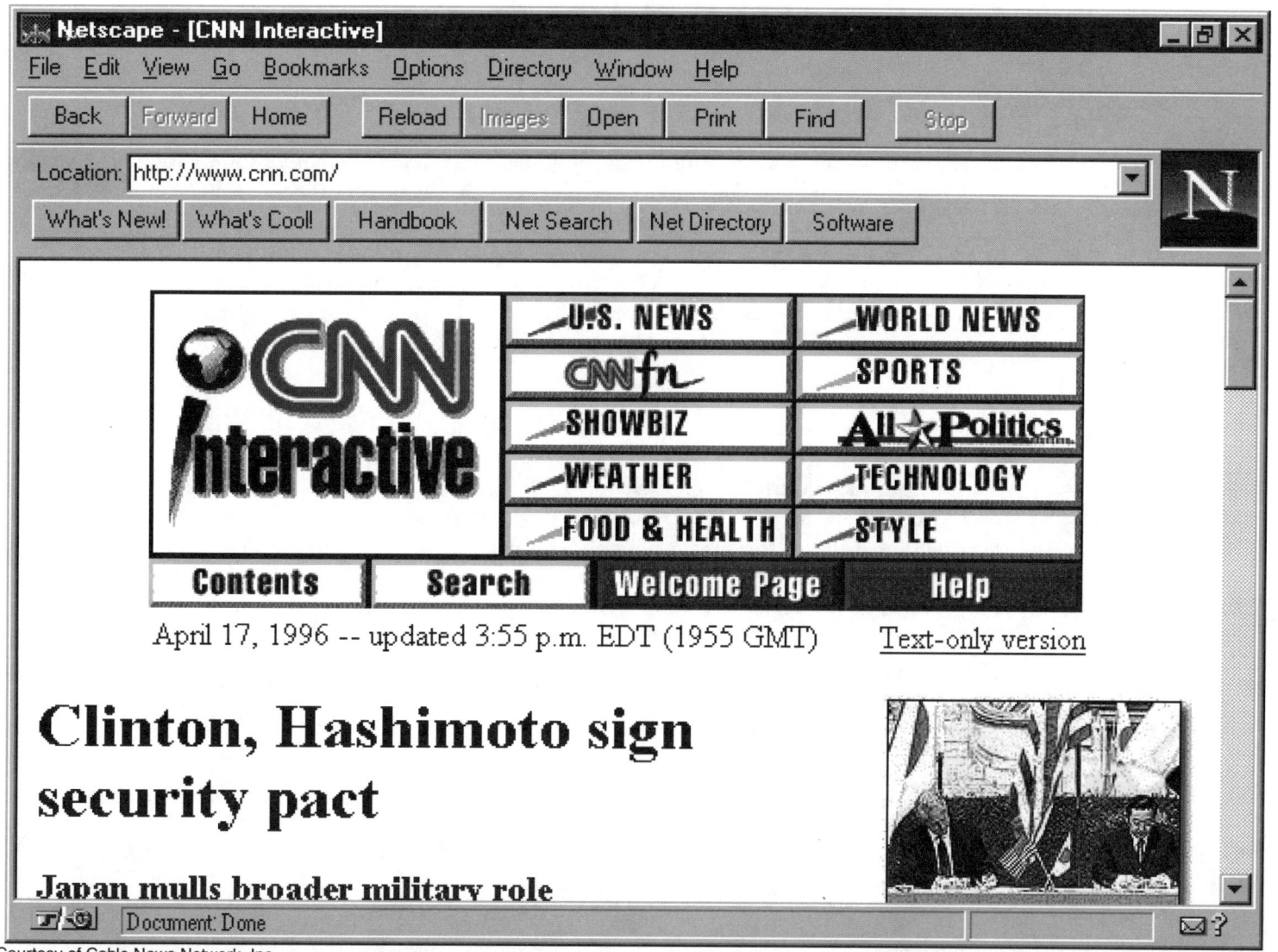

Continental Cablevision

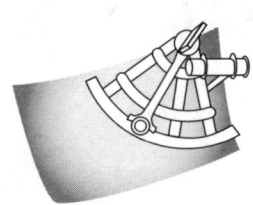

URL: `http://www.continental.com`

The Continental Cablevision Home Page simplifies their viewers' search for information or services. Each one of the nine selections on the initial image makes it easy for the visitor to learn more about the company and its services. In addition, each of the choices is explained briefly below the initial graphic. Once you select an item, you are always able to return easily to the Continental Cablevision Home Page by using the icons that are conveniently provided throughout the site. Since the site has been enhanced for those using Netscape, they have made it possible for a viewer who does not have a copy to acquire one. They have also thought about how to present their information in such a way that those without Netscape can still access it.

Key Feature

This site provides a wealth of information about Continental Cablevision and its services. It is extremely well organized and quite easy to navigate. They do an excellent job of providing clear, short explanations about the various options right on the home page, next to text hyperlinks. At the bottom of each page are a number of icons, to enable visitors to move quickly to the Continental Cablevision Home Page, their Interactive TV Listings (which are updated weekly), or to other pages.

Pitfalls and Fixes

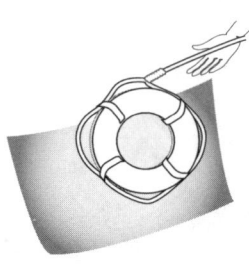

Pitfall: This site make heavy use of graphics. For those without graphics or for those with slow modems, the alternative navigational links are scattered down the page.

Fix: Repeat the text navigation links just under the graphic. Perhaps a text-only option should be offered.

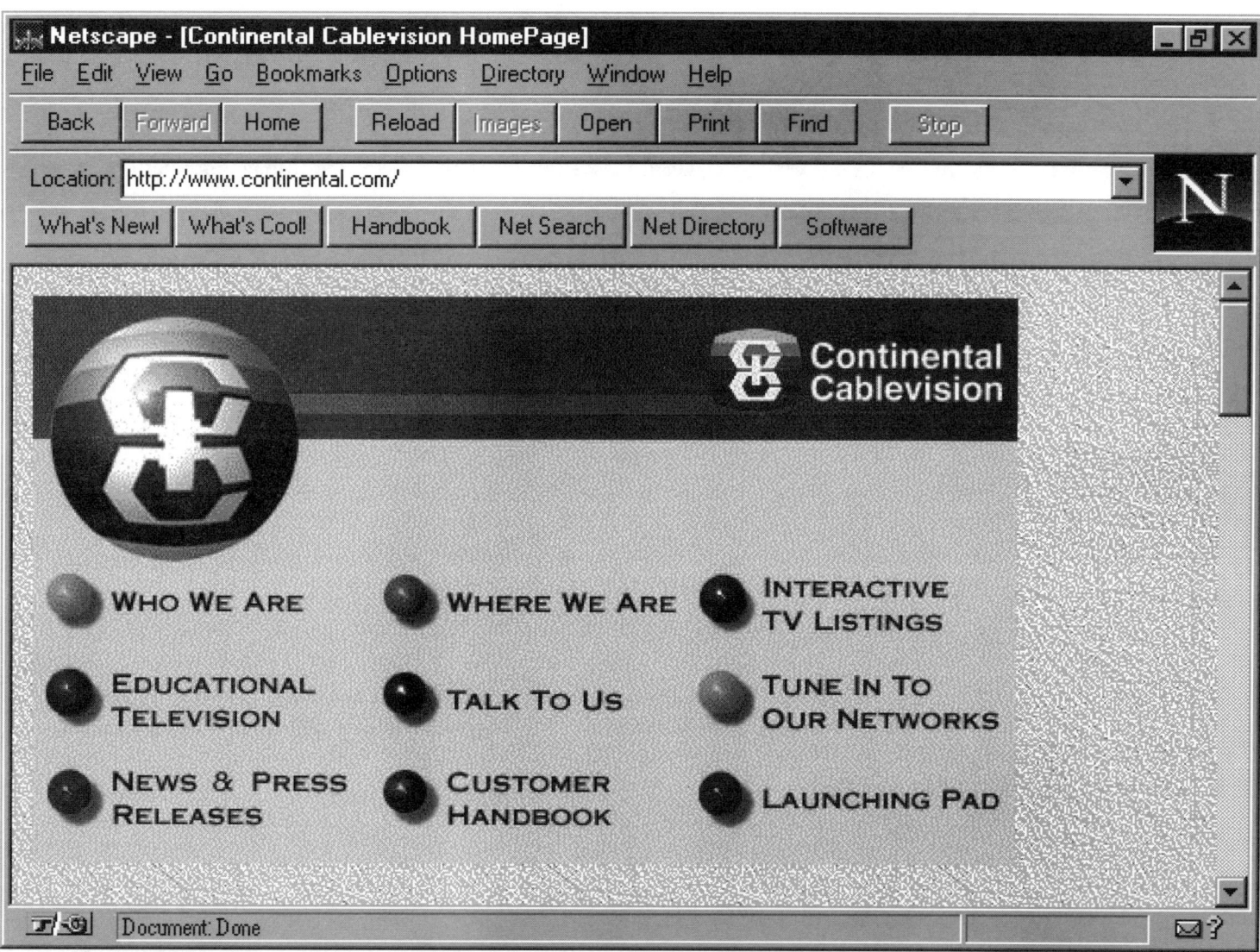

Courtesy of Continental Cablevision.

Discovery Channel Online

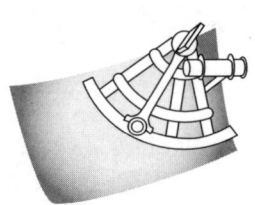

URL: `http://www.discovery.com`

Discovery Channel Online is a beautiful site filled with wonderful educational information. The site is extremely easy to navigate since the initial page of graphics also provides navigation throughout the site. Just click on Discovery World, Discovery On Air, or Discovery Tools, and you will be taken to that page. Discovery World lets you choose areas such as History, Nature, Science, People, Exploration, or Technology to explore. As they say, Discovery On Air "is the place for everything you'd ever want to know about the Discovery or Learning Channels." And Discovery Tools provides visitors with "all the navigational devices for getting around Discovery Channel Online and collecting what you want from the World Wide Web."

Key Feature

Discovery Channel Online provides a wealth of information designed to supplement its onscreen presence. The site is easy to navigate because it has clear text and graphics. The initial image is carried through to many of the following pages, even though the actual words and choices vary. It gives the site a good uniform look and feel.

Pitfalls and Fixes

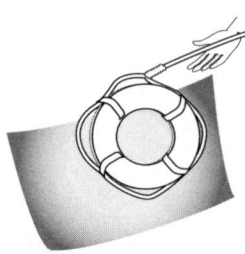

Pitfall: The use of graphics throughout this site is both the good news and the bad news. The graphics are substantial and quite beautiful. However, they load somewhat slowly over a dial-up connection, and there does not appear to be a text-only option provided.

Fix: It would be good to offer visitors a text-only option.

Courtesy of Discovery Communications, Inc.

The Internet Movie Database

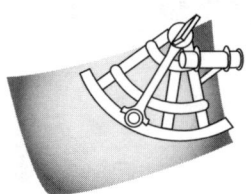

URL: `http://us.imdb.com/`

The Internet Movie Database is, as they say, "the most comprehensive free source of movie information on the Internet." The primary site for this file is the U.K., but it is also mirrored throughout the world in the U.K., Germany, Australia, and the eastern and western United States. Navigating is easy; visitors use either the small obvious icons, or the text hyperlinks right below the icons. You can search by movie title, cast/crew names, cast character names, quotes, plot summaries, soundtracks, or biographical data. All of this is done quickly and easily by using the hyperlinks found on the Internet Movie Database Search Forms page. By including the same set of icons at the top of each page at this site, as well as by making text options (Search, Help, and Index) readily available, they have made this site very useful and extremely easy to navigate.

Key Feature

The Internet Movie Database contains a very complete set of information about movies. Small, quickly loading graphics, complemented by clear, easy-to-use text icons, make this site extremely responsive to its users and wonderfully easy to navigate. The Search, Help, and Index text hyperlinks appear at the top and bottom of each screen, making it easy for viewers to always find what they want, when they want it.

Pitfalls and Fixes

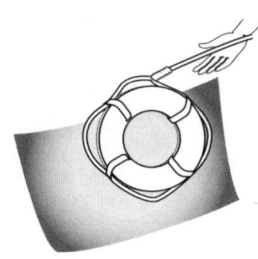

Pitfall: The one possible pitfall of this site that the site downloads slowly from its primary site in the U.K.

Fix: Fortunately, they have already remedied this with the mirrored sites in other parts of the world.

Internet Waterway Online

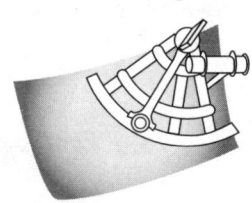

URL: http://www.iwol.com

The Internet Waterway is, according to its creators, "the newest and most innovative water sports site on the World Wide Web. We have created an ocean of information, dazzling pictures, and spectacular graphics for you to enjoy." The Internet Waterway Home Page begins with a beautiful graphic, below it are a number of hyperlinks to take visitors quickly and easily to their destinations. Clicking once on the Table of Contents hyperlink takes viewers to a page filled with navigational resources. Visitors can search for information alphabetically, categorically, by feature article, or alphabetically by author. This is extremely helpful, since this site contains a wealth of boat-related information such as a Marina Finder, Boat Finder, and a Dealer Finder, as well as lots of online images and other useful information for boating enthusiasts.

Key Feature

The Internet Waterway site is chock-full of extremely useful information for those interested in boats and boat-related activities. Navigation of the site is made easy by the well-developed Table Of Contents page and the built-in search capabilities. They have done a good job of carrying out a particular look and feel throughout the site; the image map at the top of most pages contains red boxes that provide clear choices and precise places where one should click. At the bottom of each page is a Home button.

Pitfalls and Fixes

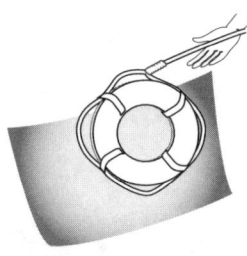

Pitfall: The hyperlink for the Table Of Contents navigational screen does not appear until the bottom of the Welcome to the Internet Waterway Home Page.

Fix: It would be more helpful if this hyperlink were to appear at the top of the home page.

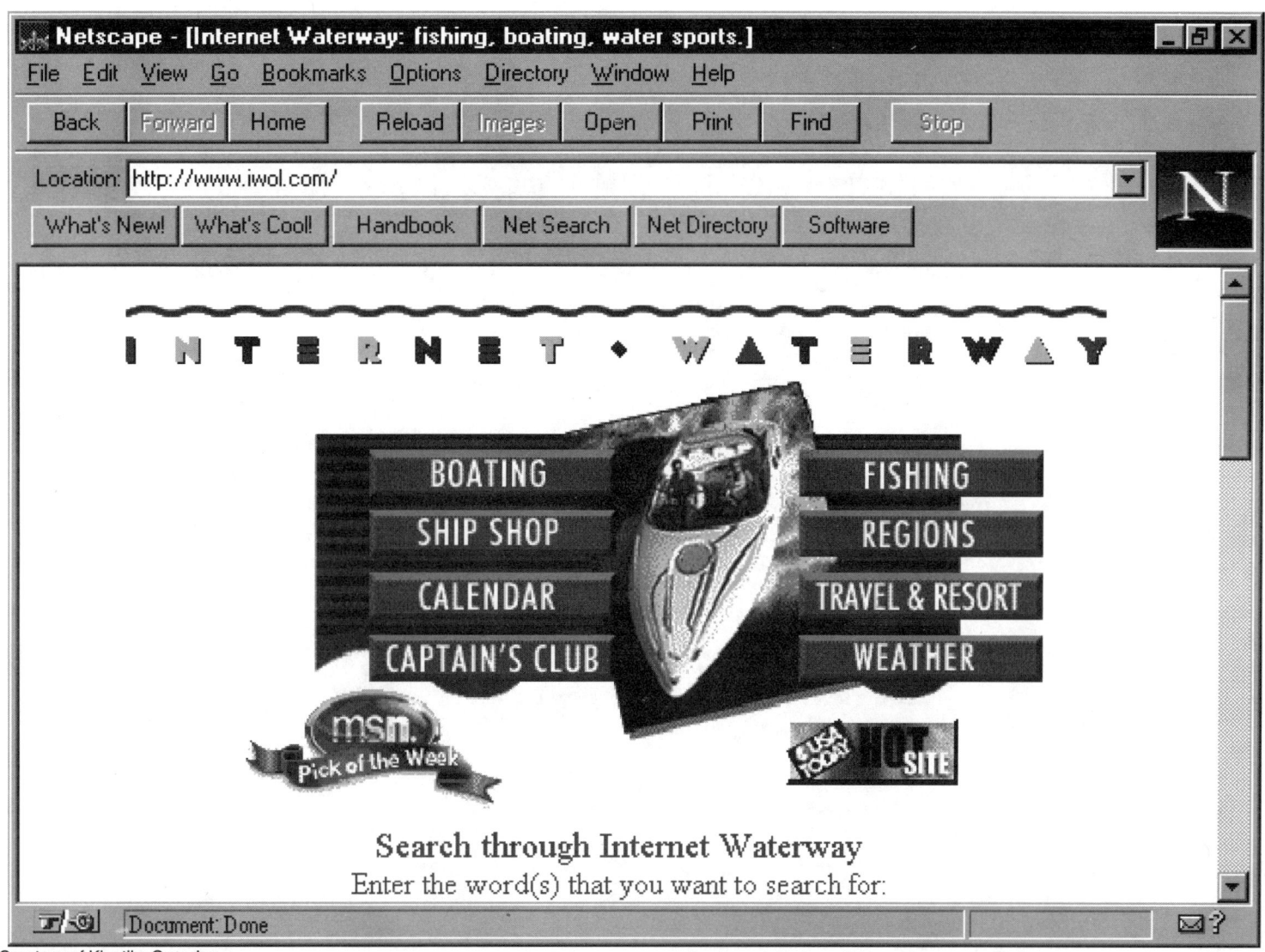

Money Magazine

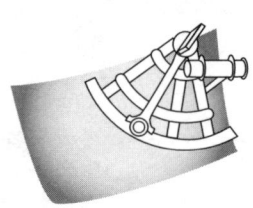

URL: http://www.pathfinder.com/money

As you might imagine, the Money Personal Finance Center is intended to complement *Money* magazine. It does an excellent job of doing so, with lots of helpful resources packed into the Welcome to Money Home Page. They include a number of useful tools designed to help you manage your finances more effectively. In addition, they have a search box that permits visitors to search an interesting (and Time Warner exclusive) database that includes *Asiaweek, Entertainment Weekly, Fortune, Money, National Review, People, Sports Illustrated,* and others.

Key Feature

The Welcome to Money site contains a lot of helpful financial information. They have done an excellent job of making navigation through it quick and easy. They have packed a lot of information into the initial image map and they also provide a "Click Here to go to the Text-based Navigator" hyperlink for those who would like to do so.

Pitfalls and Fixes

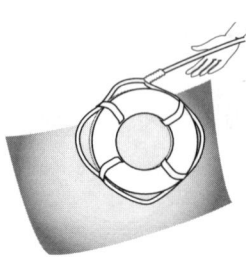

Pitfall: The text-only hyperlink is not visible on the main page without scrolling to find it.

Fix: Place the text a bit higher on the page to make it more visible.

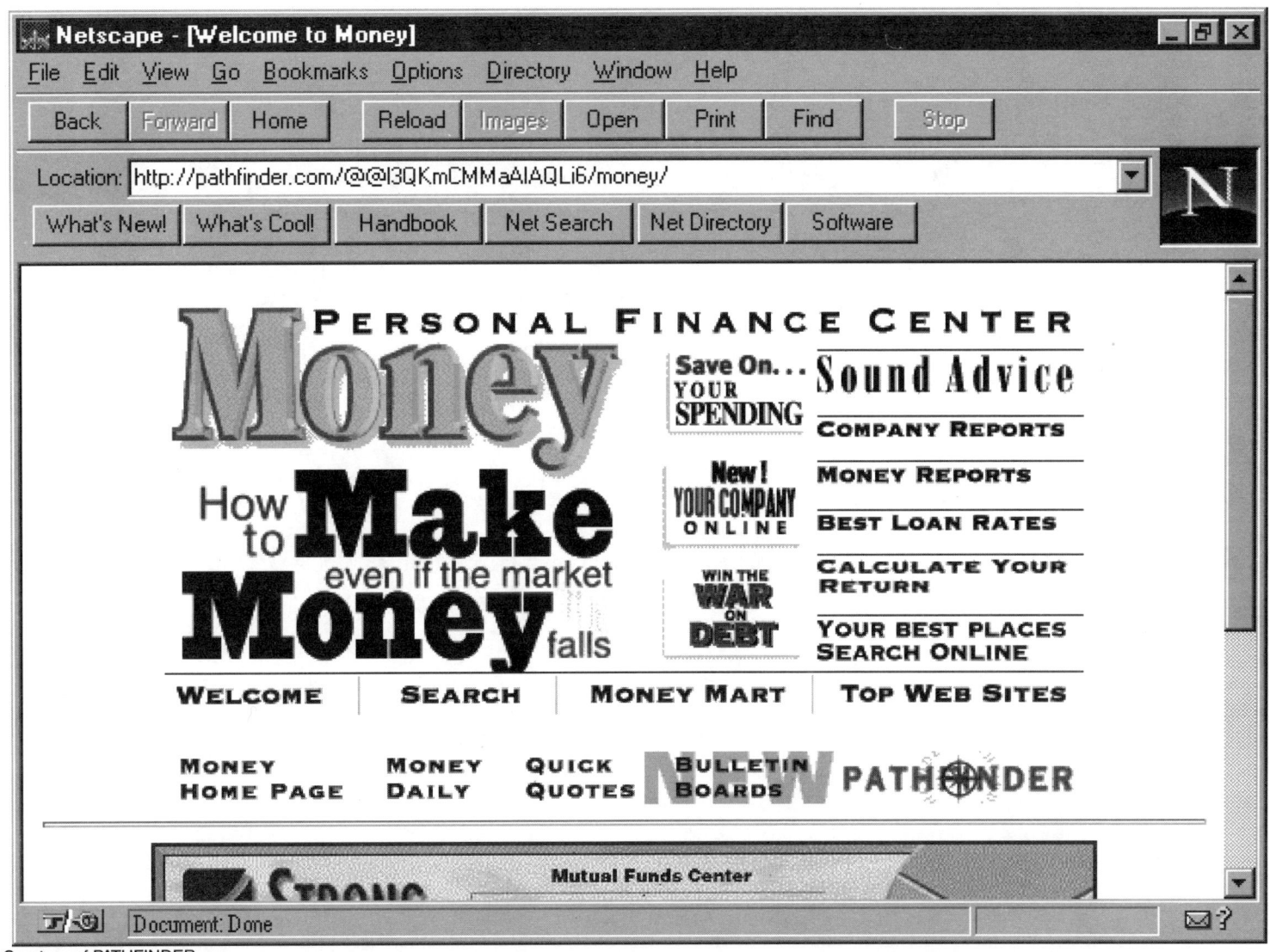

PC Computing

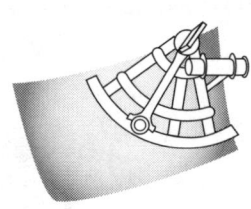

URL: `http://www.zdnet.com/~pccomp`

The PC Computing Online site is packed with wonderful resources for computer users. The six main choices on the home page (Web Map, Free Stuff, Sneak Peeks, Features, BBS, and Subscribe) with their corresponding text make it easy for the viewer to decide where they want to go as well as to have a pretty good idea of what they will find once they get there. The graphics load quickly, and moving from one page to another seems to go smoothly, even with a dial-up connection. Once you leave the home page for one of the selections, they have wisely included a small set of buttons at the bottom of the additional pages to facilitate your return to the home page, conduct a search, purchase a subscription, and look at the ad index. This site is organized logically and never loses sight of the fact that it is there to support *PC Computing* magazine.

Key Feature

PC Computing Online does an excellent job of providing information about the Internet and the World Wide Web in a well-organized and easy-to-follow fashion. Moving from one part of the site to another is easy and intuitive, and helpful icons are always there to assist!

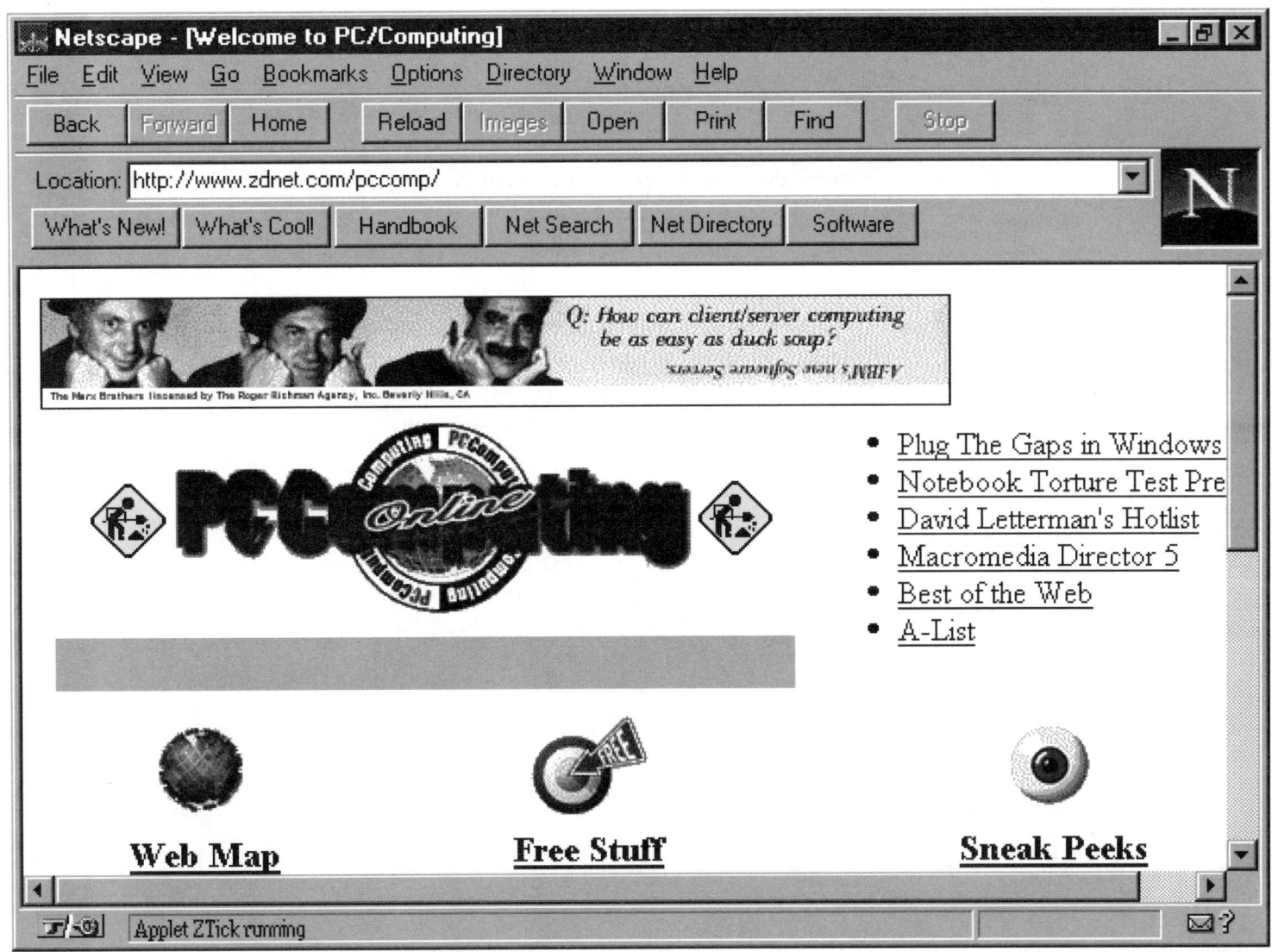

Shop.Com

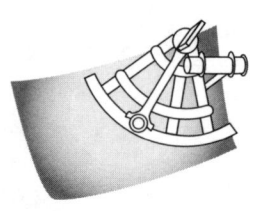

URL: `http://shop.com`

This site is an amazing resource for anyone who might be interested in shopping on the World Wide Web. Packed with information about shopping, services provided to the online shopper, a definitive list of virtual malls, information about individual virtual shops and stores, and other miscellaneous information, Shop.Com is the perfect place to begin an exploration of online shopping. Five clearly explained hyperlinks take visitors to Infomania, Services, Virtual Malls, Virtual Shops, and Diverse Sites. Most impressive, however, is the information one finds by clicking on one of these hyperlinks. Each page is filled with an alphabetical listing of the resources that are included. Each resource is a hyperlink, there is a rating system in place (a series of one to five stars below each hyperlink), and a well-written informative paragraph describing the particular site.

Key Feature

Shop.Com does an outstanding job of providing information about online shopping to visitors. Information is presented clearly, concisely, and quite completely, and the navigational tools work perfectly. Shop.Com has repeated their five-button bar (Top, Services, Mall, Shops, Diverse) at both the top and bottom of all of their pages. Navigation is never far away.

Silicon Graphics

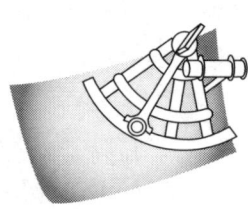

URL: `http://www.sgi.com`

The Silicon Graphics Home Page is beautiful to look at and extremely informative. Using a wonderful array of colors, and good use of space, they have created a page that is both packed with information and easy to navigate. The very large image map (71,000 bytes) that is the home page is divided into several sections, and each section has a number of different buttons that the visitor can select. Right off the bat, the visitor can select either a Java-enhanced or a text-only version, and first-time visitors are made welcome. The initial set of clearly labeled icons permits one to search for information, check on news and events, ask for help, or make purchases. Lower down on the page, you can make selections from eight more icons, and then still lower on the page, you can select from a group of four more icons. There is a lot of information here, but because they have spread all the icons out and used colors well, it never feels overwhelming or confusing.

Key Feature

Silicon Graphics has done a skillful job of presenting a large amount of information about their company and their products. They have used colors and icons extremely well; the site never feels overcrowded and yet there is a wealth of information to be found here. Navigation through this site is easy, even with all the graphics, since they have done an excellent job of repeating choices clearly throughout each part of the location.

Pitfalls and Fixes

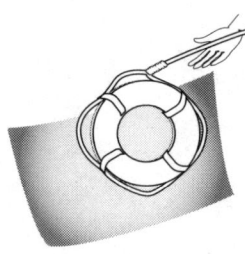

Pitfall: This site uses graphics heavily. For those who access this site through a dial-up connection, this can mean waiting quite a while until all of the images have been downloaded.

Fix: Fortunately, they have already anticipated this problem and have a text-only hyperlink at the very top of their home page. The text-only home page loads quickly and presents a quick listing of text hyperlinks taking visitors to all the same options that are available on the graphics page.

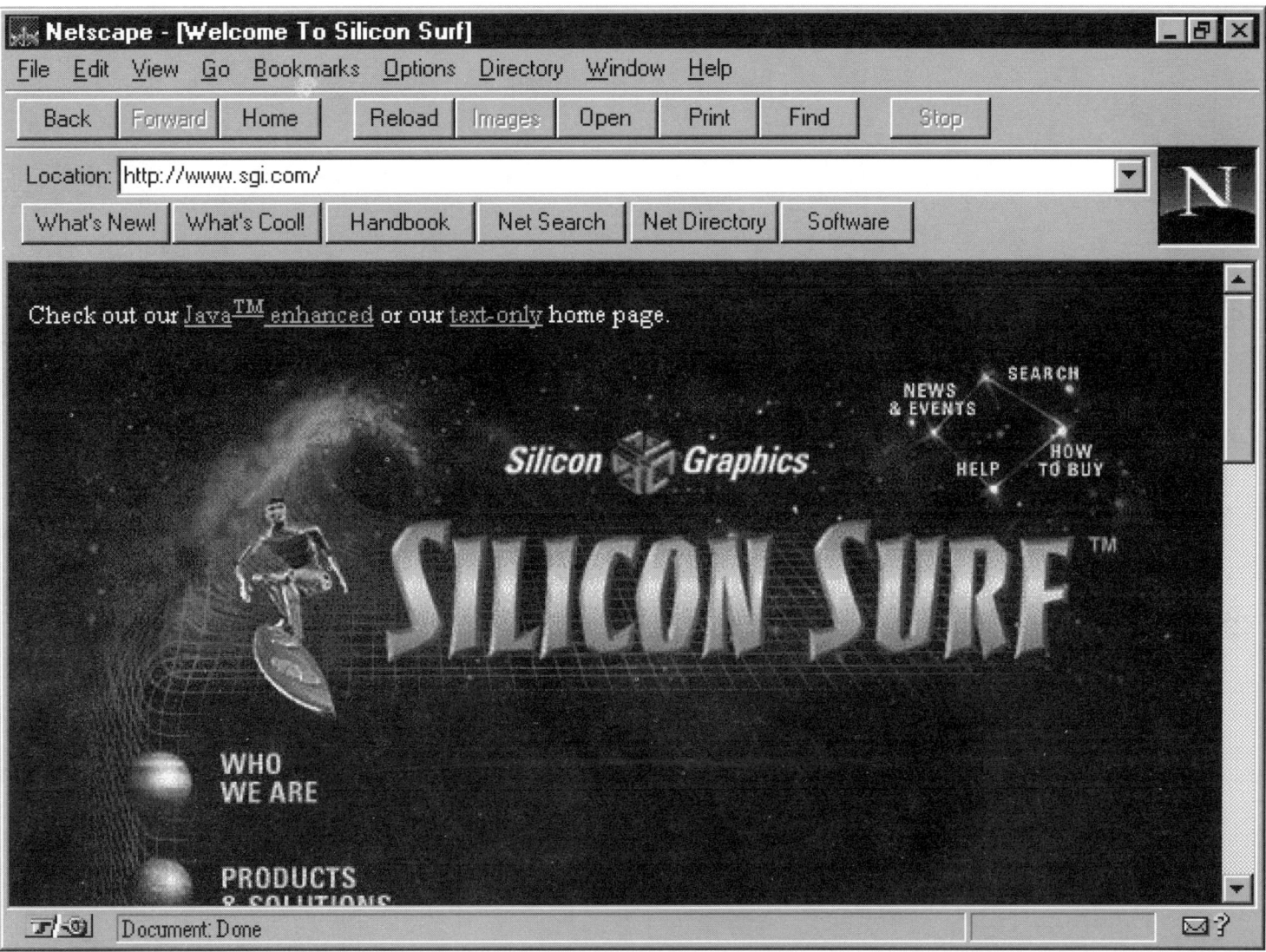

Courtesy of Silicon Graphics, Inc.

StockMaster

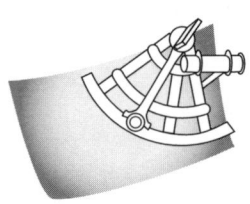

URL: `http://www.stockmaster.com`

StockMaster provides recent stock market information, including closing prices of the previous day and one-year summary graphs of prices. It is updated automatically each evening to reflect the day's closing information. Not all stocks are included; however, it is fair to say that the list of those stocks that are included is quite extensive. Mark Torrance, the Stockmaster, as he calls himself, has done a wonderful job of making navigation through this site quick and easy. Using text primarily, one is able to move quickly from one hyperlink to the next and obtain information about stock and mutual fund charts, as well as information about how the various graphs are drawn. The service has existed since 1993 and is used heavily, which indicates its success. Recently, Mark moved the service from its MIT origins to make it a commercial site.

Key Feature

StockMaster provides useful information to those interested in tracking trends in various stocks. The information is reasonably current, and navigation through the site is extremely easy. In this case, graphics are not the issue, information is, and the site achieve its goal hands down.

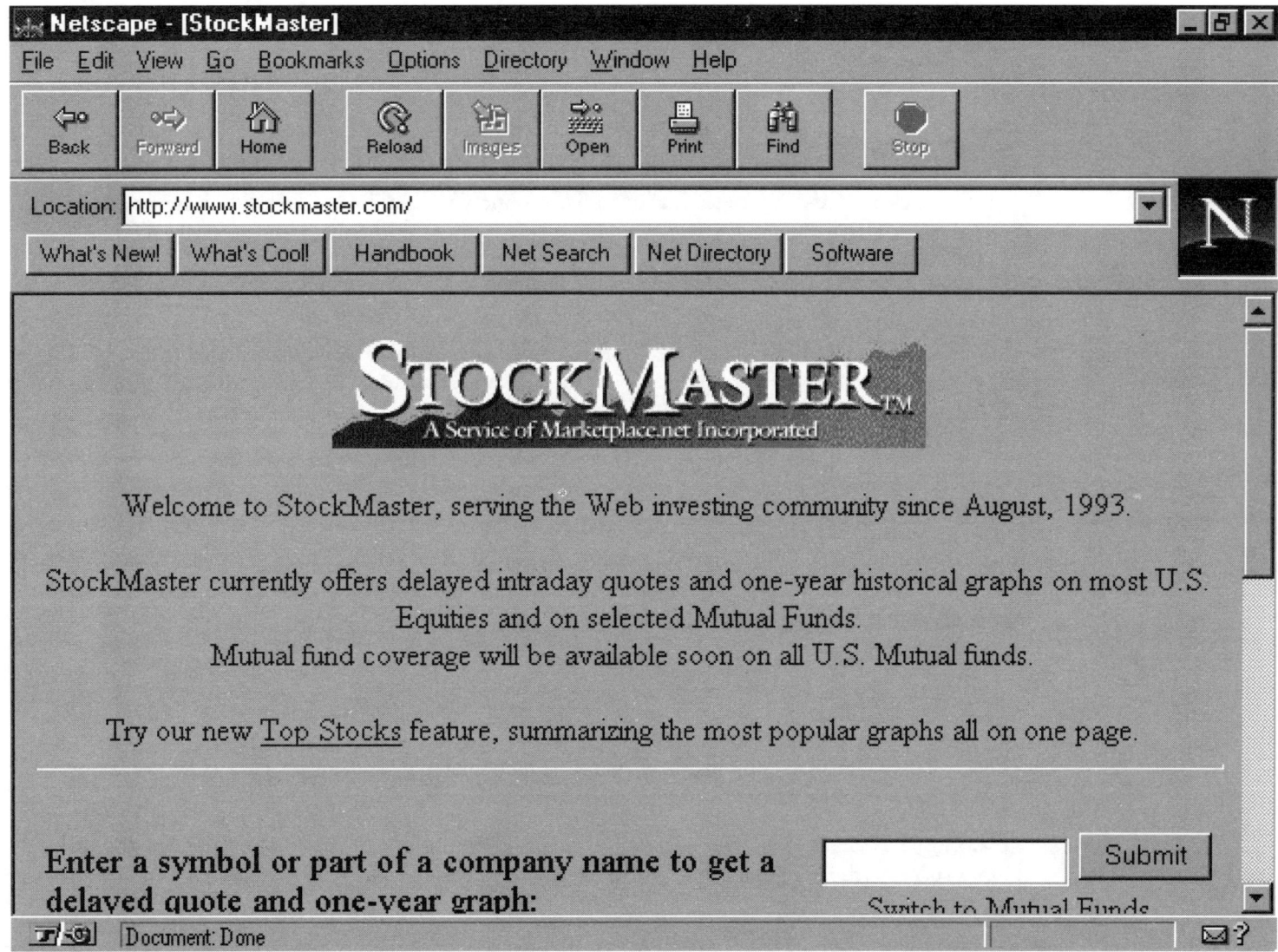

Telecom Atlas

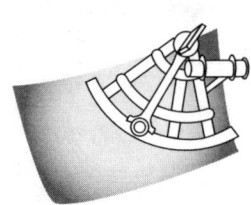

URL: http://www.wiltel.com/atlas/value.html

Telecom Atlas, the LDDS WorldCom site, provides those with a particular interest in this company with a quick and easy way to learn about their products and services. Navigation is made easy by the way that they have divided the screen. Using text hyperlinks at the top, one can easily access About LDDS WorldCom, Products and Services, Telecom Library, Feedback, and the LDDS WorldCom Home Page. A map with hyperlinks gives a graphical representation of the companies that make up LDDS WorldCom. Another set of hypertext links below the map take the visitor to the nine companies listed. Finally, we see the LDDS WorldCom Telecomm Library with nine book spines (all hyperlinks) facing us. And at the bottom of the page are some additional hypertext links (WorldCom, WhatsNew?, Services, Sales, News, Want-Ads, Library, Feedback, and Home) to some additional resources. The page is clear and crisp and presents its information well.

Key Feature

Telecom Atlas does a great job of presenting a lot of information clearly and precisely. Using space, a map, hypertext, and a library metaphor, they have done a good job of making the page interesting, accessible, and not overwhelming.

Pitfalls and Fixes

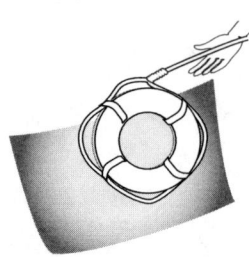

Pitfall: The image map contains, as of this writing, no default. This means visitors will get error messages (Mapping Server Error) when they click away from the indicated areas.

Fix: Create a default URL with a friendly, "Sorry there's nothing at that place" message for all the other space on the map besides the locations where you would like people to click.

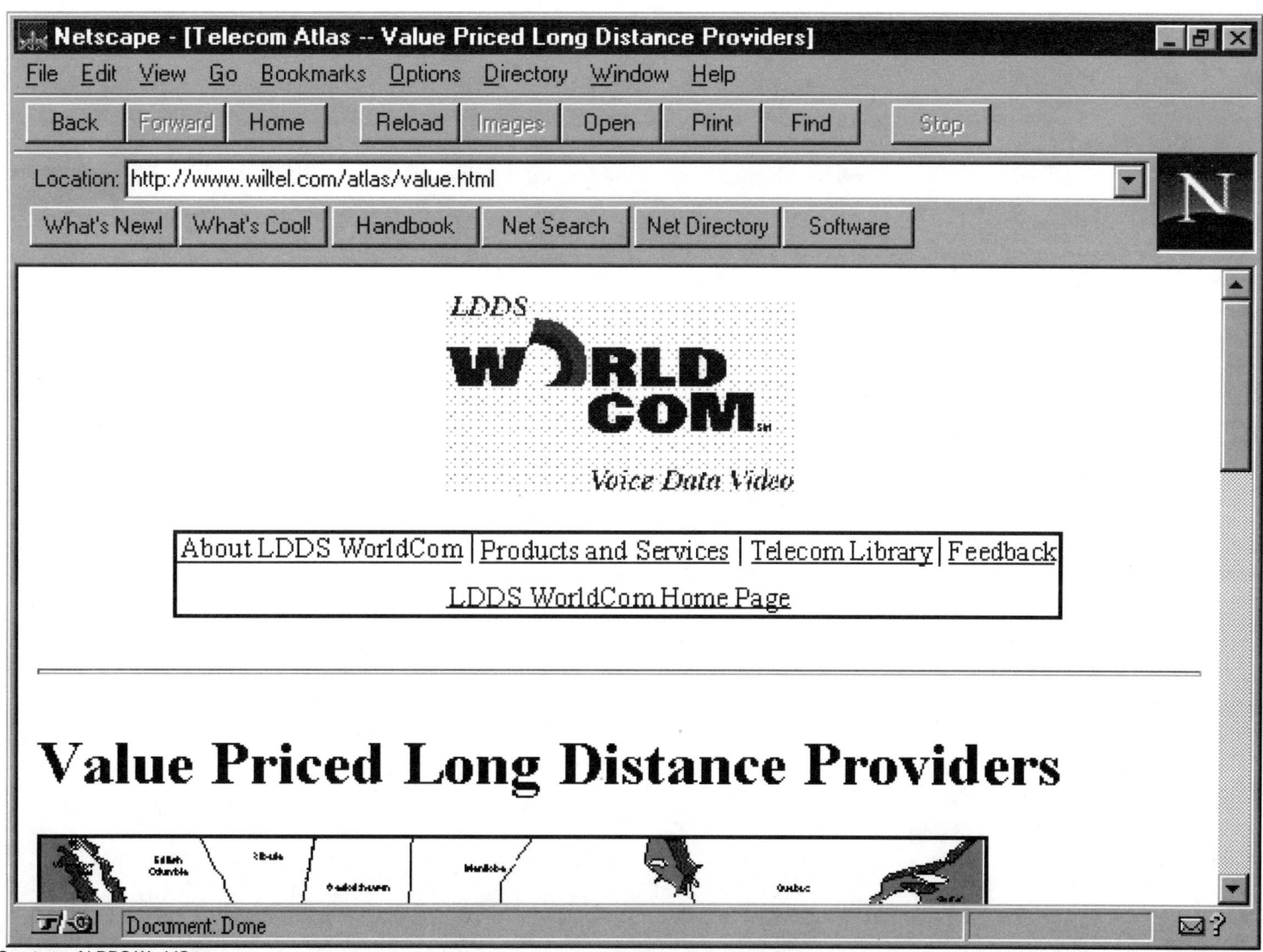

Web Review

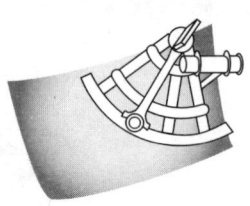

URL: `http://gnn.com/wr`

Web Review is an online publication that provides visitors with current information about the World Wide Web in a timely, interesting fashion. Web Review typically contains a Cover Story, Weekly Features, Columns, and Back Issues. In addition, they include Net Daily News, which is filled with late-breaking stories about Internet and World Wide Web happenings. One can also listen to WebTalk if RealAudio has been installed. The information is well written, and navigating through the site is a pleasure. If you are interested in being kept well informed about the Internet and World Wide Web, this would be a good site to refer to often. Navigation is quick and easy, and the information presented is timely.

Key Feature

Web Review presents timely information about the Internet and the World Wide Web. Navigation through the site is quite easy due to the clear directions and hyperlinks on each page.

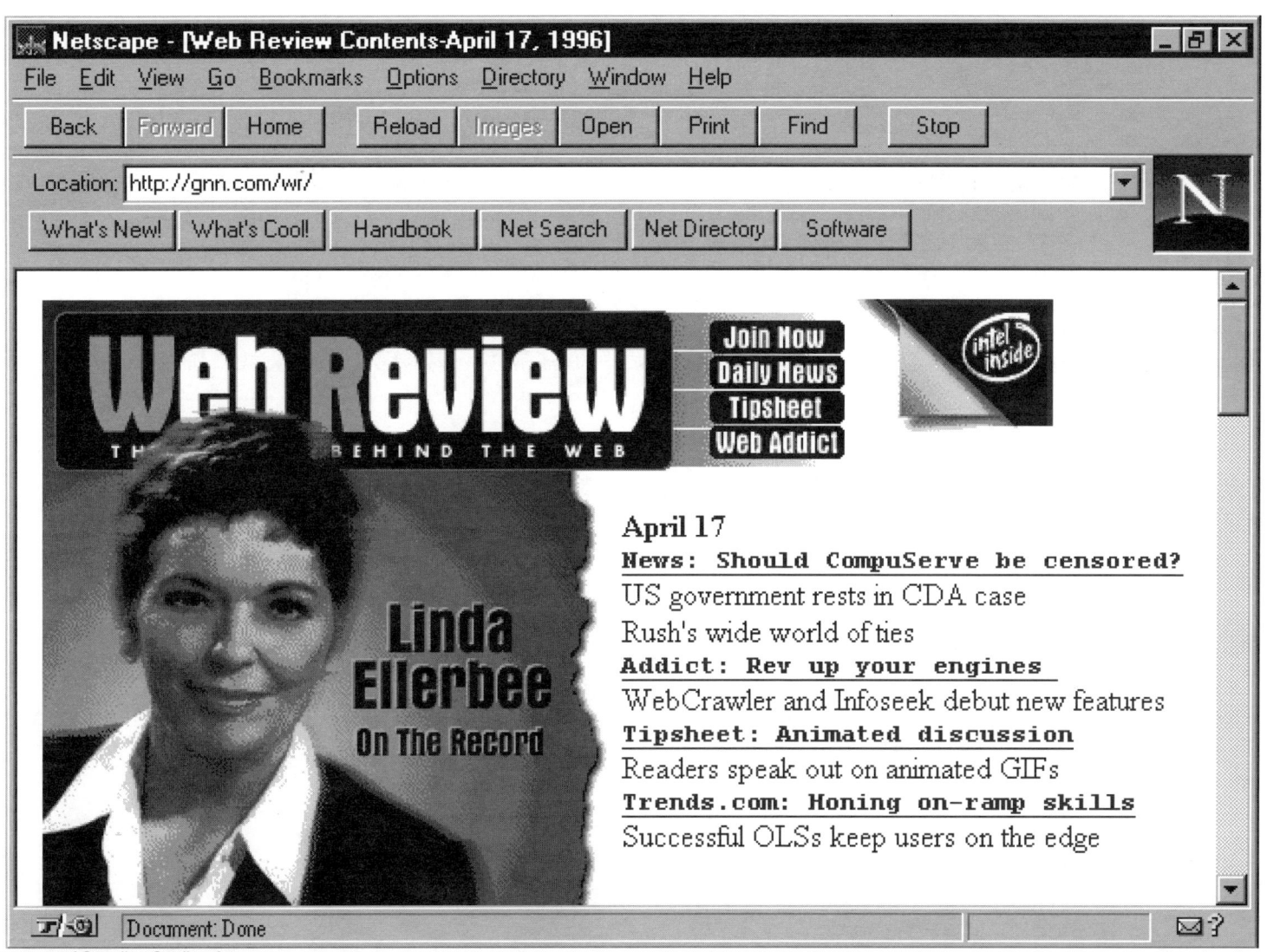

Summary

Intuitive on-page navigation is demonstrated well by the sites in this chapter. A number of different models have been employed, but it is fair to say that all of them have been very attentive to making it possible for their visitors to quickly and easily find the information or resources they are seeking. Many of the sites use visual cues that always inform viewers where they are at any given point in time, and how to find their way back to where they began. Many of the sites also do a good job of making it easy for those who want text-only access to have it. Finally, we have seen how a number of sites have used image maps quite effectively; they make it obvious where one is to click, and what information will be accessed when one does so. Intuitive on-page navigation is imperative if you want to have an effective Web site. The sites in this chapter do a good job of showing how to do that well.

Chapter 8

KEY 6:

Involve the Visitor

Introduction to Key 6 — Involve the Visitor

Key 6, Involve the Visitor, provides us with an extremely important perspective on those companies that are successfully using the World Wide Web and the Internet to enhance their business opportunities. These companies are mindful of the fact that their visitors must be actively engaged in activities at their Web site—or they will quickly leave.

This involvement can be elicited by sites that intrigue or entertain. Or perhaps a site can furnish detailed information about particular products or services to satisfy a visitor's curiosity. Involving viewers makes it easier to obtain information from them. It is not uncommon for sites to request (at a minimum) the E-mail addresses of their viewers. If viewers value the information or services being offered, they will usually provide this information. Let's see how some of the sites successfully involve their visitors.

Technical Points

Involving the user is really a two-step process. The first step is to make the visitor feel at home in a useful, fun, or friendly environment so they will want to participate. This step focuses on building site and perhaps brand loyalty. We want them to come back and visit again. In this stage we do not necessarily know who our visitors are by name or E-mail address.

The second step of involving the visitor focuses on building a customer or prospect list. Here our objective is to get a visitor's name and an E-mail address (at a minimum). This involves trust. People will be very hesitant if they believe that their names will end up on a list that may be traded or sold. Assurance must be given *and kept!* If the trust is later violated, or if a visitor believes it has been violated, the game is over. You must remember that word (and rumor) travel very fast on the Internet.

Registration

Many sites on the Internet now are asking for user registration. We have seen a number of these in earlier chapters. There are arguments for and against this practice and there are no clear answers yet.

Several methods of registration are now in use. Each one adds an increasing burden on site administration, and that burden must be thought through before beginning. Let's look at the pros and cons of each.

1. User name and password—no validation

On the pro side, this method of registration permits the site to track individual names and determine their frequency of visit and their movement while visiting It is advantageous for site management to have this knowledge.

On the con side there are several considerations. First, password files must be kept and lost password queries must be handled. If only names are required, there is no easy way to validate who the users really are. There is also the risk of duplicates, as people who have forgotten their password are more likely to register again than to ask for a new password.

2. User name and password—with E-mail validation

Again, individual users can be tracked and now there is even better assurance that their identity will be truly known, since the password is sent back by E-mail to the person who has requested it. Maintenance of password files and the re-issuance of lost passwords are still administrative burdens. However, there is a much lower risk of duplicate registrations.

On the negative side, requiring users to remember and tie in a name and password for a "free" account is user-hostile. For many of us, it is already difficult to remember all the various names and passwords we must use with different locations. If a competing service that offers the same resources opens with this "hassle," users will move away quickly. They may be very hard to recover.

3. Name, address, E-mail, and credit card per transaction or visit.

Here, we may have the best solution for online purchases. This model is well known to consumers from mail-order purchasing. As more and more people trust the Web with their credit card information, this will probably become the working model.

A Friendly Alternative

If we are not expecting people to make purchases while they are on our pages, then perhaps we should not try to identify everyone who comes in. Or if we try, we must offer them something. Next we will suggest several ideas.

Using Discussion Forums

Several of the sites in this book (and many others) have added visitor discussion forums. These are places where people can "post" their thoughts, comments, and opinions. Encouraging visitors to do this gives them the feeling that they "own" a piece of the site. This can be a very powerful builder of site loyalty.

A caution, however, about forums. If you decide to use a forum, you will want to build in a process to "screen" submissions. While most people will want to stick to the topics and behave themselves, some may become aggressive or abusive or use language you may not wish to have on your site.

Using Surveys

Another way to involve visitors is to use a survey. This can be as simple as a question or two, or it can be a complex form with many buttons, checkboxes, spin boxes, and text blocks. We recommend that if you plan a survey, you follow the time-honored principle of keeping it as simple as possible.

Using Contests or Giveaways

In our judgment, this is the fastest way there is to irritate a large number of people (or go broke or be sued). Contests are regulated in many states and countries, and before you even contemplate a contests, you should consult an attorney who is knowledgeable in this area. If you proceed, be aware that, as before, word travels very fast on the Internet. Your contest may be posted in one or more Usenet newsgroups and you probably will not even know.

If you are planning to give something away (pens, T-shirts, gimmicks, and so forth) be sure you clearly state the limits of what, when, where, and how many.

Or recommendation on contests and giveaways is simple: Don't!

Forms and CGI Scripts

Forms and CGI (common gateway interface) scripts can also be used to involve visitors. Forms and CGI scripts look deceptively simple and can be, in experienced hands. Here we suggest that you get some help from skilled programmers who have done these before. Be sure to test your forms with a variety of different browsers.

Now let's look at some sites that appear to be doing a successful job of involving the visitors.

Build-A-Card

URL: `http://buildacard.com`

This site is one that could easily have been included as a good example of Habit 2—Valuable, Useful or Fun. The site is playful and is fun to visit. However, it is important to look at this site from the perspective of a location that does a masterful job of involving the visitor. It is hard to resist the temptation to build a greeting card that can be viewed on the Web, or to take some time to see the cards others have put together. Imagine creating a custom card in which you can mix pictures and text, giving the card its own URL, and then sending it to friends or family!

Key Feature

The site is fun, engaging, and playful and does a wonderful job of involving its visitors! The site is designed so visitors can create custom greeting cards for all sorts of special events. Crated by Maximized Software, this site is a fun place where people who have time on their hands can entertain themselves by creating cards that they can send to others over the Internet.

Pitfalls and Fixes

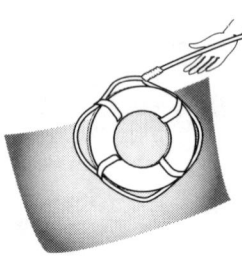

Pitfall: It takes time for the graphics to be downloaded to the user, and considerable time before the entire card is assembled.

Fix: The time delays are not a big deal, if you have lots of time (or high-speed access), but they are certainly not enhancer of productivity!

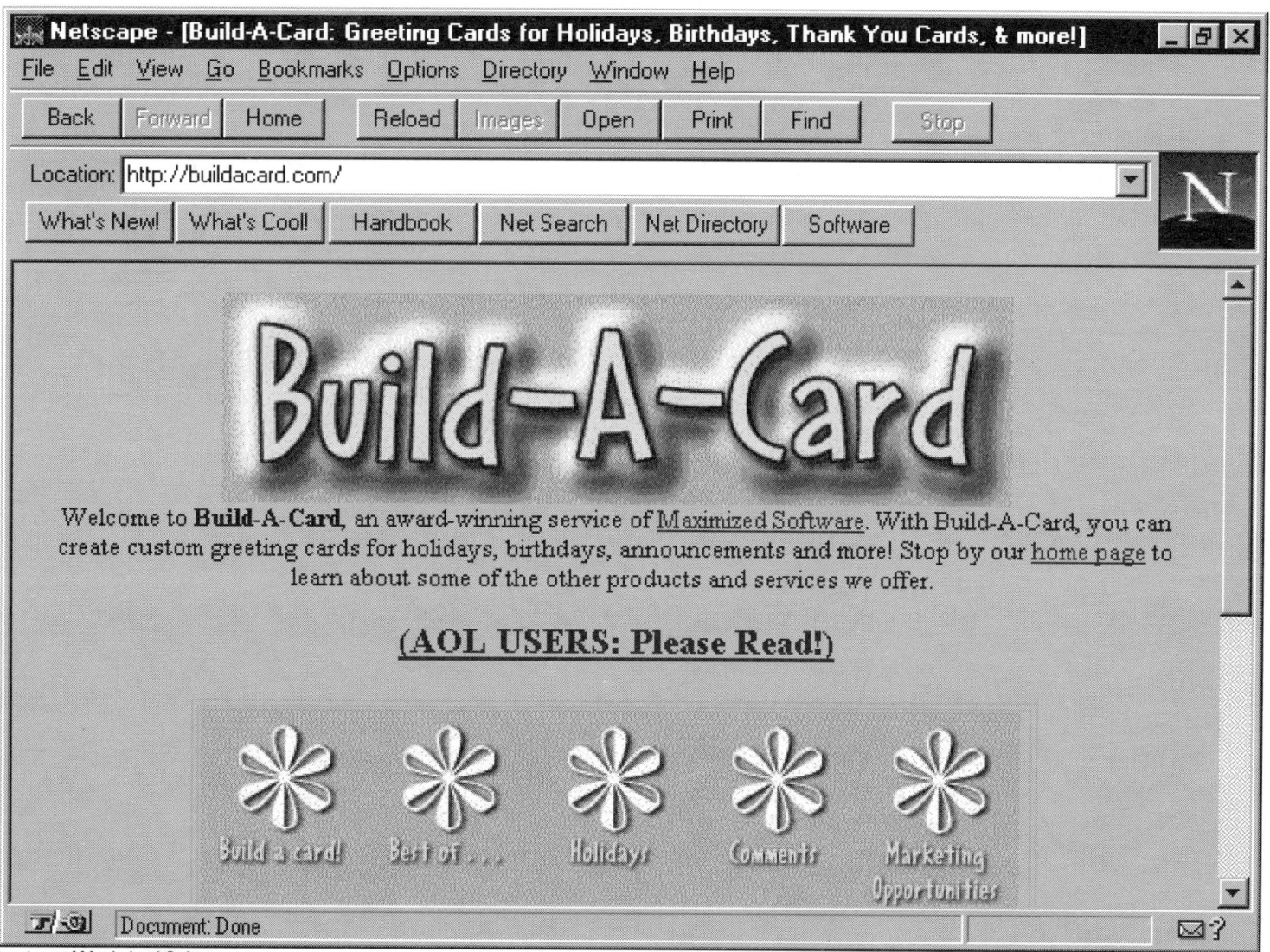

Coldwell Banker Online

URL: http://www.coldwellbanker.com

As you might imagine, the Coldwell Banker site is intended to sell homes to viewers. The involvement begins as soon as you click on "Homes For Sale." Once there, you are asked to click on the state in which you are searching. Next, you can click on the section of the state that is of interest to you, or you can enter City and State, Price Range, and Minimum Number of Bedrooms into a short questionnaire. When you click on the search button, your search begins. The search is quick, and you can view the complete listing, and in some cases see a photo, of the homes that match your search criteria. Throughout this process, the viewer is constantly involved in making decisions and obtaining information.

Key Feature

Coldwell Banker has provided an easy-to-use way to look for real estate. The viewer is actively involved in searching for a home the entire time. There is quite a bit of information available from this site, and once one finds the "perfect" home, additional information is available by calling a conveniently provided 800 number that will connect you with Coldwell Banker. They have also provided a Mortgage Calculator and a 1996 Home Price Comparison Index for those who want quick access to such information.

Pitfalls and Fixes

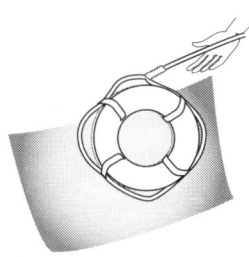

Pitfall: Text information about many homes is provided, but images are provided for only some. This means that the information is quickly obtained but might not be completely satisfactory for the visitor who might wish to have a picture of the homes that are available.

Fix: Adding more pictures of more homes would make this site more valuable.

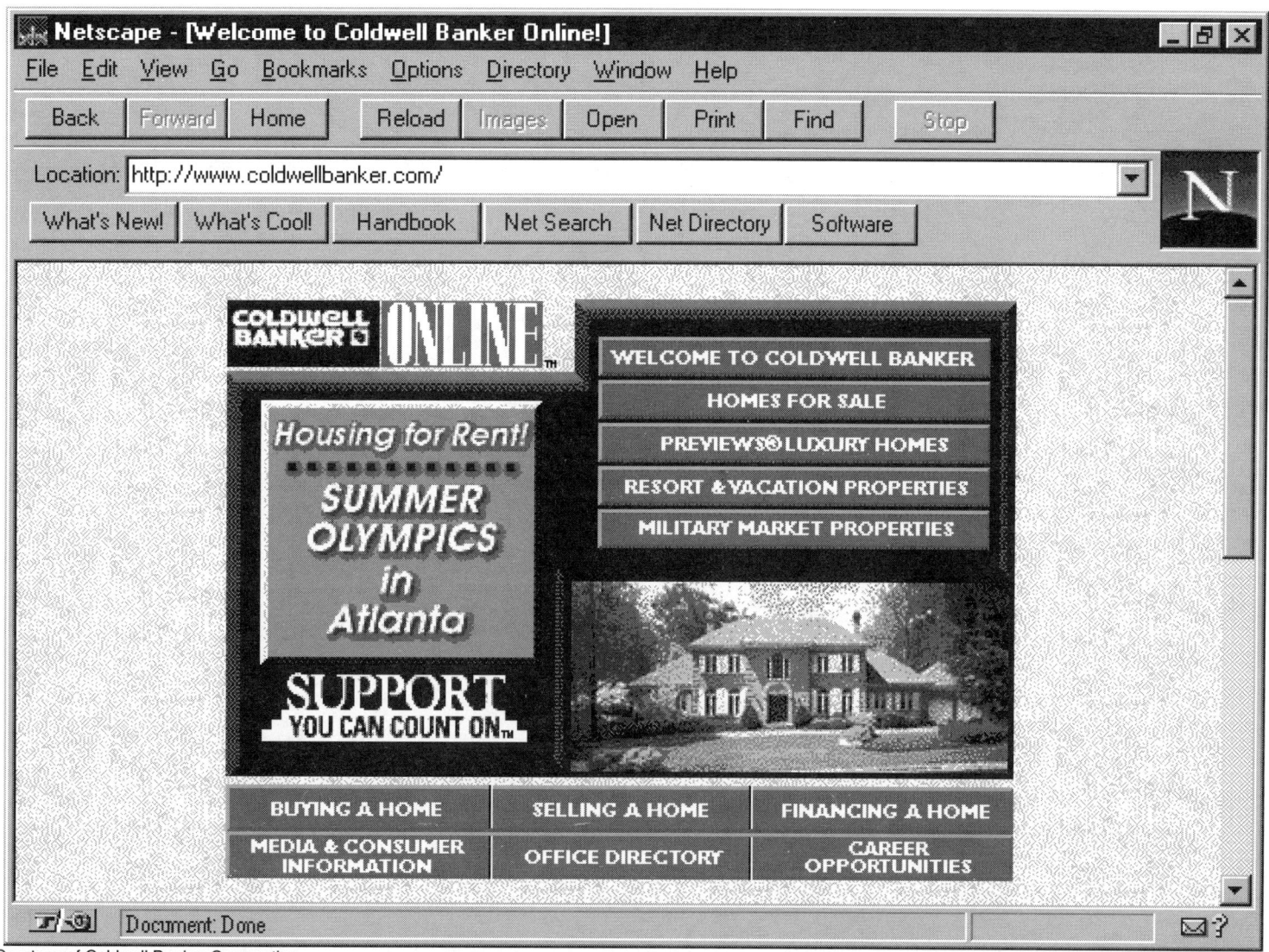

Crestar Student Lending

URL: `http://www.student-loans.com`

This site provides a very complete array of information for students, parents, and counselors who are looking for tips, information and advice about financial aid for college. Visitors will find sample applications, useful payment calculators, a financial aid planning calendar, a saving for college calculator, a paying for college calculator, as well as information about how to find the right lender. The site is chock-full of information about student loans and is a valuable resource for anyone who needs this information. Many of these pages provide easy ways for the viewer to become involved by filling in information, determining various payment plans, and actively searching for useful financial data about colleges.

Key Feature

This site provides a very complete and useful array of information to those in need of information about college loans. They make it easy to be involved in their site. They have included a number of shortcuts for those in a hurry ("All I care about is Getting a Loan Application"), and they provide more complete information for those who have time. Navigating through the site is easy, and they use six consistent choices on each page, so visitors know immediately where they are and how to get elsewhere.

Pitfalls and Fixes

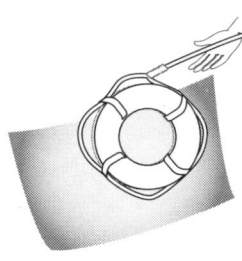

Pitfall: A minor concern has to do with the name that they have chosen for their URL. It is not intuitively obvious that one should insert a hyphen between the words "student" and "loans."

Fix: Using a name without a hyphen always helps. However, once you arrive at their site, you will be highly involved in what they have to offer.

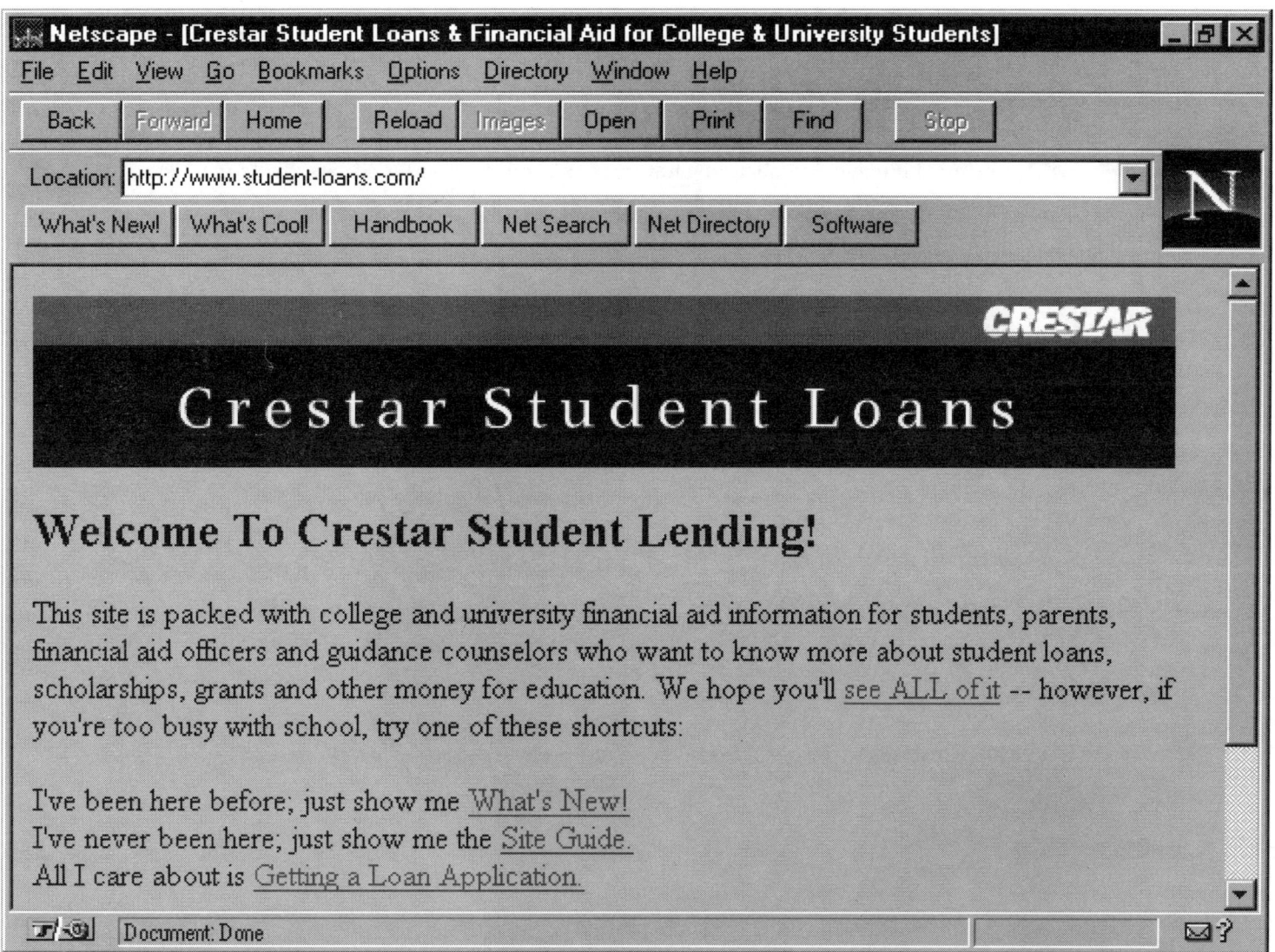

Netscape - [Crestar Student Loans & Financial Aid for College & University Students]

File Edit View Go Bookmarks Options Directory Window Help

Back Forward Home   Reload Images Open Print Find   Stop

Location: http://www.student-loans.com/

What's New! What's Cool! Handbook Net Search Net Directory Software

Crestar Student Loans

Welcome To Crestar Student Lending!

This site is packed with college and university financial aid information for students, parents, financial aid officers and guidance counselors who want to know more about student loans, scholarships, grants and other money for education. We hope you'll see ALL of it -- however, if you're too busy with school, try one of these shortcuts:

I've been here before; just show me What's New!
I've never been here; just show me the Site Guide.
All I care about is Getting a Loan Application.

Document: Done

Courtesy of Crestar Bank

DealerNet—The Virtual Showroom

URL: http://www.dealernet.com

For those interested in obtaining information about new and used cars, the DealerNet site is a wonderful repository of information. It is possible to search for dealers, new cars, used cars, or special interest vehicles, as well as to check on your credit history as recorded by Equifax, TRW, and Trans-Union. When looking for cars, you can select manufacturers, vehicle types, and your price range. There are lots of choices, lots of information is available, and the site is quite involving and useful.

Key Feature

This is a quick way to learn a lot about the cars that might match your particular criteria, as well as obtain an up-to-date credit report about yourself. The site uses graphics heavily, but also offers text hyperlinks in visible and accessible locations.

Pitfalls and Fixes

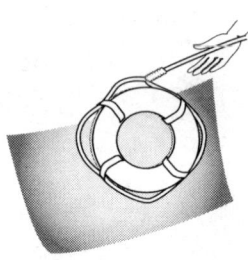

Pitfall: The initial graphic (73K) takes a long time to download, even over a high-speed modem, and the only payoff for the viewer is the chance to obtain the newest version of Netscape or the Index for DealerNet.

Fix: Perhaps a text-only option or better use of thumbnail sketches would assist those with slower modems or those who are in a hurry to get to the desired information.

FedEx

URL: http://www.fedex.com

The FedEx site is filled with interesting and useful information about their services. Most important (and most involving) is the FedEx Airbill Tracking Form. Any time of day, anywhere in the world, even while your package is in transit, just enter the FedEx Airbill Tracking Number and the Destination Country, click once on Request Tracking Info, and you will be provided instantly with the latest information about your package. This is a wonderful, useful resource in which the visitor is involved easily and powerfully in finding the information that is desired.

Key Feature

Involvement is quick and easy and visitors are given exactly what they need, when they need it. This site has designed an easy-to-use resource for their customers and provides them with the information they need with impressive speed and accuracy. FedEx reports that amazing numbers of people from all over the globe use this resource on a daily basis. The information is reliable, accessible, and requires no additional help or support. It is impossible not to be involved in this process, since you have to enter the requested data.

Pitfalls and Fixes

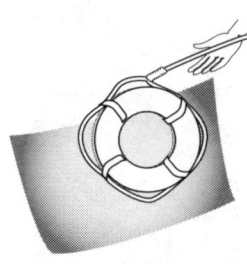

Pitfall: The latest version of this site now has an image map as the first page. It is significantly larger (39 Kbytes) than their previous images, and takes longer to download than one might prefer. A second concern has to do with the use of the color black; as mentioned earlier, not all people find that color appealing.

Fix: Using smaller images would speed up the download time for this page. Perhaps a different (lighter) choice of colors would make this page somewhat more visually appealing.

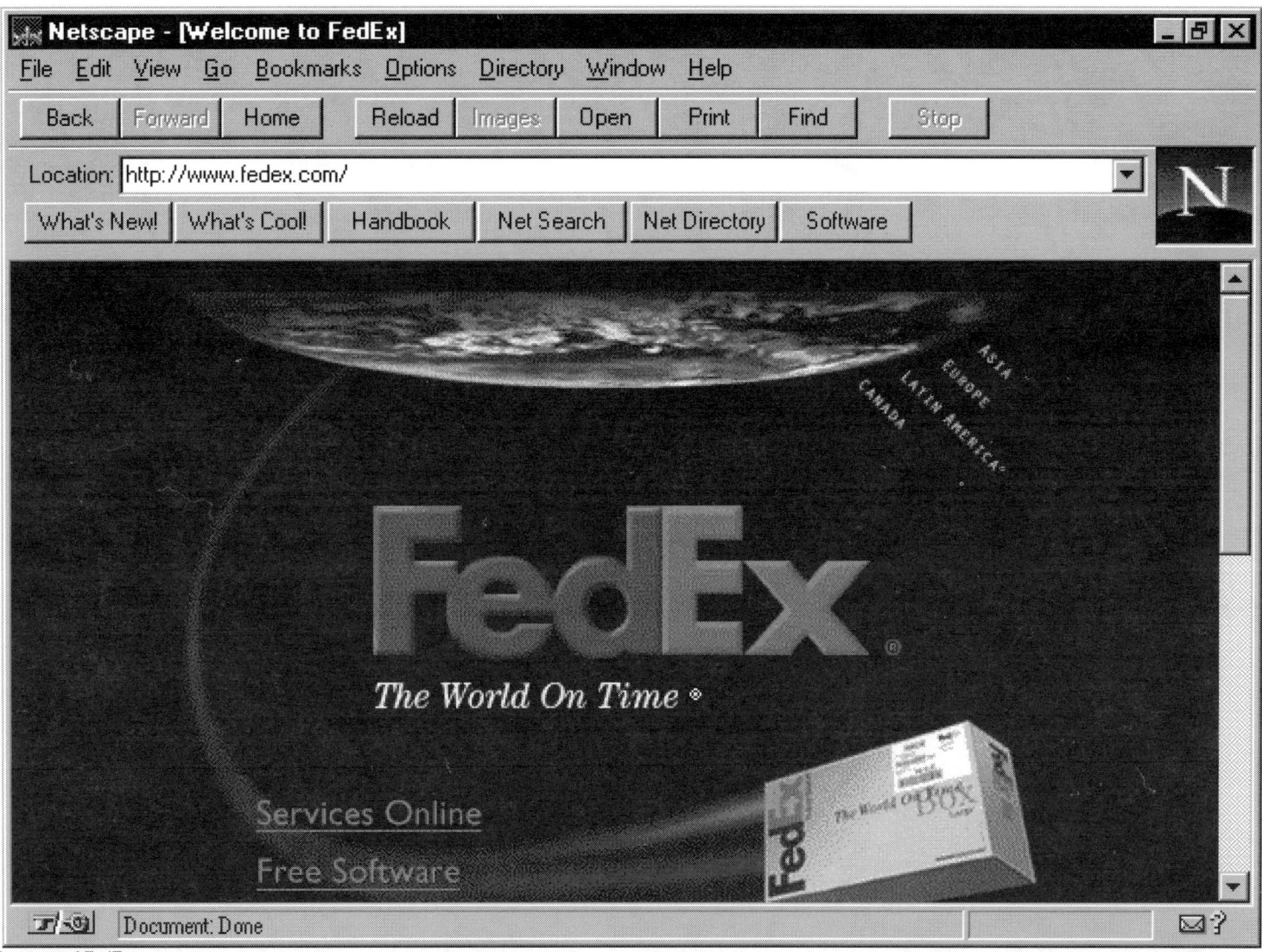

Freeways by Alamo Rent A Car

URL: `http://www.freeways.com`

This site is the Alamo Rent A Car reservation and travel information service. They have done an excellent job of furnishing information that travelers need, including detailed travel directions, kids' games, coupons, and, of course, the ability to rent a car. Their forms are clear and make it easy for the visitor to enter the requested information. In addition, the support information they offer for travelers, makes the site both valuable and useful. They have focused on the notion of involving the viewer every step of the way. You can find out about the locations and availability of the car that you might like and then book it. You can find directions you will need for your travel. And, they have created a space in which visitors can see what others have liked and disliked about the site and then add their own comments.

Key Feature

This site is engaging, clear in its objectives, and provides much useful information. There is good, clear navigation throughout the site; for example, when you are on the Find It page, a clear graphic at the top of the page tells you your location, and an icon at the bottom with the word "home" on it permits you to return to the home page. They use color and graphics sparingly, so the various pages load quickly; their goal is to be helpful and informative and they are on every page. It should be noted that the use of graphics on these pages is particularly good. They use thumbnail sketches which download quickly, and the graphics play a supportive role, not a dominant one. They are very sensitive to the speed with which graphics download and have done a great job of using them effectively.

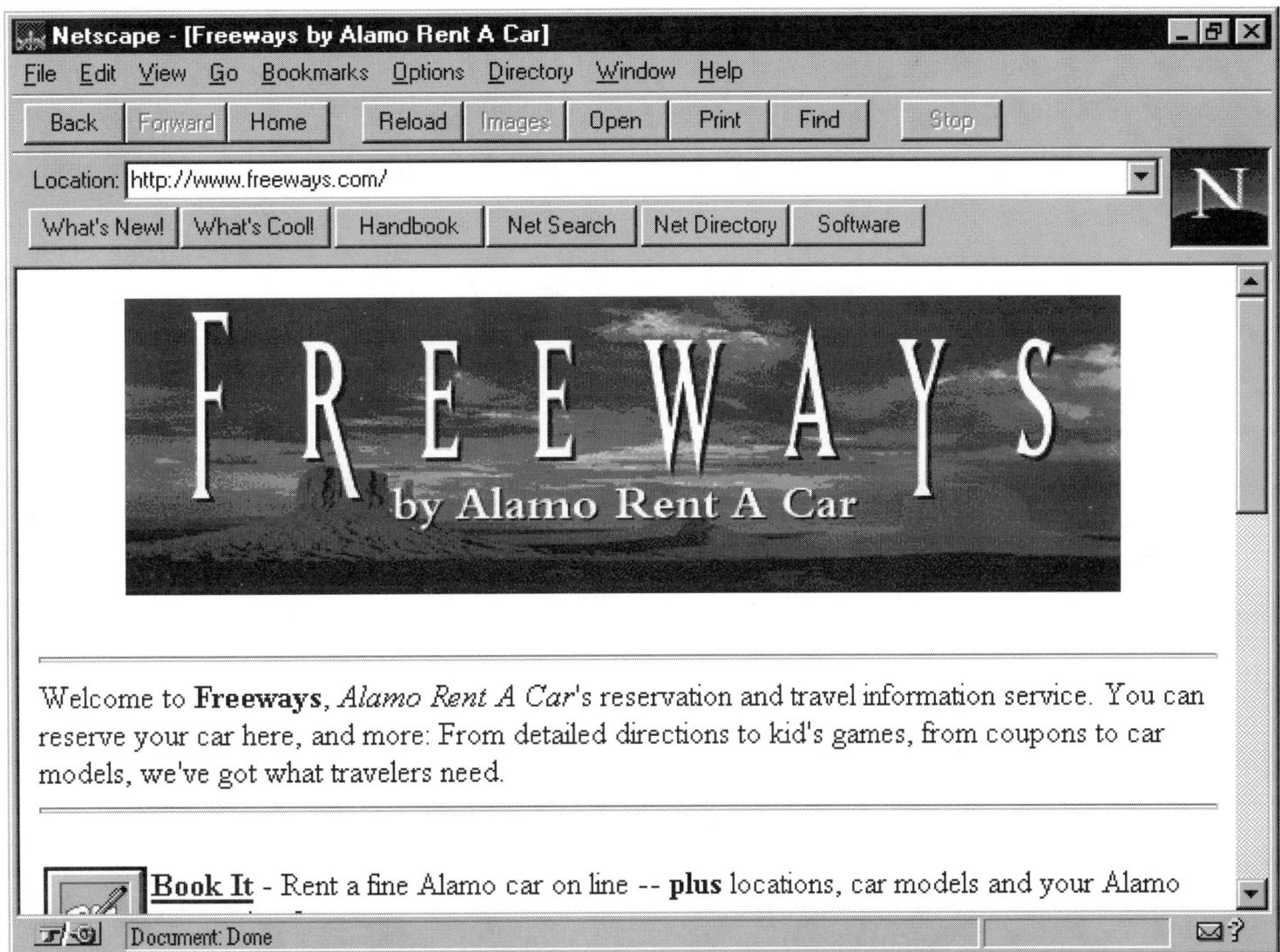

Netscape - [Freeways by Alamo Rent A Car]

File   Edit   View   Go   Bookmarks   Options   Directory   Window   Help

| Back | Forward | Home | | Reload | Images | Open | Print | Find | | Stop |

Location: http://www.freeways.com/

| What's New! | What's Cool! | Handbook | Net Search | Net Directory | Software |

FREEWAYS
by Alamo Rent A Car

Welcome to **Freeways**, *Alamo Rent A Car*'s reservation and travel information service. You can reserve your car here, and more: From detailed directions to kid's games, from coupons to car models, we've got what travelers need.

Book It - Rent a fine Alamo car on line -- **plus** locations, car models and your Alamo

Document: Done

The Golf Circuit

URL: `http://www.golfcircuit.com`

The Golf Circuit™ is a site devoted to golf and golf resources. They have provided viewers with lots to see and do at this site including information about Golf Courses, Golf Tips, a Pro Shop, Classifieds, and current Golf News. In addition, they have thought about ways to keep their viewers interested and involved. Primarily, they have a Golf Giveaway, in which the viewer has to fill out an easy-to-complete entry form. In return for a chance to win two dozen golf balls, visitors must provide their E-mail address, name and address, day and evening phone numbers, as well as their sex and age. Viewers are also offered an opportunity to join a confidential mailing list.

Key Feature

This site provides a wealth of information about golf. In addition, The Golf Circuit's contest is a clever way to involve their viewers in the site as well as to provide The Golf Circuit with a lot of information about the demographics of their visitors.

Courtesy of THE GOLF CIRCUIT

PC Travel

URL: `http://www.pctravel.com`

PC Travel, a site that focuses on air travel, does a good job of providing the information that airline travelers need in an easy-to-use fashion. PC Travel does a wonderful job of providing forms that are clear and precise about what information is required. The viewer is involved right from the beginning in making a series of decisions that lead to particular results. PC Travel wisely offers different selections to new and registered users, so repeat users do not have to enter the same information each time they return to this site. They use SSL security, but include good warnings throughout the site about the security and transmittal of information. They also make it possible for users to enter credit card information using an 800 number or a fax number.

Key Feature

The PC Travel site does an excellent job of guiding new and repeat users through their site. The forms they provide are intuitive, and they have wonderful advice built into the site along the way. They make good use of graphics; enough are included to make the site interesting, but not so many as to overwhelm a visitor. The visitor is totally involved in this site, since information has to be entered every step of the way.

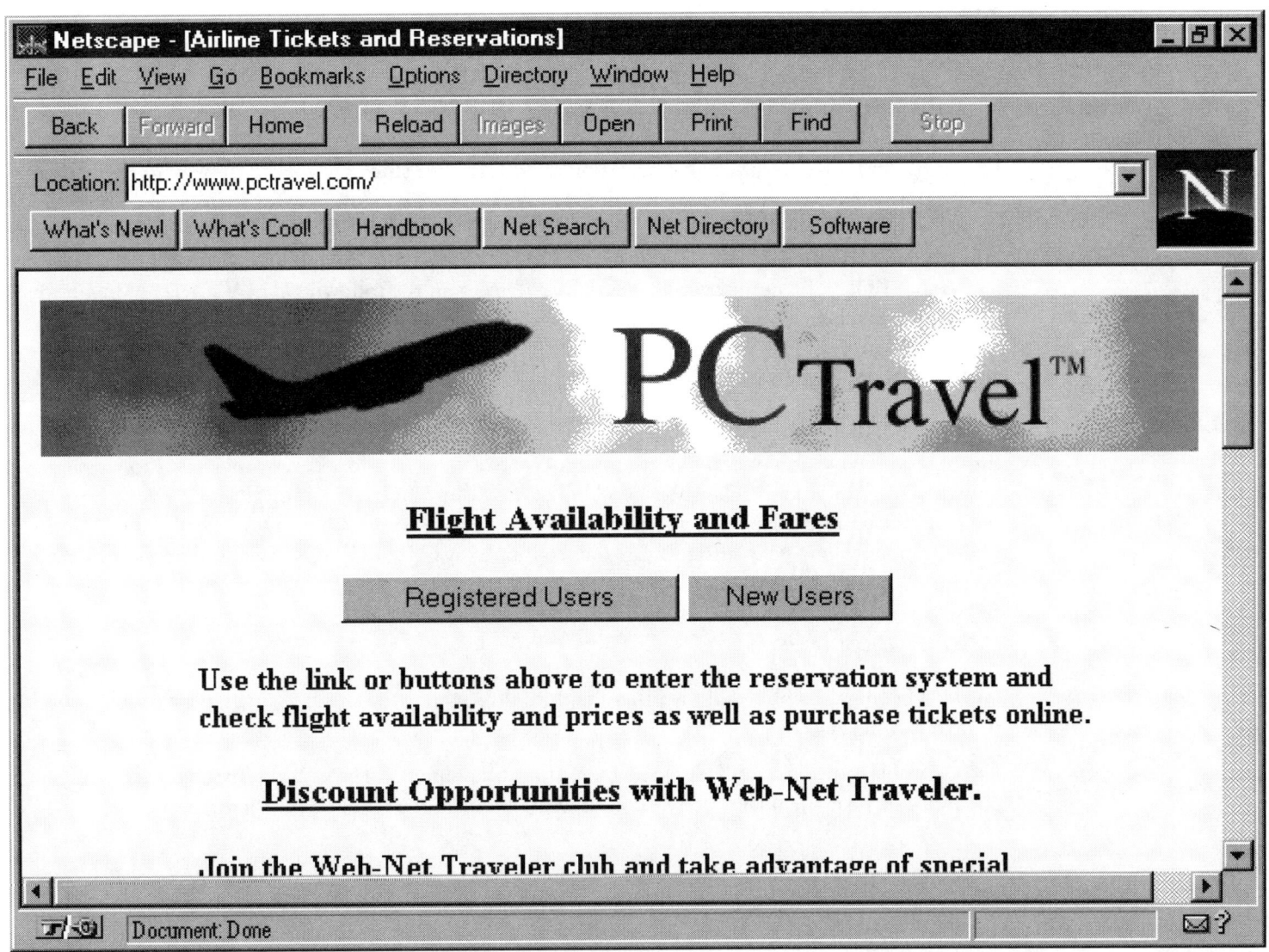

PhotoDisc Index

URL: `http://www.photodisc.com`

PhotoDisc Index is a very valuable repository of royalty-free stock photos for those who need to purchase such items. Viewers can search online for the image they want, pay for it electronically, and download it immediately. Their system allows viewers to enter a keyword and to browse through their library of images. Viewers can either purchase a single image and download it immediately, or else have a CD ROM of a number of images delivered to them the following day. Viewers are involved as they search for their particular images and as they choose the method for delivery and payment.

Key Feature

PhotoDisc Index provides a quick and easy way for visitors to obtain images. Viewers are involved throughout their visit in making decisions about what they want to see, how they want to view it, and how they want to order it. They do a good job of providing navigational images and words throughout the site. The options are consistent and include: Press Tour, About Photo Disc, The Design Mind, Photographers Alley, Web Surfer, Image Collection, Image Finder, FAQs, Sales and Service, Site Map, Write to Us, and License Info.

Pitfalls and Fixes

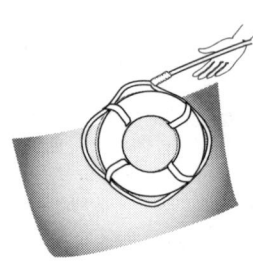

Pitfall: The initial graphic and the other graphics throughout the site are quite large and take a bit of time to download.

Fix: A simple solution would be to use more thumbnail images that would provide viewers with a good idea of what the images are without making them wait so long to see them.

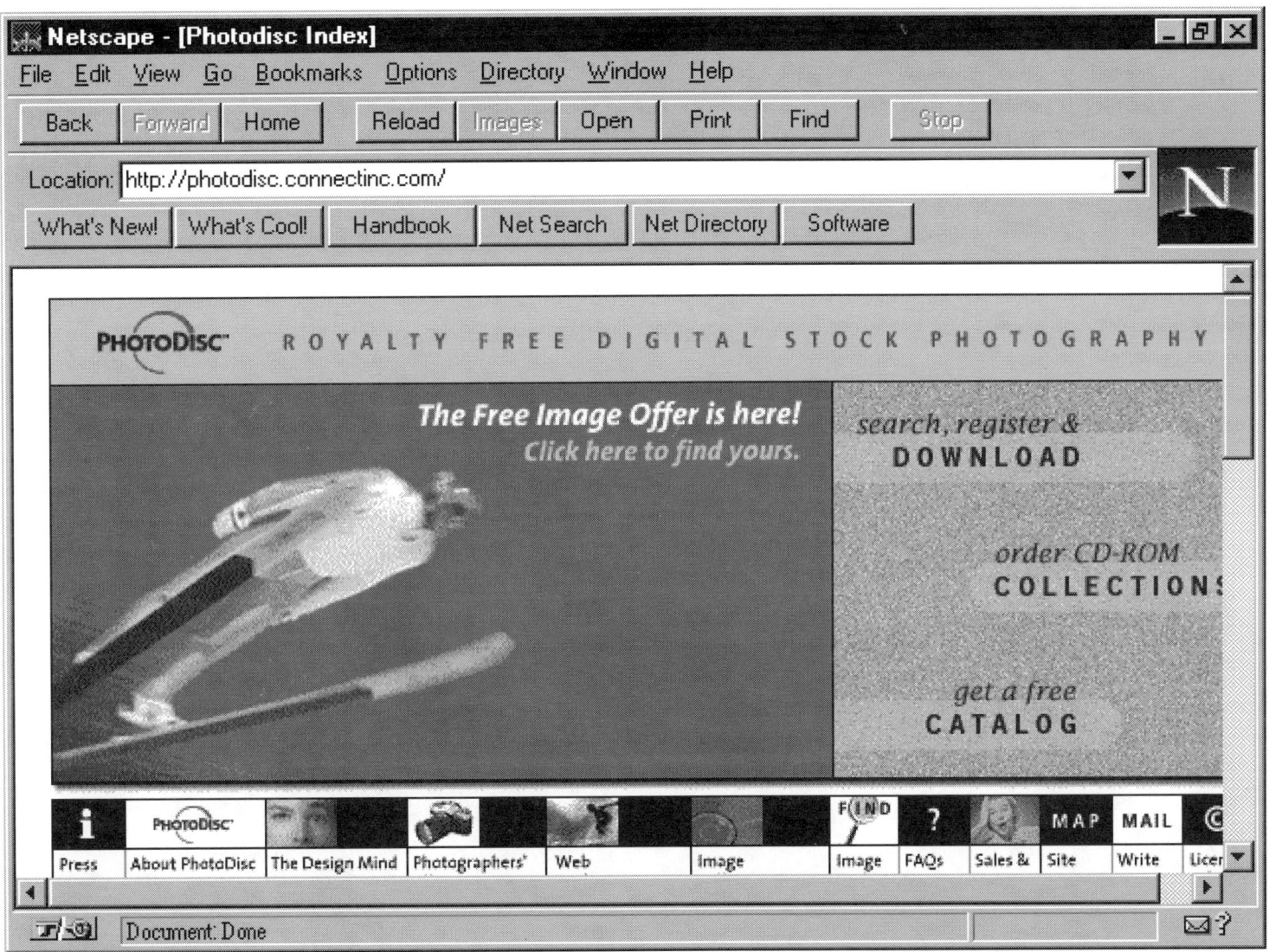

Courtesy of PhotoDisc, Inc.

Progressive Farmer Online

URL: http://www.pathfinder.com/PF

This site does an excellent job of furnishing farming techniques, hunting tips, and farming studies—even new recipes. Hosted by *Progressive Farmer* magazine, this site does a good job of offering current information in a friendly and easy-to-use fashion. The involvement at this site is simple. All you have to do is to fill out a questionnaire with nine questions on it, and you will be eligible to win the miniature boom box that is awarded each month. The questions are clear and straightforward, and would probably not take more than a few minutes to complete.

Key Feature

This site does a good job of providing information to farmers and outdoors people. The graphics are used well throughout, and the questionnaire is clear, to the point, and well done. Progressive Farmer Online immediately gives viewers a text-only option right at the beginning of their home page. Their questionnaire is long enough to be useful and short enough to be answered in a timely fashion. And, the have a prize waiting for those who choose to register with them!

San Francisco Reservations

URL: http://www.hotelres.com

The San Francisco Reservations site is extremely well done and very engaging. Visitors to this site can review hotel locations, prices, types of hotels and accommodations, and availability easily and efficiently. San Francisco Reservations involves their viewers in making a series of selections about the various hotels they have listed using clickable maps for the location. At the same time, they are sensitive to those who might not have the ability to use clickable maps and they provide a search box option. The site holds your attention with an excellent use of graphics throughout; there are lots of thumbnail sketches, and the viewer always has the option of choosing to see the larger versions. There is good attention to detail, and the information is timely within a few hours of when it is requested. For those bound for San Francisco, this is an extremely valuable and involving resource.

Key Feature

San Francisco Reservations is a wonderful resource for those wishing to obtain hotel accommodations in San Francisco. The site is engaging and informative, and the visitor is immediately involved in a number of decisions that pertain to the information they desire. In addition this site does an outstanding job of integrating text and images. Thumbnail images provide a sense of the information that can be obtained, and the viewer always has the option about whether or not to obtain it. Navigation is easy because the same text hyperlinks (Top, Location, Price, Type, Key, and Availability) appear on every screen.

Sandra Gering Gallery

URL: `http://www.users.interport.net/~gering`

The Sandra Gering Gallery involves visitors in a way that is different from any we have seen before. We Both Belong, a World Wide Web project by Ben Kinmont, is interactive art—he and visitors to the Sandra Gering Gallery have created a piece of art, together! As we move from the Home Page of this site through the six pages behind it, we are told by Ben Kinmont: "I invite your participation in a project of exchange and interaction, a project where we will make a sculpture gift as two points of reference on either end of our shared sculpture. The piece will be two photographs of domestic moments, one of you washing your dishes, and one of me washing mine, framed as a diptych and given to you in appreciation for your willingness to get involved." It is necessary to move through all six pages of the Ben Kinmont project in order to appreciate what he has attempted to do. Even though the project had ended when we visited there, we fully expect to find many more interactive projects such as this one in the future.

Key Feature

Sandra Gering Gallery provides a good first look at the possibilities artists might explore with the interactive nature of the World Wide Web. This site does a really outstanding job of engaging the visitor. Even though the project has officially ended, it is interesting to move through Ben Kinmont's pages and to see what he has intended for us to do.

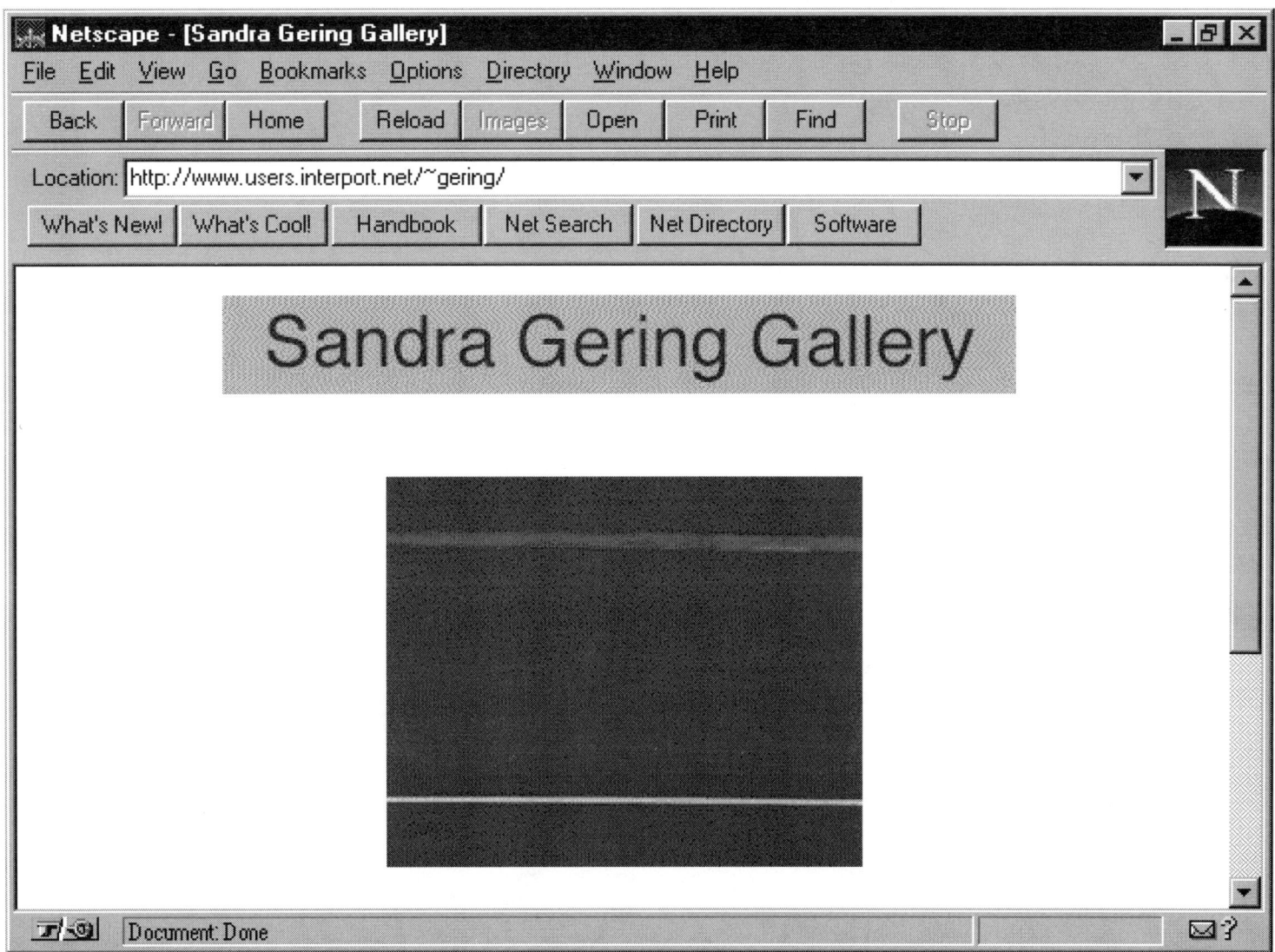

Speak To Me Catalog

URL: `http://www.clickshop.com/`

The Speak To Me Catalog is available from ClickShop.Com, a mall that offers not only this catalog, but also access to gourmet foods, home office supplies, pet supplies, and coffee beans. One is immediately involved in the Speak To Me Catalog, since almost every item that is presented will actually talk! When we chose Teddy Bears, we were presented with the Teddy Sez Talking Bear, the Animated Singing Happy Birthday Bear, and Teach Me Teddy. Selecting Teach Me Teddy permits the viewer to sample demo sounds for the eyes, ears, feet, hands, head, mouth and nose. These are all small files that download quickly and easily. The site involves the visitor from the outset, and the sample sounds make a purchasing decision much easier.

Key Feature

Speak To Me Catalog provides a highly involving experience. One is intrigued by the idea of hearing the sounds that the items for sale will actually make, and the sample sounds are small and download quickly. This site does a really good job of arousing interest in their wares and providing samples of what the viewer might wish to purchase. Small sounds that download quickly work well no matter what the access speed, and are remarkably lifelike!

UPS

URL: `http://www.ups.com`

The United Parcel Service site is well done, easy to use, and makes effective use of graphics. Most importantly, the site does an excellent job of enabling UPS users to obtain accurate information about their shipments. Viewers are involved instantly in the package tracking, the primary reason many visit this site. It is easy to track packages. Just click on the words "Package Tracking" along the top of the UPS home page, and you will quickly be taken to their UPS Package Tracking form. Just enter your tracking number and you will have the desired information!

Key Feature

The involvement here is very simple because the site has been designed to enable users to quickly and easily locate the information that they wish to have. In addition they have made it remarkably easy for visitors to who prefer a text-only option to have one; across the top of the UPS Home Page are text links for Using UPS, Package Tracking, About UPS, New Contacts, What's New, and Contents. One could not ask for a more user-friendly or clearer way to access these resources. This site does an excellent job of being both visually interesting as well as nonintrusive. Text-based choices across the top of the initial screen make it easy for viewers to find what they want, when they want it. And, their form is a model of simplicity.

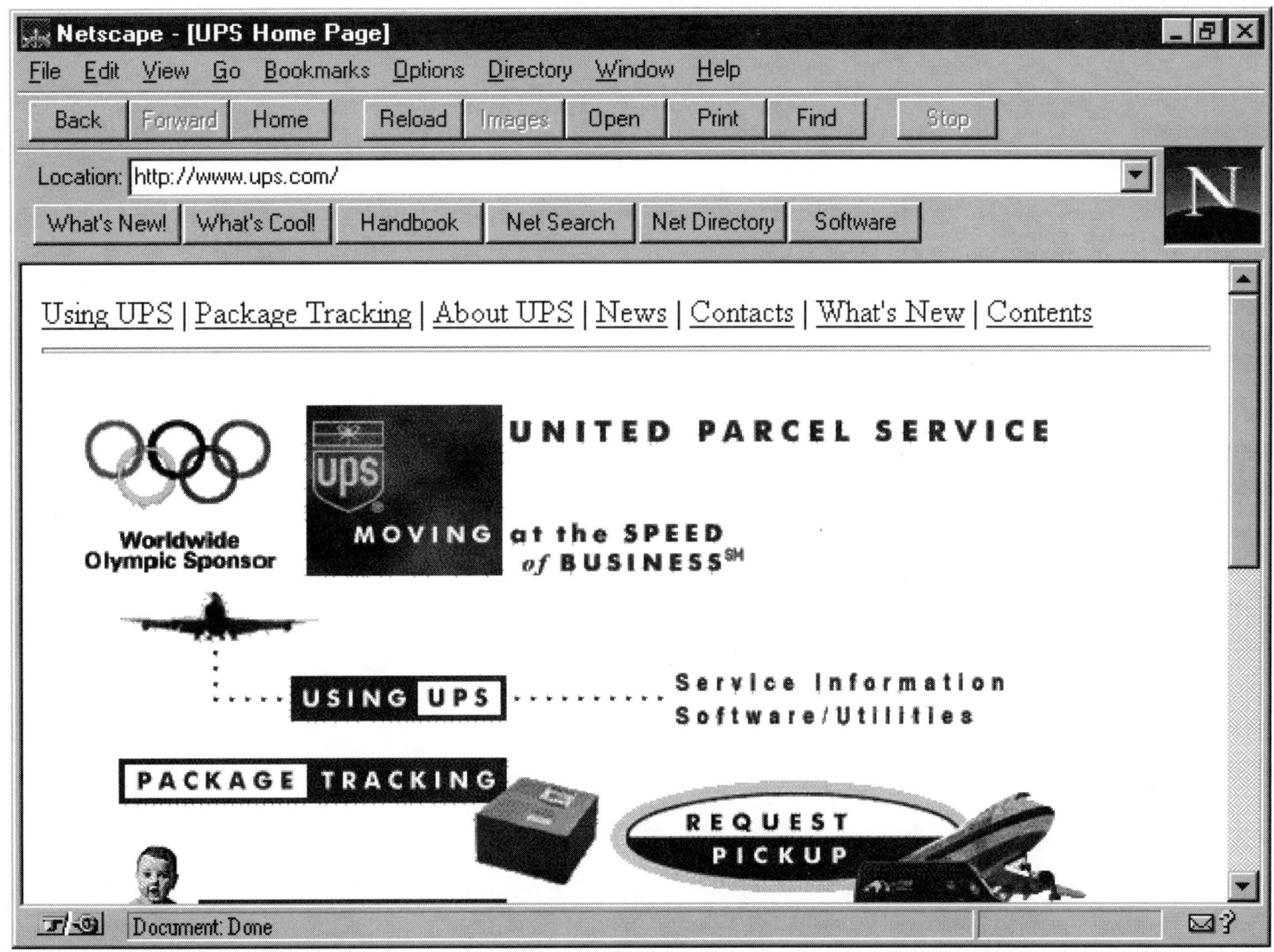

Courtesy of United Parcel Service of America, Inc.

Windham Hill Records

URL: `http://www.windham.com/`

Windham Hill Records is a good example of a site that involves its visitors in a way that correlates exactly to the product they sell. That is, one would imagine that visitors to this site are interested in hearing the music of the Windham Hill recording artists. You can go quickly from the Windham Hill Home Page to Our Music to The Listening Room. Once there, you will find almost 70 selections from which to choose. Each sound clip will play for about 30 seconds and has a file size of approximately 300,000 bytes. What a wonderful way to get a good sense of the Windham Hill artists and their music!

Key Feature

Windham Hill Records presents a site that is involving and informative. Sound clips are long enough to provide the viewer with a good sense of what the artist is all about, yet short enough that they download reasonably quickly, even over a modem.

Pitfalls and Fixes

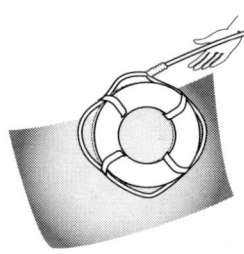

Pitfall: This initial graphic for this site is very beautiful, but it is large and adds little value to the information that is waiting behind it. One wishes for a smaller graphic and quicker access to the (wonderful) information that is available on all of the following pages.

Fix: An obvious solution would be to make the graphic smaller.

Courtesy of Windham Hill

Summary

The sites in this chapter represent a variety of ways in which to involve visitors. While their methods may vary, their goal is identical. The want visitors to come to their sites and stay for a while. There is much evidence to support the fact that those who go to a site and stay for a while or those who return there frequently are more likely to purchase goods or services from that site. There is clearly no one "best" way in which to involve visitors in a site, but it is clearly an important consideration when designing one. What will your visitor do once they are "inside the door" of your location? How involved will they be? How often will they return? Hopefully, these sites have given you a sense of how to proceed in making your particular site more involving for potential visitors.

Chapter

KEY 7:

Responsive to Its Users

Introduction to Key 7 — Responsive To Its Users

Key 7 provides us with an opportunity to think about how our site is responsive to its users or visitors. Do visitors have an easy way to send E-mail to the Webmaster? Are suggestions from visitors actively solicited? Does the site make an active attempt to learn more about the visitors? Is there a questionnaire, or feedback form, or set of questions, or contest, or registration form that will permit the Webmaster to learn more about the visitors?

Feedback forms and questionnaires serve a multitude of purposes. They set a tone that says that those managing the site are interested in knowing more about their visitors. They also provide a wonderful opportunity for "fine-tuning" of the site; if you can learn more about those who are visiting your site, then you might be tempted to make some changes in what is or is not being presented there. And, if you have many thousands of people looking at the site, perhaps some of them might have some helpful suggestions for ways to make the site better.

As you will soon see, different sites have adopted different models of feedback. While there is no "right" answer, it is clear that each one of these sites, in a nonintrusive way, manages to make it clear that they are interested in learning more about their visitors and are actively soliciting information from them.

We have included sites which provide a wide array of feedback forms and sites that continuously change in response to their users. We feel they are all good examples of responsive sites. A key feature of many of these sites was expressed years ago in French: "*Plus ça change, plus c'est la même chose*." (The more things change, the more they are the same.) For a Web site, this means retaining the basic "look and feel" while continuously refreshing that "look and feel" in response to users.

Technical Points

Placement of Text and Graphics Options

As Web sites mature and become more sensitive to user needs, they tend to move away from the large, flashy initial graphic toward a better use of smaller graphic files that download more quickly. This is most apparent in the placement and size of text and graphic options. Some good examples were presented in earlier chapters. They include Classroom Connect's use of an opening page to give the visitor choices, or others, such as IBM and Yahoo! which now use many smaller graphics than they originally did on their initial home pages to speed viewing.

If you offer a text-only or minimum graphics choice, it should be located near the top of your page. Visitors respond well to choices if they are offered early.

Offering Language or Geographic Options

Web sites intended for audiences outside of a single area or country do well to offer choices. As you will soon see, the IBM site does this well by offering many different country versions of its home page.

Different languages present another opportunity and also a challenge. Languages using the basic Roman alphabet display well on most browsers. Languages requiring specialized characters such as French, or German, or the Scandinavian set, may not display well on all browsers. Ideographic languages, such as those from Asia, are only slowly getting support and standards on the Web. If you plan to offer multiple languages, test them carefully with many different browsers. Offer hyperlinks to the ones that support your choices.

E-mail Feedback

All sites should follow the convention of providing an E-mail hyperlink somewhere on their home page. This means visitors should always be offered the option of sending E-mail to the "`web-master@...`" That's the easy part. The hard part is having a plan to deal with the E-mail that comes in. You have several choices depending on your resources.

Autoresponders or mail-bots will return a "Thank You for your note..." automatically (and almost instantly) for each incoming electronic note. Mail-bot responses, however, just give you breathing space. People who take the time to send you mail deserve a personal response if you can manage it. The original mail-bot note should contain some hint about what will happen next. Be sure you check your mail-bot regularly by sending it mail. Also, read the response carefully and see if what you put in some months back is still accurate at the current time.

Requesting comments places two responsibilities on you. First, you must answer all notes. Second, you must consider objectively and without prejudice if the comment has merit. We say without prejudice because none of us likes criticism. If we want to be responsive to our visitors, we will have to listen to them fairly.

Questions and Surveys

Plan well ahead before launching a questionnaire or survey. Ask yourself the following questions:

> Why you are doing this survey?
>
> Why should visitors choose to participate?
>
> What you will offer people who respond?
>
> What you will do with the survey results?
>
> Will you post or E-mail the results to participants?
>
> Will you put time limits on the survey?
>
> Will you take visible actions based on survey results?

Survey Forms

If you decide to use surveys, review the examples from this chapter and pick the best one (or ones) that match your concepts. Then edit it (them). You may never know how many people will start your survey and abandon it if they become bored or tired. Keep your forms short, sweet and simple. Remember, you are not the U.S. Census bureau.

Anonymous "Button" Surveys

Be cautious of using survey techniques that allow anonymous responses. Keep in mind that the Internet is, and will always be, an open frontier with mostly good people, but also a few "bad guys." Don't expose your site to pranks or hoaxes. Each survey participant should provide you with their E-mail address. Your autoresponder should send out thank you notes and should also automatically log those which are undeliverable. The responses from the undeliverable ones should be removed before tabulation.

Changing the Site to Accommodate Responses

If you ask for comments about changing your site, move slowly when implementing the changes. More than one Webmaster has been bombarded by unhappy visitors after a change to the site has been made. Introduce changes deliberately and keep them in place long enough for the comments to come in. Avoid doing a drastic change in the "look and feel" of your site without a lot of prior testing.

One solution is to set up a secondary test site with the changes and put a link from the current site, such as, "Try our new look and let us know..." This gives you a way to judge reactions without jeopardizing your current visitor set.

Having said all this, let's now go look at a number of sites that do a good job of being responsive to their users.

Apple Feedback Page

URL: `http://support.info.apple.com/feedback/feedback.html`

The Apple Feedback Page is a good model of how to effectively solicit feedback from visitors to a site. They ask a few demographic questions (First Name, Last Name, E-mail address) and then move to a short set of seven questions that can be answered quickly and easily by most people. Additional demographic questions at the bottom of the page are strictly voluntary. In addition, they make it clear that these questions are for feedback only. If a visitor would like additional technical support, there are several hyperlinks and an 800 number to provide that.

The Apple Feedback Page does a good job; it sets a tone that says that they are interested in knowing more about those who visit the site, it does not overwhelm you with questions, and it asks for a minimum of demographic information.

Key Feature

The Apple Feedback Page is a really good example of how to effectively elicit feedback from visitors. They indicate clearly that "we are constantly looking for ways to improve these services and we need your help in making them better." The questions are limited, the demographic information is nonintrusive, and additional resources are indicated with hyperlinks and an 800 number.

Pitfalls and Fixes

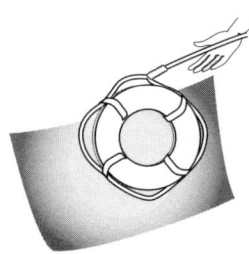

Pitfall: The use of a toll-free 800 number allows response from only the Untied States.

Fix: For overseas visitors who really want to call, put in a number they can reach from their countries. Use the form +1-321-555-1234.

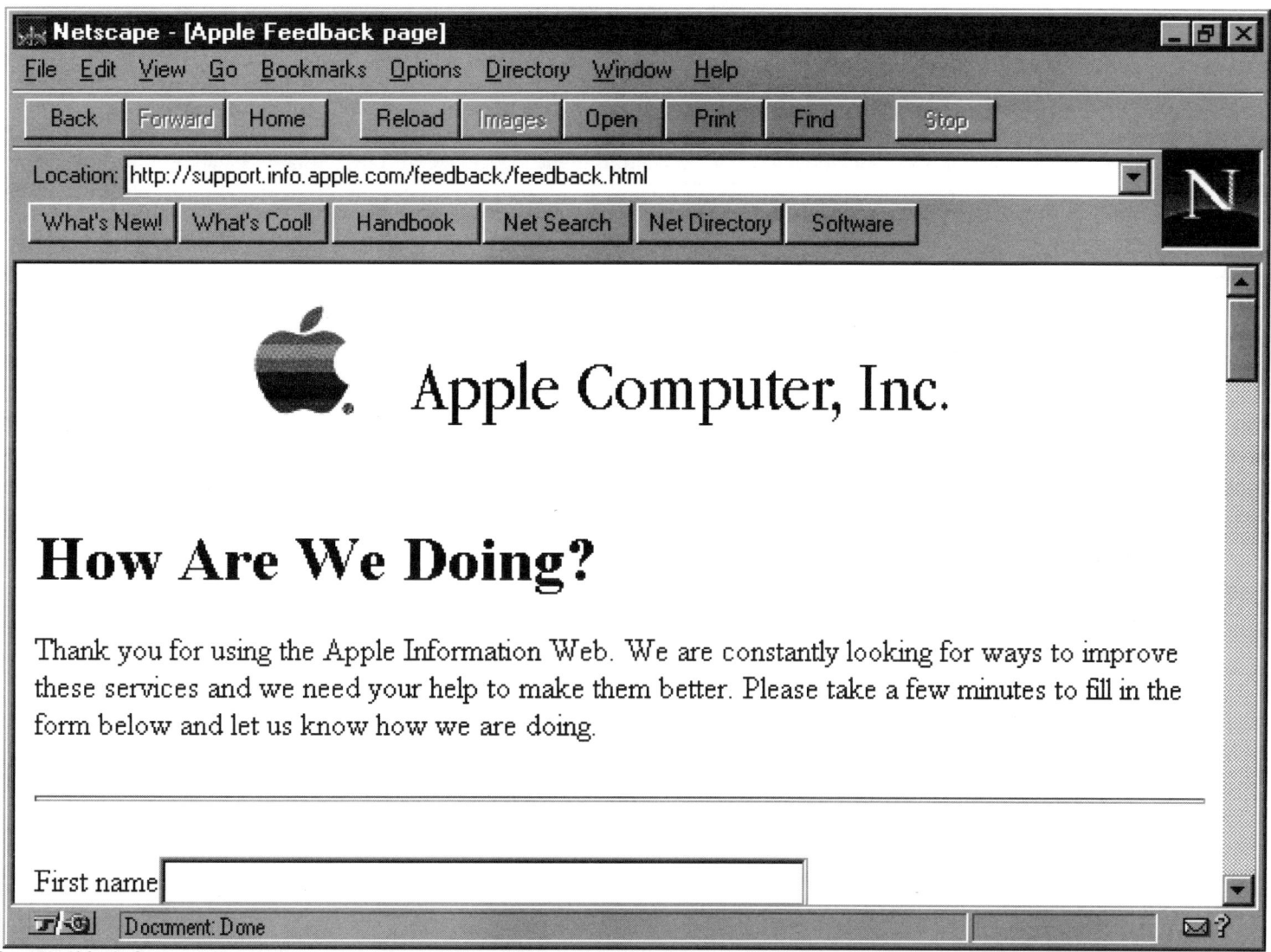

Black Box On-Line Catalog

URL: `http://www.blackbox.com`

Black Box "is a globally recognized brand name associated with high quality data communication and telecommunications products." What is most impressive about the Black Box Home Page is how easy they make it for their visitors to communicate with them. For comments and questions, you just have to click on the hyperlink `info@blackbox.com`. For comments and questions about the Black Box Online Catalog, you just click on the hyperlink `webmaster@blackbox.com`. If you wish to search for a particular item, there is an easy-to-use search engine with an appropriate hyperlink (`Search the Black Box On-Line Catalog`) included. And, perhaps most importantly, one of the very first hyperlinks on the home page asks visitors to complete their user survey before leaving. The Black Box On-Line Catalog User Survey is a model of clarity. And, it is also a good example of how a company can use a directed set of questions to help them serve their customers better.

Key Feature

The Black Box Home Page sets a tone from the outset that says that they are interested in being responsive to their visitors. Multiple opportunities are provided for visitors to submit comments, questions, and information about how to make the Online Catalog more useful.

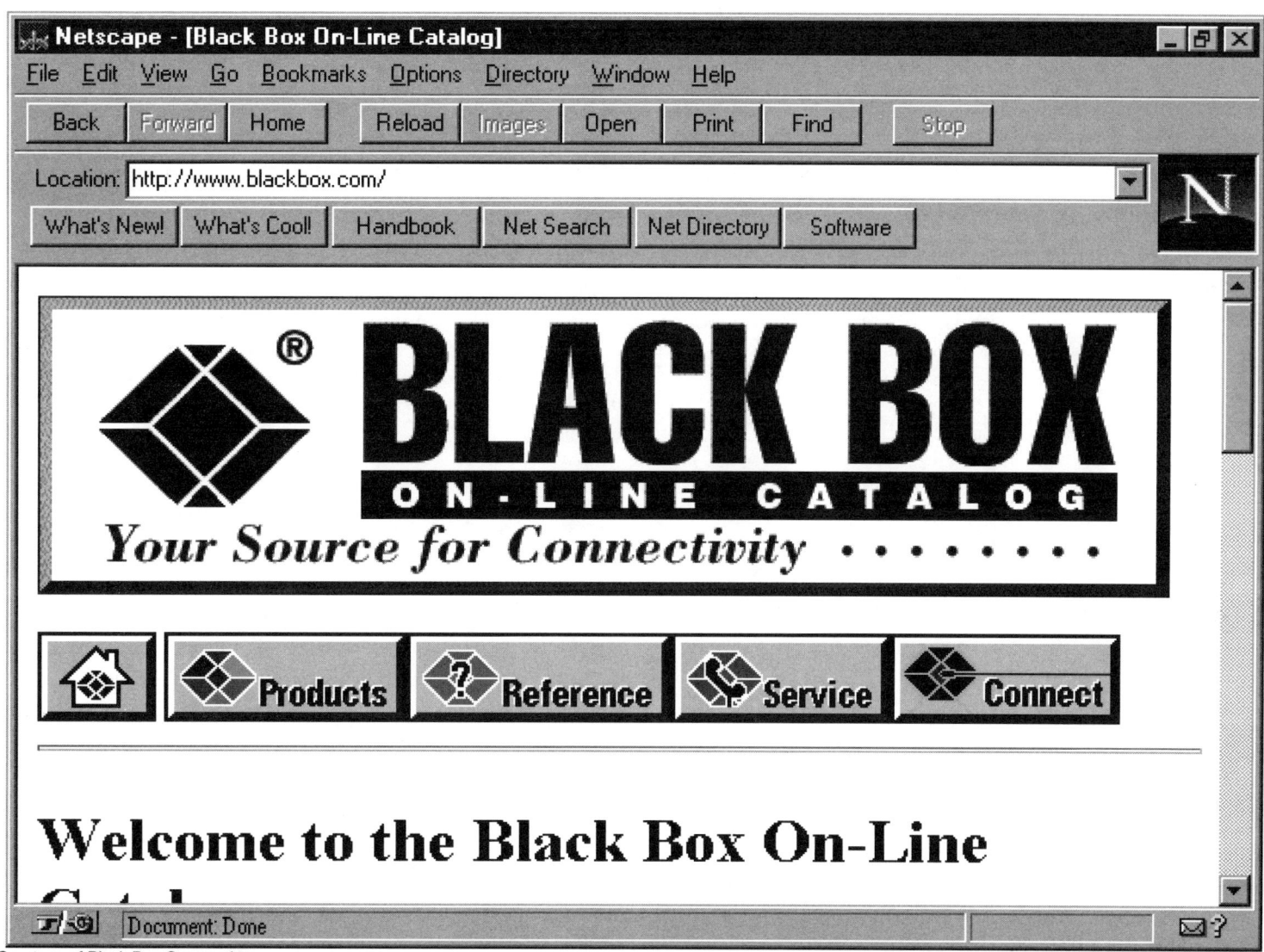

c|net online

URL: `http://www.cnet.com`

c|net online is a wonderful site for those interested in current computer information. c|net has a good clear home page that make it easy for visitors to find their way around. Our focus here, however, their method of getting information from (and consequently providing information to) their visitors who choose to join. Two icons on the c|net online Home Page enable you to "join now." When you do so, you are taken to their registration form and are told that "c|net online is a free, advertiser supported service for its members. While there is no cost to becoming a member, we do ask that you register."

Registration is a simple process that can be completed in a minute or less. There are only a few questions, and a very clear Privacy Notice makes it clear that the information is for their internal use only. They state that the information will help them "to customize the service for each individual member's preferences" as well as enable them to provide their advertisers (and themselves) with the demographic profile of their membership. Other than some quick demographic questions about age and gender, the primary focus of the questions is on the software, connectivity speed, and hardware used by the visitor. At the end of the registration process, visitors will have a user name for the c|net online service, and a password.

Key Feature

c|net online is a good example of how it is possible to use a registration process to obtain accurate demographic information from those visiting a site. They state clearly that the information will be kept private and that the information requested is to enable them to provide better customized service for users of c|net online.

Pitfalls and Fixes

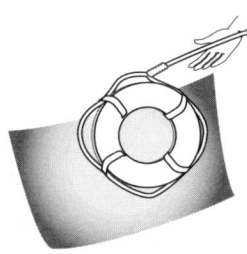

Pitfall: As we have noted before, registration entails some risk of losing visitors and, in addition, creates an administration load for the site.

Fix: Some sites have decided that other ways of eliciting information about visitors are less intrusive and perhaps less burdensome.

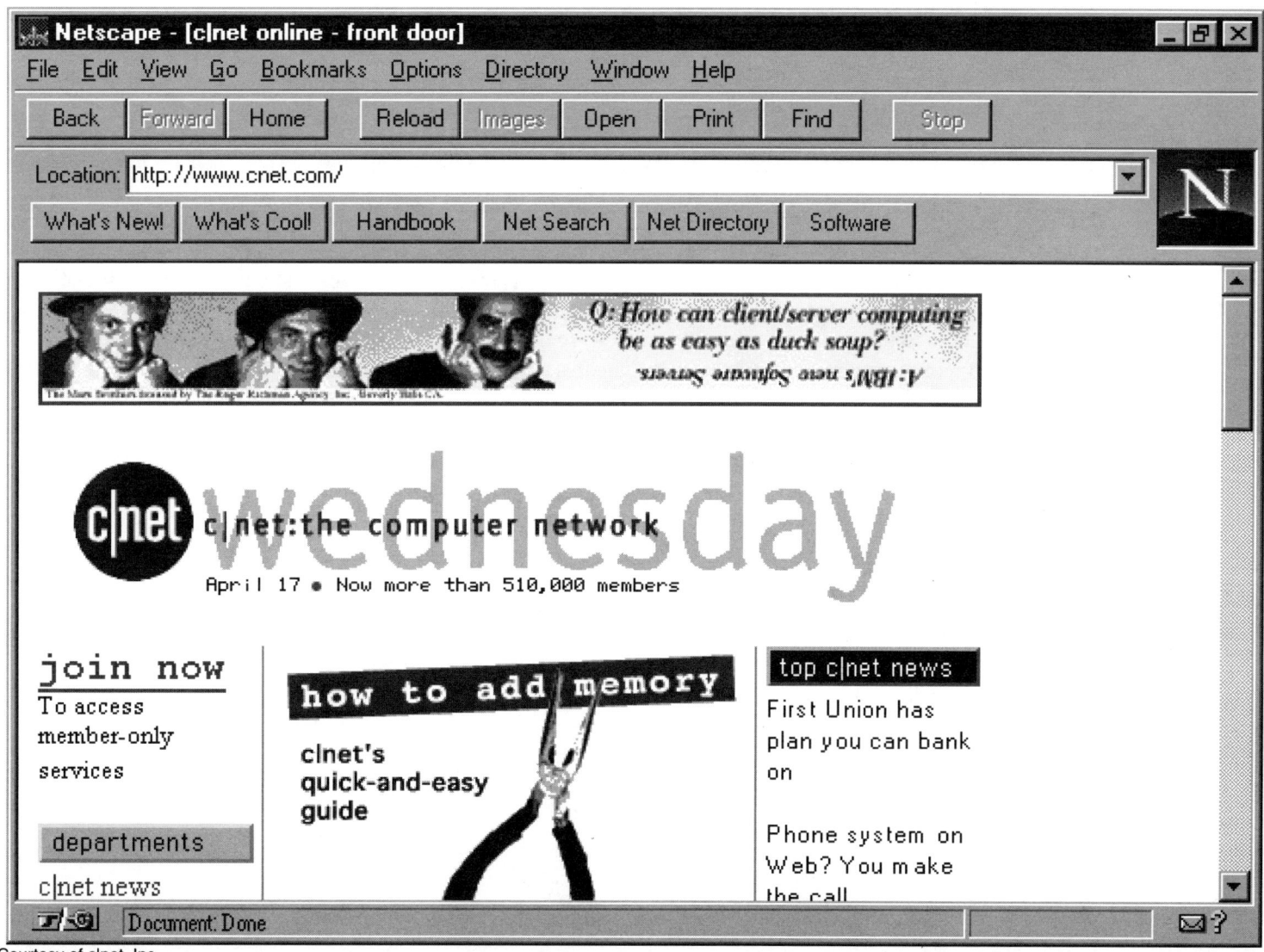

Cyberian Outpost

URL: `http://www.cybout.com`

Cyberian Outpost is, as they say "the cool place to shop for computer products." Their initial graphics on the Cyberian Outpost Home Page set a friendly, inviting, folksy tone. In addition, they make it easy for visitors to find what they want with a convenient and very powerful full featured search form. They also provide a newsletter (*The Cyberian Express Newsletter*) for their customers (and potential customers) that can be had by just entering your E-mail address. This is a great way for Cyberian Outpost to collect information about visitors to their site, and it is a non-threatening and simple way for visitors to provide them with information. In addition, Cyberian Outpost actively solicits feedback from its visitors by using a convenient feedback page that consists of nothing more complicated than a hyperlink enabling one to "Send feedback to Cyberian Outpost" (mailto:`feed-back@cybout.com`). While it's impossible to tell how much feedback they do receive, it was interesting to read the feedback that had been posted.

Key Feature

Cyberian Outpost sets an inviting tone with its graphics and folksy manner. The site actively solicits feedback, and also provides a free newsletter for the price of your E-mail address. This seems to be a clever idea. The newsletter appears on a more (or less) regular basis and is filled with news about the industry as well as Cyberian Outpost. They now have a listing of the E-mail addresses of those who have requested it as well as some demographic information about visitors to the site.

Courtesy of Cyberian Outpost

IBM Corporation

URL: `http://www.ibm.com`

The IBM Corporation Home Page illustrates the importance of responding to visitors from all over the world. IBM, which clearly has a global presence, now makes its information available in a multitude of languages to those who visit its site. Notice in particular the box labeled IBM Planetwide (below the figure that is shown) in which the words "Choose a country" can be seen. When you click on the down arrow, you are offered an array (today) of 20 different countries, including Argentina, Australia, Austria, Belgium, Brazil, Chile, Israel, Italy, Japan, Peru, and Switzerland. When you click on the Go! button to the right of the "Choose A Country" box, the IBM World Wide Web Home Page disappears and you are taken to a page that has been prepared in the language of that country.

Notice also several other features that make this page particularly responsive to its users. At the bottom of the page are hyperlinks for text-only, HTML 2.0, and HTML 3.0 versions. In addition, there is a self-contained search engine that is easily accessible by a hyperlink. There is also a hyperlink that permits you to `Contact IBM`. When you click on it, you are taken to a page entitled `Personal Help From IBM` and hyperlinks permit you to send E-mail easily to `askibm@info.ibm.com` or to `web-master@www.ibm.com`. You are also given phone numbers for both US-based and international phone calls.

Key Feature

Of particular note is how the information is presented in special versions for visitors from different countries. The "look and feel" of the different pages remains the same, but the languages change instantly, and visitors who would prefer to receive information in their native tongue are now afforded an opportunity to have it that way. This is a really fine example of how to be responsive to one's users! It should also be noted that visitors are provided with a text-only hyperlink at the bottom of the home page.

Pitfalls and Fixes

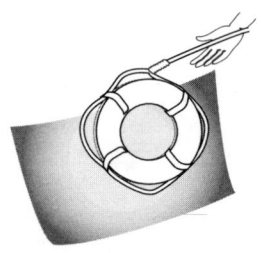

Pitfall: At the bottom o f the home page, visitors are provided with a sentence that states: "Text-only, HTML 2.0 and HTML 3.0 versions of this page a re available." While offering the choice HTML 2.0 and 3.0 is admirable, it is possible that many visitors may not understand the differences between HTML 2.0 and 3.0 or which version of HTML is supported by their particular browser.

Fix: It would be more complex to manage, but a "Browser Recognizer" could offer a statement such as: "We see you are using the so-and-so browser. Would you like to see the features we offer for that browser?"

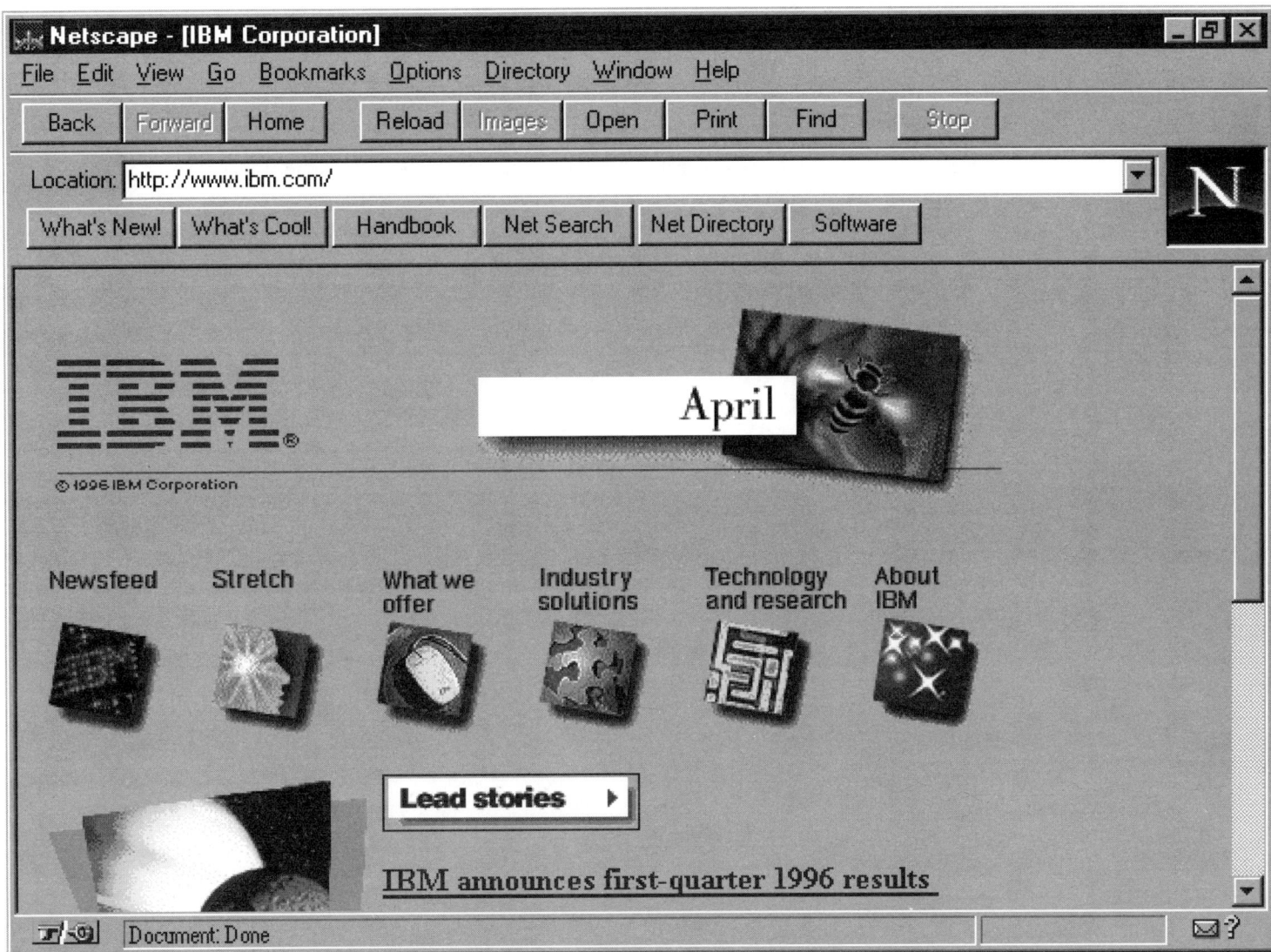

Courtesy of IBM Corporation

Internet Business Reply

URL: `http://www.ip.net/cgi-bin/ibr/icc`

Internet Business Reply™ is a really clever idea. It was developed by the Internet Presence and Publishing Corporation (`http://www.ip.net`), a provider of Internet connectivity and electronic publishing services. The Internet Business Reply form makes it quick and easy for visitors to communicate their need for information or their comments to a company. Shown here is the card used by the International Communications Corp. It asks for the customary name, company, address, city, state, zip, phone, E-mail and fax that we see in the "real" world. There are three simple checkboxes at the bottom of the form, as well as a place where additional comments can be entered. The Internet Business Reply card is sent to the International Communications Corp. just by clicking when you have entered the information, and no postage is necessary!

Key Feature

The Internet Business Reply card cleverly takes a metaphor known by all and converts it into an electronic version. The card is quick and easy to complete and collects a reasonable amount of information in a short amount of time. This form feels very nonintrusive, and the visitor is able to make some choices about what should happen next, quickly and easily. If you would like to receive a phone call, or additional information, or be added to their mailing list, the choice is yours. And, if there are additional comments to be made, there is a very simple and easy-to-use box into which to enter them. All of us have completed similar postcards at one time or another; doing so electronically seems to be familiar, easy, and nonthreatening.

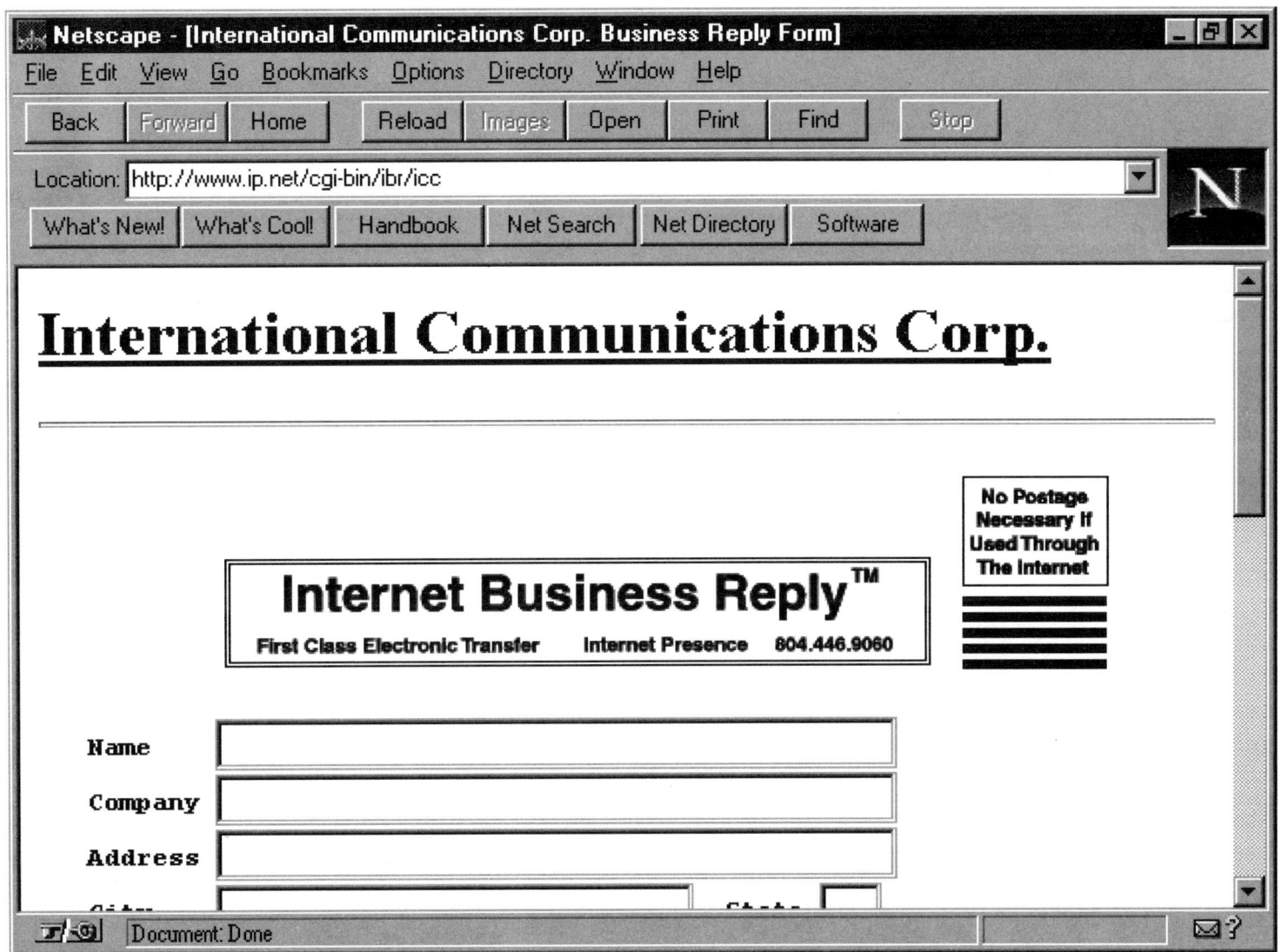

Jim Knopf—The Father of Shareware

URL: `http://www.halcyon.com/knopf/jim.html`

In some respects, there is probably nothing more responsive to its users than the idea of shareware. Creating software and then sharing it with others for free, in the hope that they will like it and buy it after they have tried it, are certainly an acts of faith, and for some, a wonderful way to be in business. One of the most (if not the most) successful creators of shareware is a man named Jim Knopf. This site is a testament to his success that began in 1982, as well as a wonderful repository of shareware and other resources. Notice how friendly the words and images are. In addition, it is so easy to find information, or to send feedback to Jim Knopf and we are encouraged to do so. We are guided through the shareware selections that Jim thinks we should have, to other selections for shareware distributors, creators, and others. The style throughout is folksy and we are told clearly that he solicits our: "Comments, Suggestions for improvement, corrections (bad links) - Please Help!, Links to be added - Please help!, and Words of encouragement." With a note such as "Send email to me (Jim, the big guy). I'd love to hear from you." who could resist?

Key Feature

Jim Knopf's site is friendly, easygoing, inviting, informative, and full of wonderful information about, and access to shareware. The site makes it easy for visitors to find what they want, and clearly encourages visitors to share their thoughts. Comments such as "This is a User Supported Home Page. It'll only be as good as You and I make it!" set the tone that pervades the site. Jim Knopf has been very successful in the shareware business; with this sort of attitude, it is easy to see why he has.

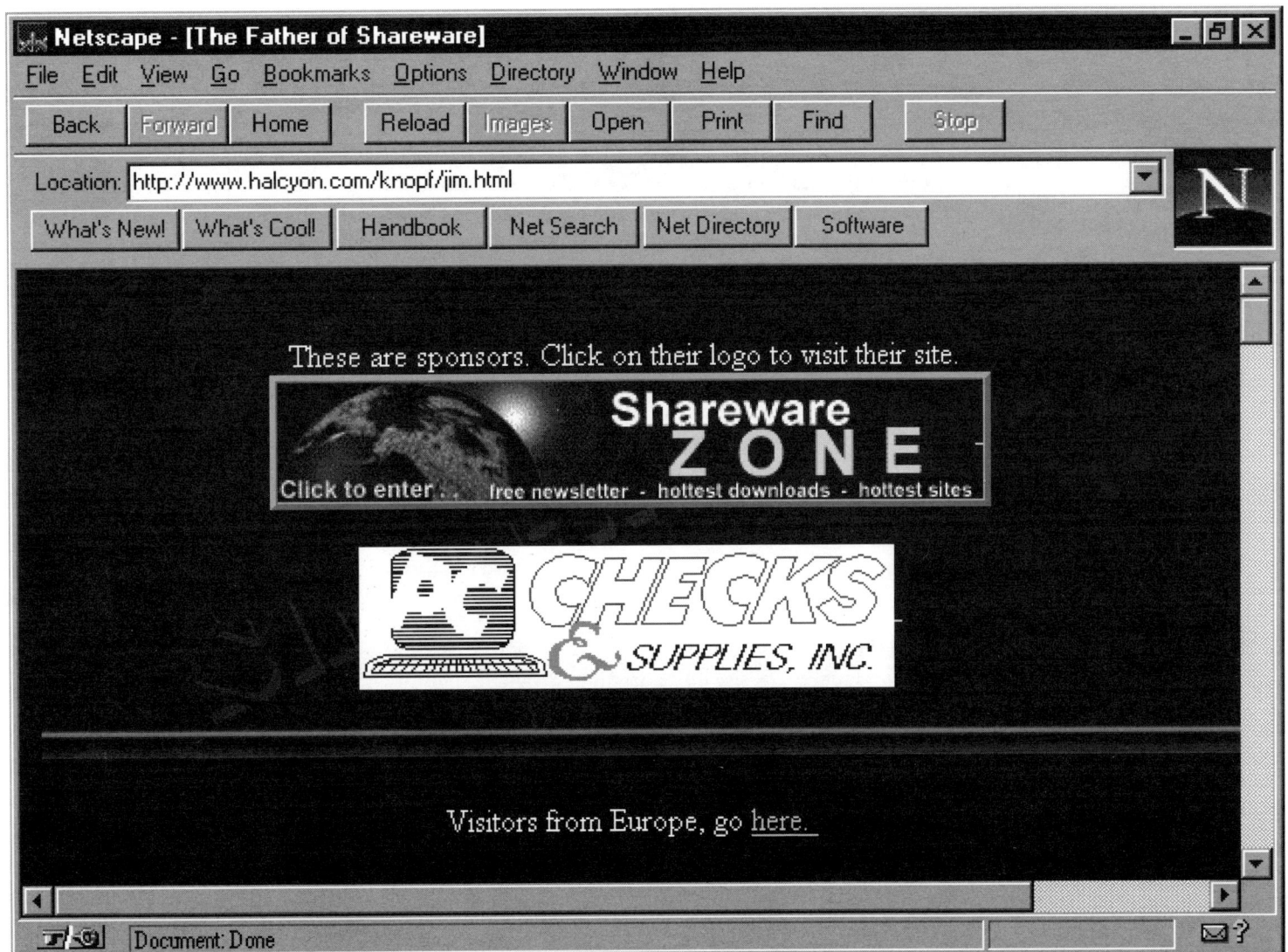

Lycos, Inc.

URL: `http://www.lycos.com`

Lycos is one of the best known of the Web search engines and is often visited. Visitors may not realize how Lycos has been continuously evolving since its early Carnegie-Mellon University days. The site has maintained its basic look and feel but has been rearranged slightly in response to visitor comments. The search form is presented quickly near the top of the page for those in a hurry. For more complex searches, the "Enhance your search" hyperlink takes us to another more detailed page. Offers of other new and interesting links keep the page fresh.

Lycos now offers a new directory service called A2Z. This new feature appeared only recently, and has been provided in response to visitor requests. There are also opportunities to quickly and easily access the New Top 5% reviews on Point, and a support for those who are new to the Internet and the World Wide Web is provided as well.

Key Feature

The basic design of this Web site has been retained over time, but it has been slowly modified to suit the needs of its visitors better. Lycos exists to help people find information and resources on the Internet and the World Wide Web. Good navigation, easy to follow menus, and continuous support for their visitors make this site quite useful and valued. The site has always been a good one to visit; now it is even better!

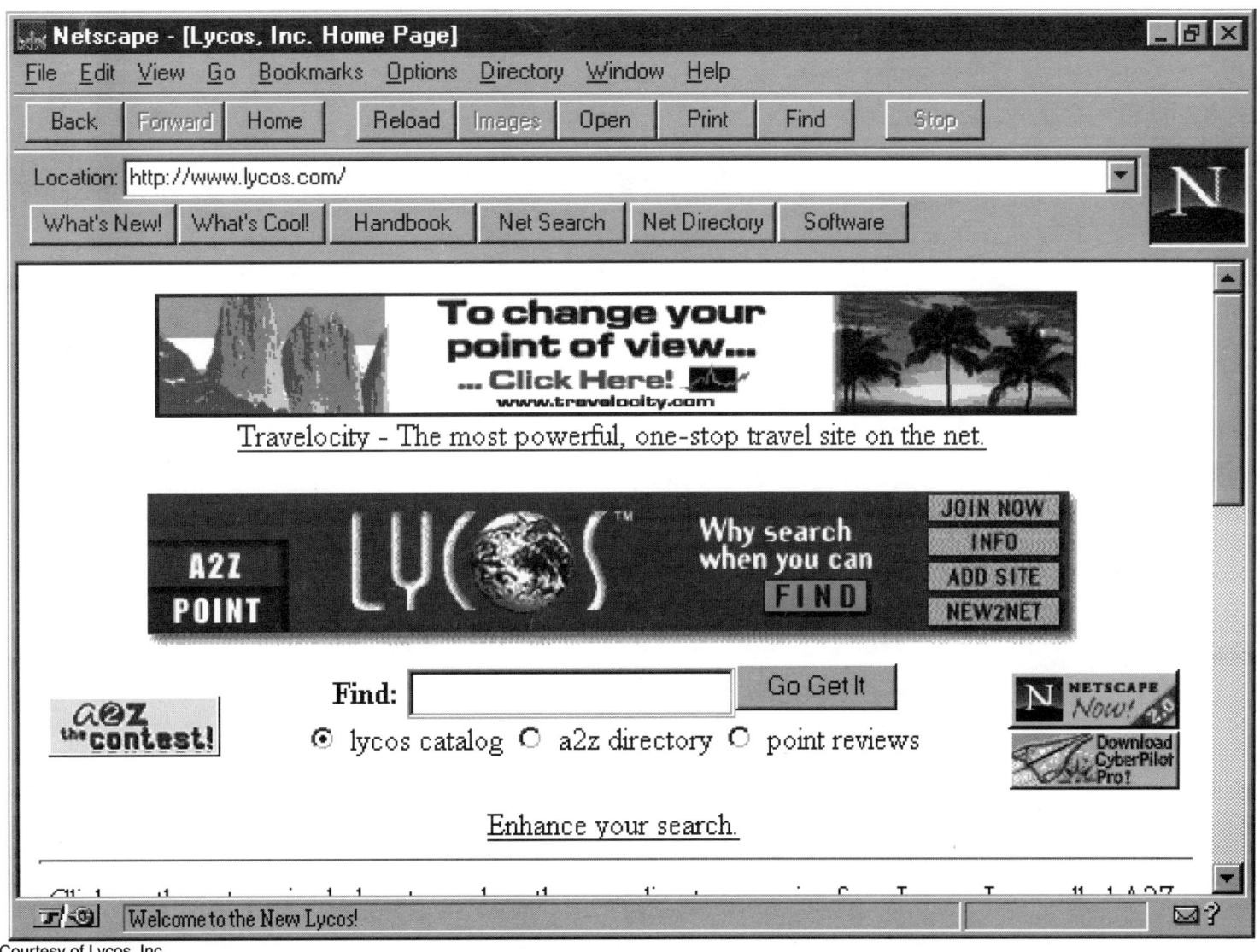

Mama's Cucina

URL: http://www.eat.com/

Mama's Cucina is a wonderfully engaging site to visit. Its atmosphere is one of family and home and all the various aspects of the site support that feeling. There are many entertaining aspects to the site; be sure not to miss Mama's Soap Opera: *As The Lasagna Bakes* and Mama's Tour of Little Italy. However, we will focus our attention on the two parts of the site that are most purposefully responsive to the site's users: *Mama Wants to Know....* and *Talk to Mama.*

A survey is presented in the *Mama Wants to Know* section. It begins: "The nice kids at Ragu wanted me to ask you a few questions so they could know you better and know how to make better sauces for you. They're even holding a drawing every week for all the people who answer the questions. If you win, those nice kids at Ragu will send you a special gift—I'll send you email if you win. So what are you waiting for?" The survey asks questions about the visitor's perceptions About The Site, About Food, and About You. It takes a few minutes to complete and will certainly provide the "nice kids at Ragu" with a lot of useful information. *Talk to Mama* prompts visitors to "Tell me what's on your mind. Don't be shy, eh!" and then advises them how to easily send Mama some E-mail.

Key Feature

Mama's Cucina creates a warm and inviting feeling for visitors. *Mama Wants to Know...* is a detailed survey about the site, the products, and the visitors. *Talk to Mama* makes it easy to send E-mail. This is an excellent example of making visitors feel welcome and at ease. It is also a good example of how to actively elicit feedback from those who visit a site While completing the detailed survey may be more than some of us want to take the time and effort to do, the fact of the matter is that there is a survey, and a tone of actively soliciting feedback has been set. In addition, they make it quick and easy to communicate by E-mail with those responsible for the site.

Courtesy of Van den Bergh Foods, Inc.

McAfee Network Security & Management

URL: `http://www.mcafee.com/`

McAfee has always been a name associated with virus protection software that was available as shareware. You could quickly and easily download the current copy of their well-known SCAN virus protection software and be reasonably assured that your computer was safe from harm. The company has been quite successful and has now expanded into Network Security & Management. However, they still make it easy for visitors to their site to find and download the latest version of their virus protection software. There is a hyperlink on the home page entitled `Download Files from McAfee's FTP Site`. Clicking on it once takes you to the Download McAfee page, where visitors are told that "Fully functional, evaluation copies of all McAfee software packages are available from these McAfee Associates FTP servers." They provide hyperlinks that make it easy for the visitor to Download McAfee Products or to Download Third Party Products. If you click on Download McAfee Products, you will be taken to the directory of their ftp file server, where you can easily click on the hyperlink for antivirus. Doing so takes you to the antivirus subdirectory, where you can easily download the latest copy (scn-229e.zip as of this writing) of SCAN.

Key Feature

The McAfee Network Security & Management Home Page continues their fine tradition of making it quick and easy to obtain evaluation copies of their antivirus software. They obviously offer a great many other products these days, but they have continued to take good care of their loyal customers with an easy-to-use set of hyperlinks leading visitors to the desired products. The site is valued for the software the company provides, and they also offer a wealth of information on the topic of virus protection. There is an Internet Support Forum for those who have questions about viruses, or any of the McAfee products.

Another hyperlink provides access to a Guest Book in which visitors can sign. The Guest Book begins with the usual demographic information (name, company, E-mail, and so forth) and then asks a limited number of questions about reasons for visiting the site, products being used, and particular information being requested. The Guest Book idea works well; the amount of time to fill it out can be measured in minutes, and McAfee is extremely attentive to responding quickly to requests for information. The McAfee site provides several models of responsiveness to users than could be emulated by others: they provide fully functional working copies of their software for others to try, and they actively solicit feedback and information about their visitors.

Courtesy of McAfee

NetMind Free Services

URL: `http://www.netmind.com/`

The NetMind Free Services Home Page is an interesting example of being responsive to one's users. As we are told, "The objective of this page is to provide hyperlinks to free services available on the Web. To be included on this page, a free service must do more than provide on-line information; it must perform a customized service for the user. Services on this page don't just tell you something, or let you tell someone else something; they do something for you. Most importantly, they do it for free. Net-Mind is dedicated to keeping useful and entertaining Internet-based services free to end users." How much more responsive could one be?

The NetMind Free Services Home Page includes a Free Services List that includes E-Mail Robots, Media Changers, Synthesizers, Calculators, and Personal Processors. As you might imagine, they make it easy to navigate through their site. In addition, they encourage visitors to provide them with their E-mail address so that they can be notified when the page is updated. They also provide a NetMind Suggestion Form where visitors are encouraged to provide NetMind with comments and suggestions.

Key Feature

NetMind Free Services Home Page is a terrific example of how to make a site useful for visitors. It is chock-full of useful hyperlinks, is easy to navigate, provides a free update service, and welcomes comments and suggestions. One could hardly ask for more!

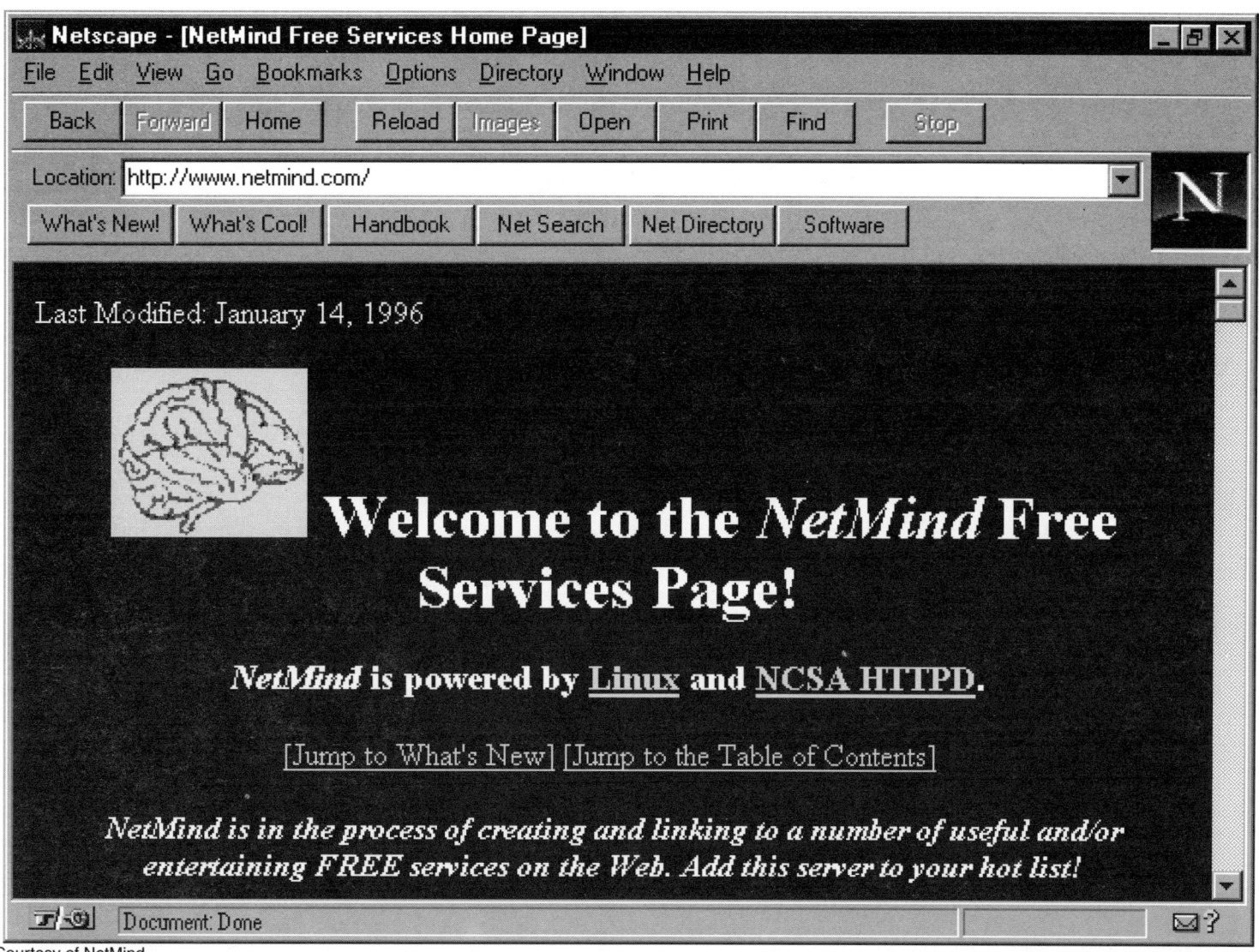

Paperless Guide to NYC

URL: `http://www.mediabridge.com/nyc/`

Paperless Guide to NYC is a wonderful repository of information about New York City. In addition to providing many useful resources, they have also done a good job of making their site easy to navigate. They provide visitors with a hyperlink (`nyc@mediabridge.com`) for submitting E-mail suggestions and contributions and have included an easy-to-use Feedback Form. On this Evaluation and Mailing List Request Form, visitors are told that "We appreciate your feedback about our site, and ideas on how to improve the content within the guide. In order to stay in touch with us, and to receive announcements about new changes, please fill out your E-mail address." The feedback form asks only a few questions, which makes it quick and easy to fill out.

Key Feature

Paperless Guide to New York City provides useful information for those who want to know a lot about New York City (particularly Manhattan). They make it easy for visitors to correspond with them via E-mail and also provide a short feedback form that encourages suggestions and ongoing correspondence. There is an interesting nice touch at the bottom of the home page—a hyperlink called "contributions" tells visitors about those who have made the page successful. There is nothing profound about this, but it does add a nice human touch.

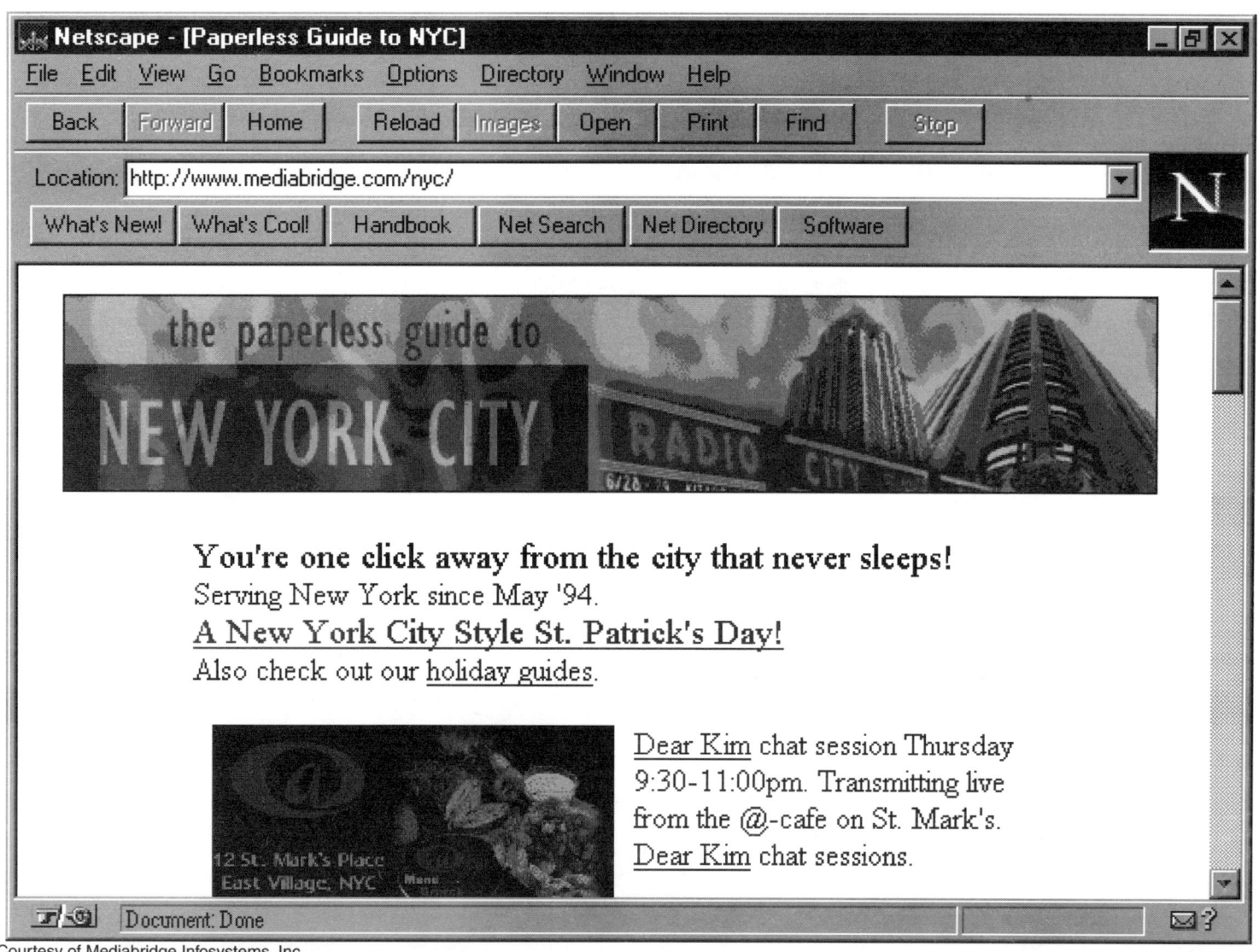

Virtual Vineyards

URL: `http://www.virtualvin.com`

Virtual Vineyards has done a marvelous job of creating a site that is full of information and that is extremely responsive to its users. They provide a tasting chart to help visitors select wines that match their individual tastes and they have an E-mail List that lets visitors stay in touch with Virtual Vineyards. They do a good job of discussing Internet Security, and they also permit visitors to create a personal account. Registering for this personal account allows visitors to "take advantage of special personalization features that help to: 1. Remind you which items you like by maintaining a history of your previous purchases; 2. Keep you own personal tasting notes about your favorite purchases; 3. Tailor the presentation and products we offer according to your preferences." All of these features serve to make visitors feel welcome and cared for as well as provide Virtual Vineyards with lots of personal information about their visitors. Comments and suggestions are encouraged and are easily sent using the hyperlink that has been provided. Visitors are told that "we read and appreciate all of them."

Key Feature

Virtual Vineyards does a great job of providing visitors with lots of personalized information about wine. The registration form enables visitors to create their own profile (complete with billing information) and attention is paid to any concerns about Internet security that visitors might have. Virtual Vineyards has created a site that is focused on what it does, why it does it, and how to do it well. There is also a hyperlink permitting visitors to sign in, but we are clearly told that this optional. And, in fact, visitors are made to feel welcome to enter, browse, and buy whether or not they have an account. That is a clever idea—one we wish more companies could copy.

Pitfalls and Fixes

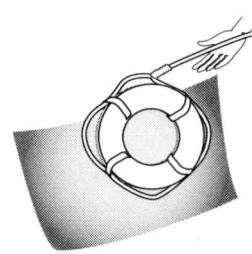

Pitfall: Earlier pages from Virtual Vineyards contained large graphics.

Fix: A responsive fix has already been applied to reduce graphics sizes in response to the needs of users, while retaining an attractive look.

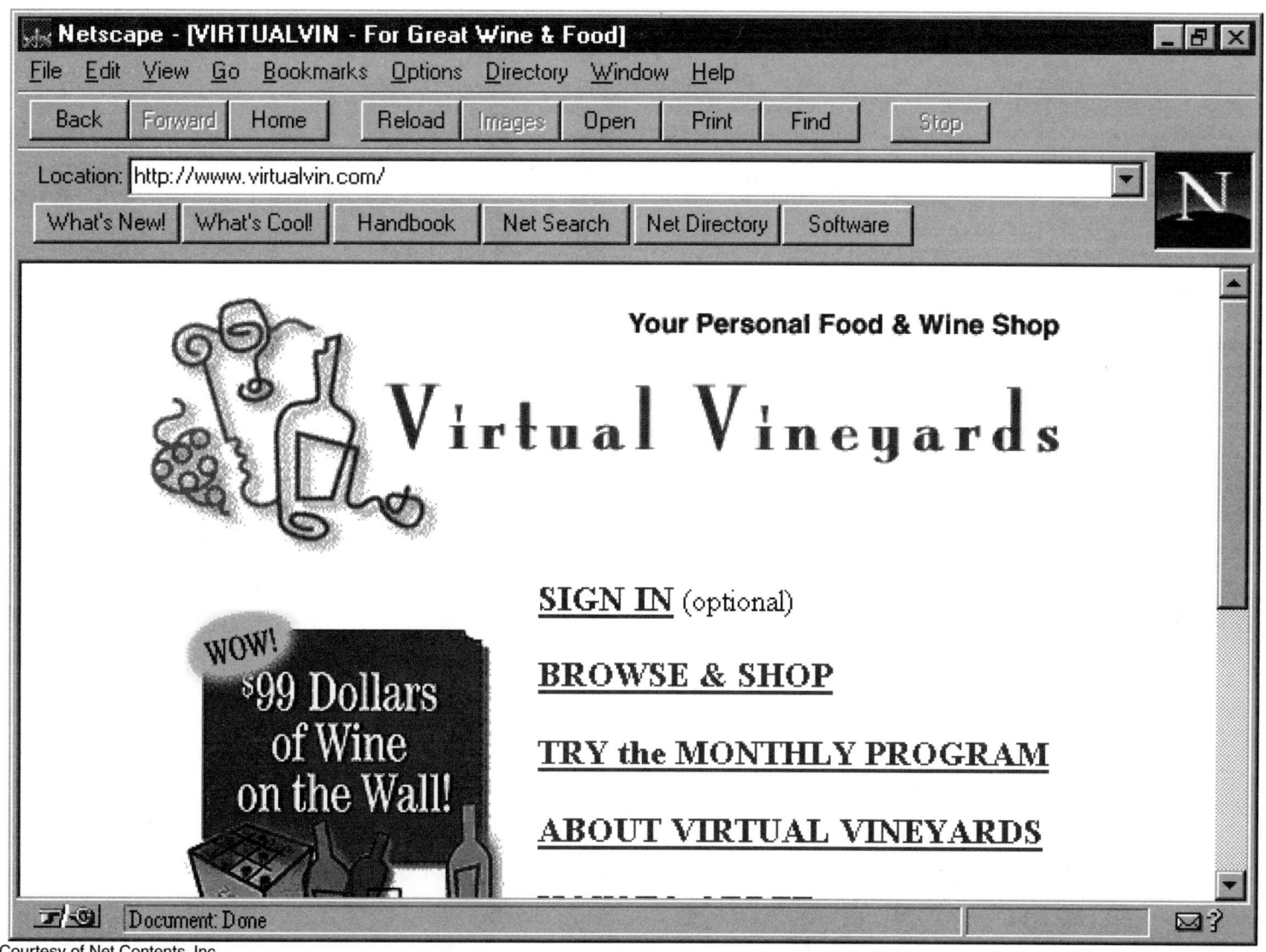

Yahoo!

URL: `http://www.yahoo.com`

Perhaps no other Web directory will ever be as famous as Yahoo! But its continued popularity is due to a lot of very hard work by its people. The basic look has changed only two or three times since its inception and the current overall appearance has been constant for some time. But each time we visit, we find some small iconic changes, such as a color change, or some new current offerings or features, such as Web Launch. The original hierarchical directory structure has been kept with two levels visible. By offering both the directory heading and a search form, Yahoo! remains very responsive and thus extremely popular.

Creative minds are continually working on these pages to help users and to help Yahoo! as well. The new Yahoo Quick Access suggests putting a Yahoo! link or even a Yahoo! search form on your own site and shows you how to do it. What a wonderful combination of user responsiveness and creative marketing!

Key Feature

Yahoo! provides a clean, easy-to-use directory with constant enhancements. The site has always had a well-deserved reputation for providing good search tools. And now they have refined the site so that it is clearer and easier to use. There is a text-only option provided at the bottom of the home page, as well as a hyperlink inviting readers to "Write Us." When you click on it, you are taken to a page that begins: "We are always looking for ways to improve Yahoo. Give us your comments, feedback, and suggestions!" Again, this invitation to participate in making a site better sets a tone that we think should be taken by all; they are actively looking for both positive as well as negative comments (Eeks, a Bug?! and Dead Links are two good examples) and they make it easy to report such information to them. Yahoo! has a really good reputation. With this kind of active solicitation of visitor feedback, it is easy to see why.

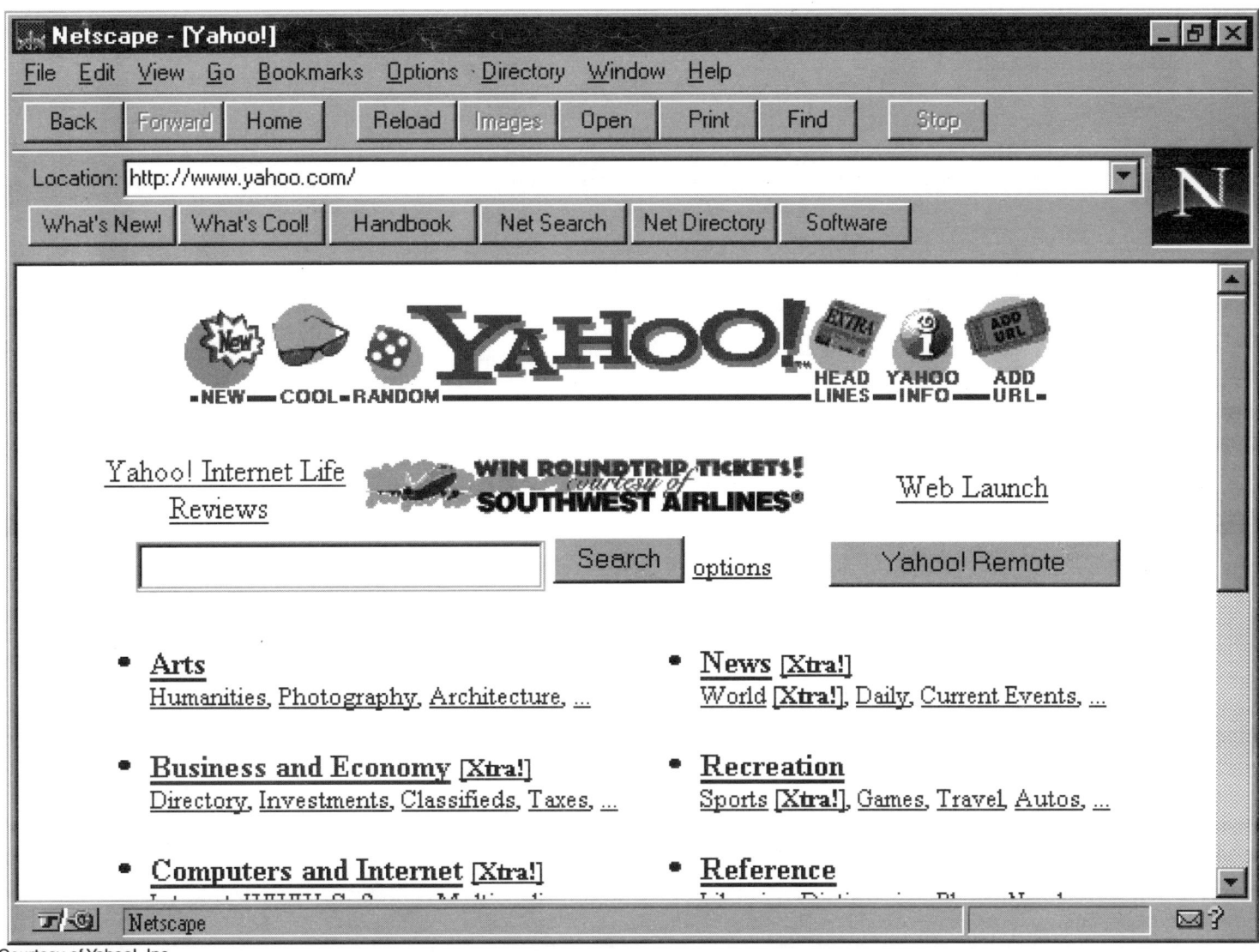

Courtesy of Yahoo!, Inc.

Summary

What we have seen in this chapter are a number of sites that do an exemplary job of being responsive to their visitors. The sites do this in a variety of ways, and some are more or less formal than others. However, all of them do an outstanding job of actively soliciting feedback from their visitors, and then using that feedback to improve themselves or their services. It is clear that people have committed time, energy, and financial resources to making themselves responsive. One would like to believe that they are pleased with the results of having done so. Certainly the responsiveness of some of these sites has been made evident in the changes we have seen over time: their graphics download better (because their file sizes are smaller), it is easier to find information (because they are better organized), new features are present (because visitors have requested them), or new and better resources are available from their site (because they did so well with the original ones and decided to add more). All of these examples illustrate well the notion of being responsive to visitors and all of them carry forward the spirit that has pervaded the Internet since its inception.

Chapter 10

New and Emerging Web Features

Introduction to New and Emerging Web Features

In this chapter we will briefly review some of the expected major trends in Web software, features, and languages. Some are already becoming well established, some are contenders, and many are hopeful "wannabees." In attempting to look toward the future, we must remember that the Web as we know it today was really born during the winter of 1993–1994. That makes it an infant. As it grows up it will, perhaps, head off in unanticipated directions.

Webmasters will have to make difficult choices about when and how to adopt the new features while continuing to support the current and the old. Which ones shall we adopt and when shall we adopt them?

Now we enter the realm of sheer speculation. The speculation is not about all the marvelous new and emerging features for the World Wide Web, but about which ones will survive.

The Problem for Webmasters

On the current Netscape Plug-ins page alone, there are more than 20 different helper applications or plug-ins. They all do the most wonderful job of presenting information in exciting new ways and include options that range from audio to virtual reality. Beyond these are literally hundreds of software applications you can add to your site to get really things jumping.

Implications for Webmasters

Which ones will you assume your visitors can use? Which new player applications should you carry as download links? Can you afford to maintain many multiple copies of pages destined for differing user capabilities? How will you know the "right answer"? While we do not have any solid answers, we will make some suggestions and more than a few guesses. First, let us separate the Intranets from the Internet.

Intranet Sites

Webmasters in Intranet environments may have more control over the browsers being used, the plug-ins that are running, and those to be adopted in their closed environments in the future. We say some control, because you must remember that your closed internal user group may have other browsers and plug-ins in other parts of their lives.

That will put some pressure on you to adopt someone's favorites. In an Intranet, you are able to exercise some degree of control. On the open Internet, you must make more difficult choices.

Internet Sites

For sites on the open Internet, decisions will have to be made based on the factors we discussed in Chapter 2. That is, who are our customers and prospects and what browsers (and browser features) do they have? As more and more specialized plug-ins and helper applications appear in the market, each Webmaster will have to decide which ones to support, when to support them, and when to drop support.

User migration assumptions

Unlike an Intranet, open Internet sites cannot control what the users have, but they can use the techniques described in the previous chapters to find out. You can also use "browser counters," such as Browser Counter 1.1.1, found at the following URL:

URL: `http://www.netimages.com/~snowhare/utilities/browsercounter.html`

The figure on the facing page shows the top part of the summary output from this perl script. There is an immense amount of data below this with every version of every browser available.

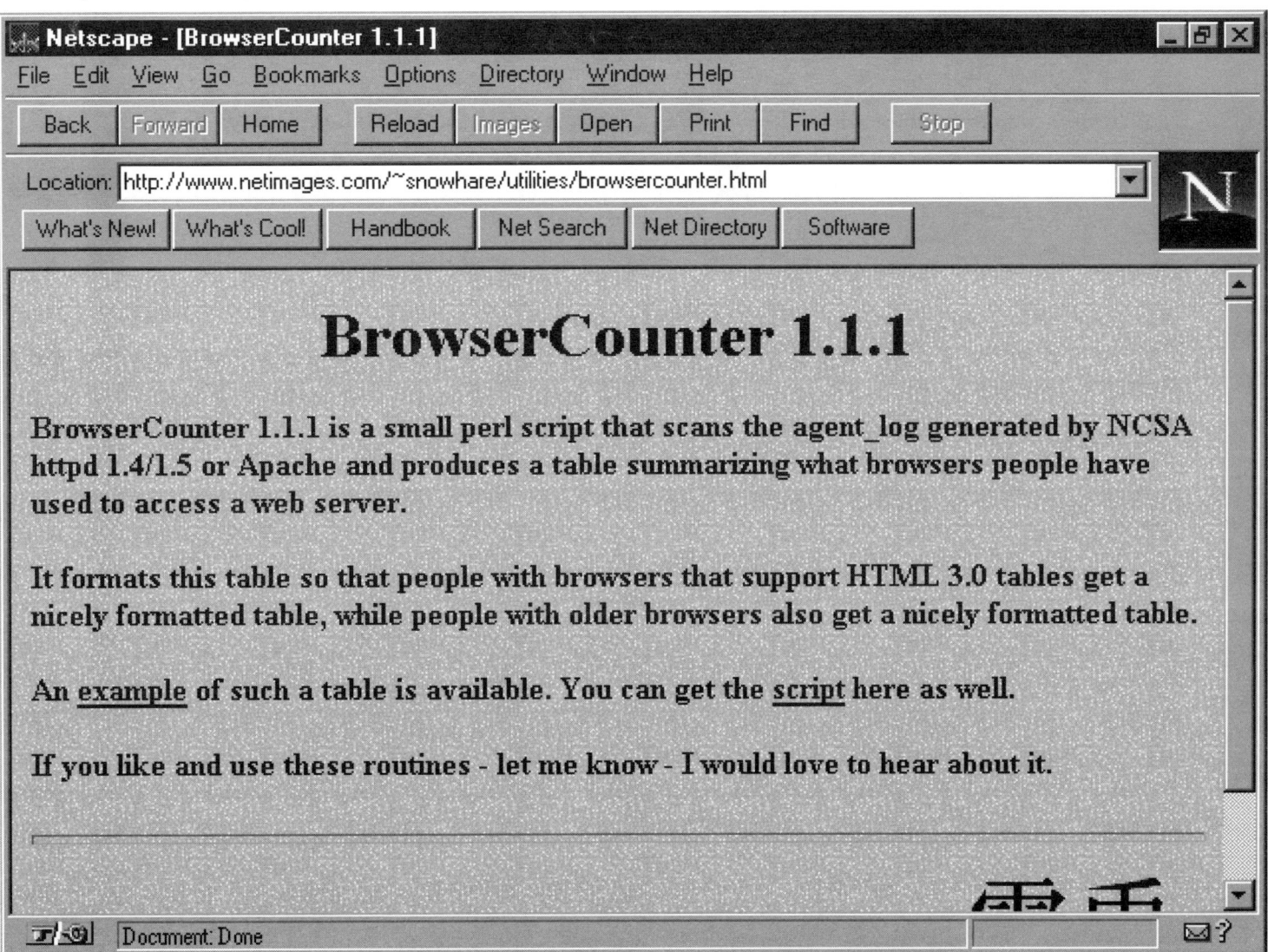

BrowserCounter 1.1.1

BrowserCounter 1.1.1 is a small perl script that scans the agent_log generated by NCSA httpd 1.4/1.5 or Apache and produces a table summarizing what browsers people have used to access a web server.

It formats this table so that people with browsers that support HTML 3.0 tables get a nicely formatted table, while people with older browsers also get a nicely formatted table.

An example of such a table is available. You can get the script here as well.

If you like and use these routines - let me know - I would love to hear about it.

Courtesy of Net Images

With this data about your visitors, you may be able to judge what to support and what to ignore. You will need to look at this information regularly to keep up with changes. You can also use logs and log analysis tools to see where your visitors are going once they arrive at your site. For instance, if you have a "plain vanilla" home page with links to pages with Acrobat, Java, RealAudio, or VRML content, you can use your logs to count how many visitors actually select those options once they are at your site. This specific data may help you decide which software packages you can begin to count on.

Alternatives for Nonmigrated Users

One key decision you will need to make and make again is what that "plain vanilla" page should contain. Will it be like the IBM page which offers visitors a choice of text only, HTML 2.0, and HTML 3.0? Or will it be a somewhat plain page with a few graphics and links to the more exotic features? Another key decision has to do with what you should do with users who have not migrated to the newer tools. For example, browsers on the legacy information services (Prodigy or CompuServe) do not adopt new features as quickly as the competitive browsers do. Another example is the people who got a browser with an operating system and don't know how (or don't want) to upgrade. If these users are in your constituent set, you will need to maintain "older" (meaning less feature rich) pages for them.

The hardest decisions will be which "basic" innovations to support. If you decide to offer a new feature, be sure to include hyperlinks so your visitors can easily obtain the plug-ins. Most plug-ins offer a "Logo" button on their pages for you to place on yours.

We will make a few guesses here based on the culture and heritage of the Internet. The Internet's culture and heritage can be characterized as open, nonproprietary, world-wide, and, generally, free. Where we find free viewers and plug-ins for the browsers, there we will at least find contenders for common usage.

As we look at the new and emerging features, applications and languages, some of them fit into this culture pretty well. Others are trying hard to fit. In alphabetical order, here is our best guess list of eight new features that will be widely used in the near future.

They are:

Acrobat, HTML 3.2 and higher, Java, JavaScript, QuickTime, RealAudio, ShockWave, and VRML.

Perhaps other multimedia and three-dimension standards will emerge during the next few years, but at this time, we see at least this basic set of new software taking hold. Now let's take a brief look at each.

Adobe Acrobat

URL: `http://w1000.mv.us.adobe.com/Acrobat/Acrobat0.html`

While calling this document viewer "The Universal Electronic Publishing Tool" may be a bit of marketing hyperbole, it has been catching on for a number of reasons. In keeping with our Internet culture, the viewer is provided free of charge, although document creators must pay to acquire Adobe software. The file format is called PDF, for Portable Document Format. It has several advantages over HTML. With PDF, the document creator has complete and exact control over the document's appearance. In HTML, as we have all discovered, the browser software "interprets" the appearance of the incoming HTL file. Once committed to PDF a document may be copied, but not altered.

Newer versions of Acrobat are now becoming available that will link seamlessly to browsers such as Netscape. Browsers may soon directly incorporate PDF format, so that the viewer will not even be aware of the fact that PDF is somewhat different from HTML. The documents can contain almost any form of information, including active hyperlinks.

Where document control is necessary, Acrobat has few real competitors on the Web.

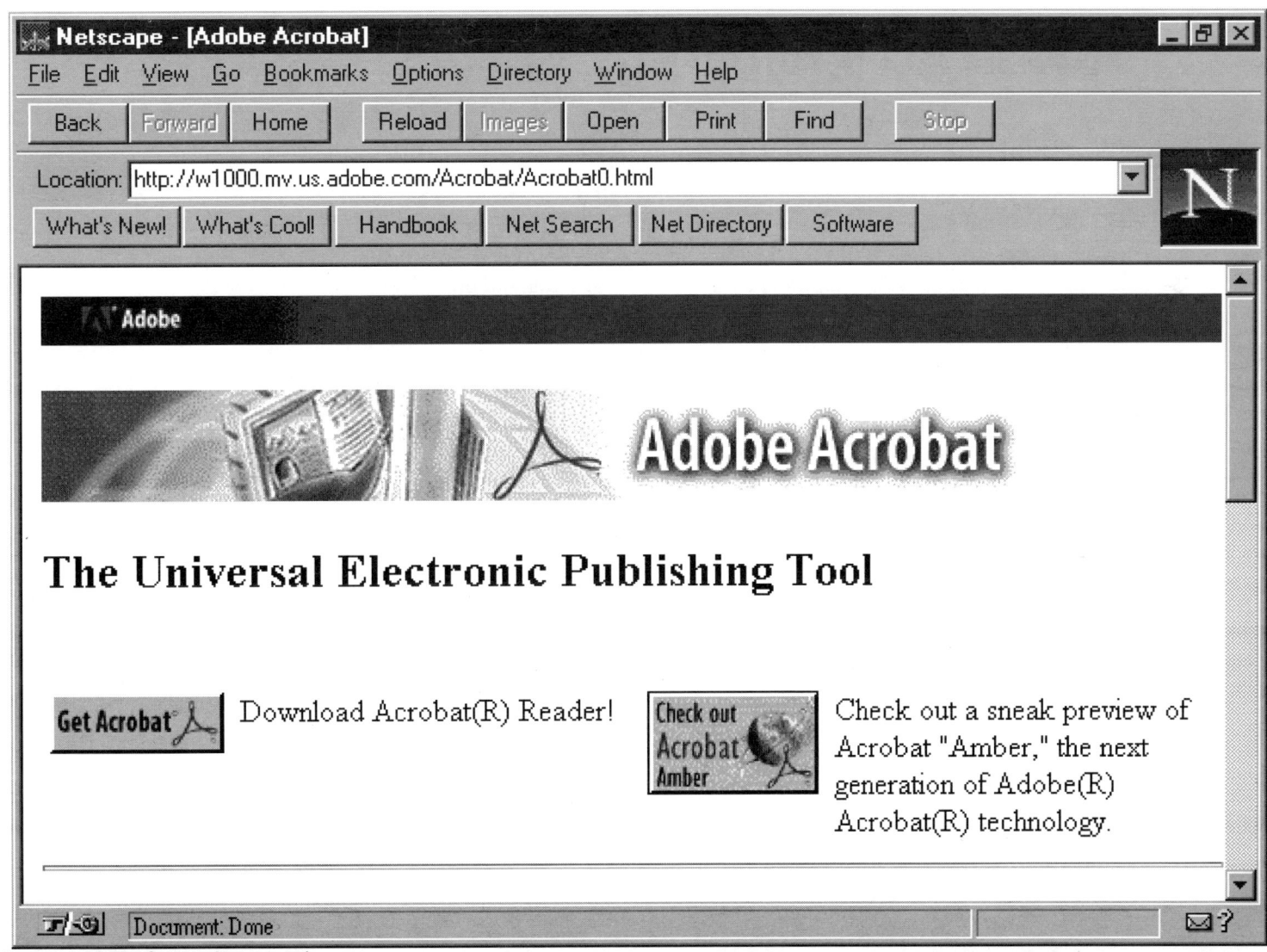

HTML 3.0 — HyperText Markup Language

URL: `http://www.w3.org/pub/WWW/MarkUp/#specs`

HyperText Markup Language is, of course, what we all use to create Web pages. Why do we list it here in New and Emerging? A significant reason has to do with the fact that it has several attributes that make it continuously new. In keeping with Internet culture, HTML is a free and open standard that anyone can use. It is also vendor and platform (read computer and operating system) independent and completely standard. Or, at least each release is standard when finally released as an Internet standards track RFC (Request for Comment).

Although Netscape, Microsoft, and others will continue to offer "extensions" to the HyperText Markup Language, the Internet's HTML is the real standard. As HTML moves from HTML 2.0 to HTML 3.0 and beyond, pages written in the standard will be usable everywhere on the Web, not just with Netscape Navigator or Microsoft Internet Explorer.

As with any other standard, efforts are continuously underway to incorporate various extensions into the standard. HTML may lag a bit in time over the proprietary extensions, but all browsers will have to follow it.

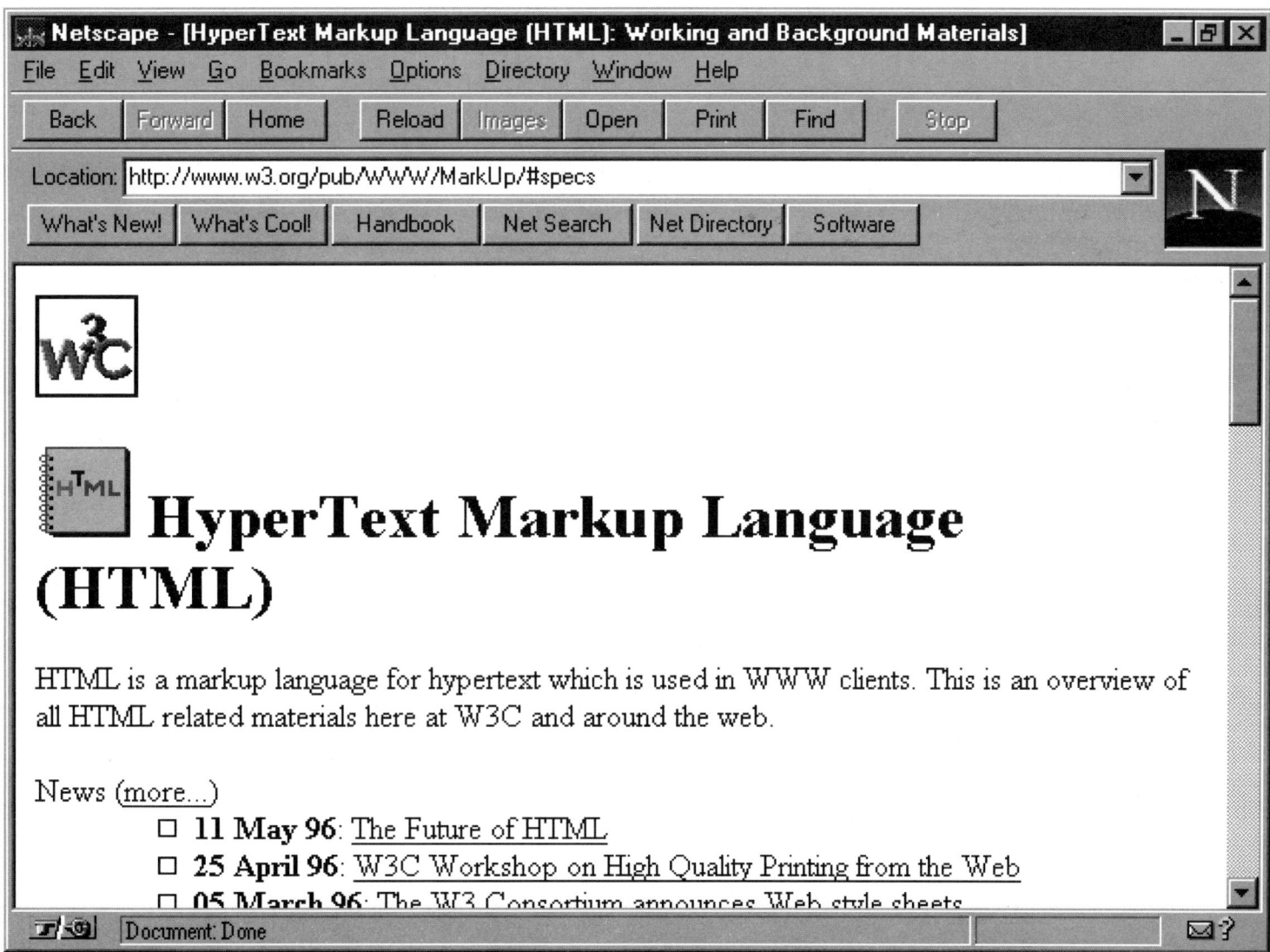

Sun Microsystems' Java Language

URL: `http://java.sun.com/`

Java adds motion and animation to Web pages. That is probably understating the impact of Java-enabled pages. They really come to life! It is more than just coffee steaming out of a cup. It is stock market ticker tapes and moving images running right on your browser screen. Java adds an entire new dimension to the Web. It delivers these images across the Internet not as GIFs or JPEGs or QuickTime movies. It delivers them as brief code packages called *applets*. These applets then run in the client- or browser-end computer without further intervention from the Web site.

Java, as we write this, is rapidly entering the entire Web. Netscape now supports Java on many flavors of UNIX, IBM's AIX, Windows NT and Windows 95. Support for the Macintosh and Windows 3.1 is being released.

According to Netscape, "Java applets allow expert graphics rendering, real-time interaction with users, live information updating, and instant interaction with servers over the network." Security has been closely addressed by Sun, and Java is believed to be free of many of the security problems of executable code on public networks.

Make no mistake about it: Java will be a potent force in extending browser and Web capabilities. Because many browsers will not support Java for some time to come, Webmasters will be forced to offer at least two versions of their pages.

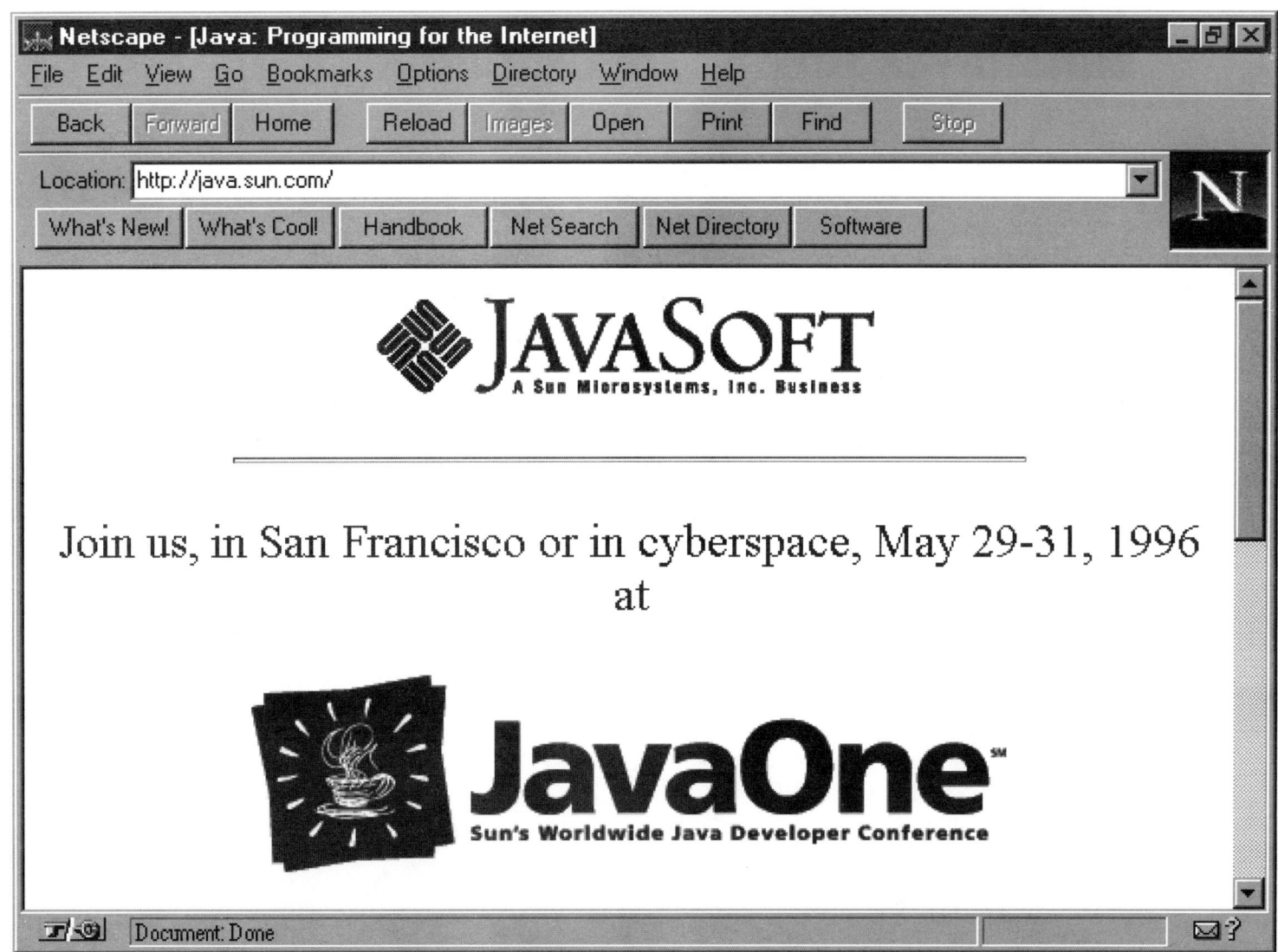

Netscape's JavaScript Language

URL: `http://home.netscape.com/`

JavaScript, a language originated by Netscape, is a simpler, almost HTML-like language. JavaScript is used to do simple management tasks at the browser. It can respond to user actions, such as mouse clicks and the beginning and ending of page loading. Netscape calls it the "glue" to be used to tie Java applets, HTML, and the plug-ins together. Due to its simplicity, many HTML writers can be expected to use it more quickly than they might use Java.

Some examples of JavaScript are already circulating on the Web. One creates a "banner" that scrolls across the status bar after a page has been loaded. The scroll continues until the visitor moves on to another page. Small icons in motion are now appearing thanks to JavaScript.

It can be expected that JavaScript will evolve rapidly as other browsers pick up the ability to use it. Eventually, it will probably be an Internet standard, although Netscape will be "extending" it.

QuickTime from Apple

URL: `http://quicktime.apple.com/`

QuickTime from Apple is rapidly becoming the de-facto "standard" for short movie clips on the Internet. Major movie companies and *Playbill* distribute short previews of films and shows for Quick-Time players. Although originally designed for the Mac, QuickTime players are now available for Windows-based PCs. Like the plug-ins and helper applications discussed earlier, the player is free and available easily over the Internet.

The only major downside to QuickTime is the size of the movie files. If you plan to distribute Quick-Time film clips, be aware of the file sizes and make your viewers aware. Well-designed sites indicate not only the file sizes but also provide estimated download times in minutes at various line speeds.

The clips themselves, as played on most computers, are a bit grainy but will clearly improve over time. QuickTime movies seem to have won the immediate battle over MPEG for video clip distribution. The video war may not, however, be over. Several other potential solutions are now entering the Web. These promise to offer closer to realtime, streaming delivery rather than making viewers wait for and entire file to download before the images can be seen.

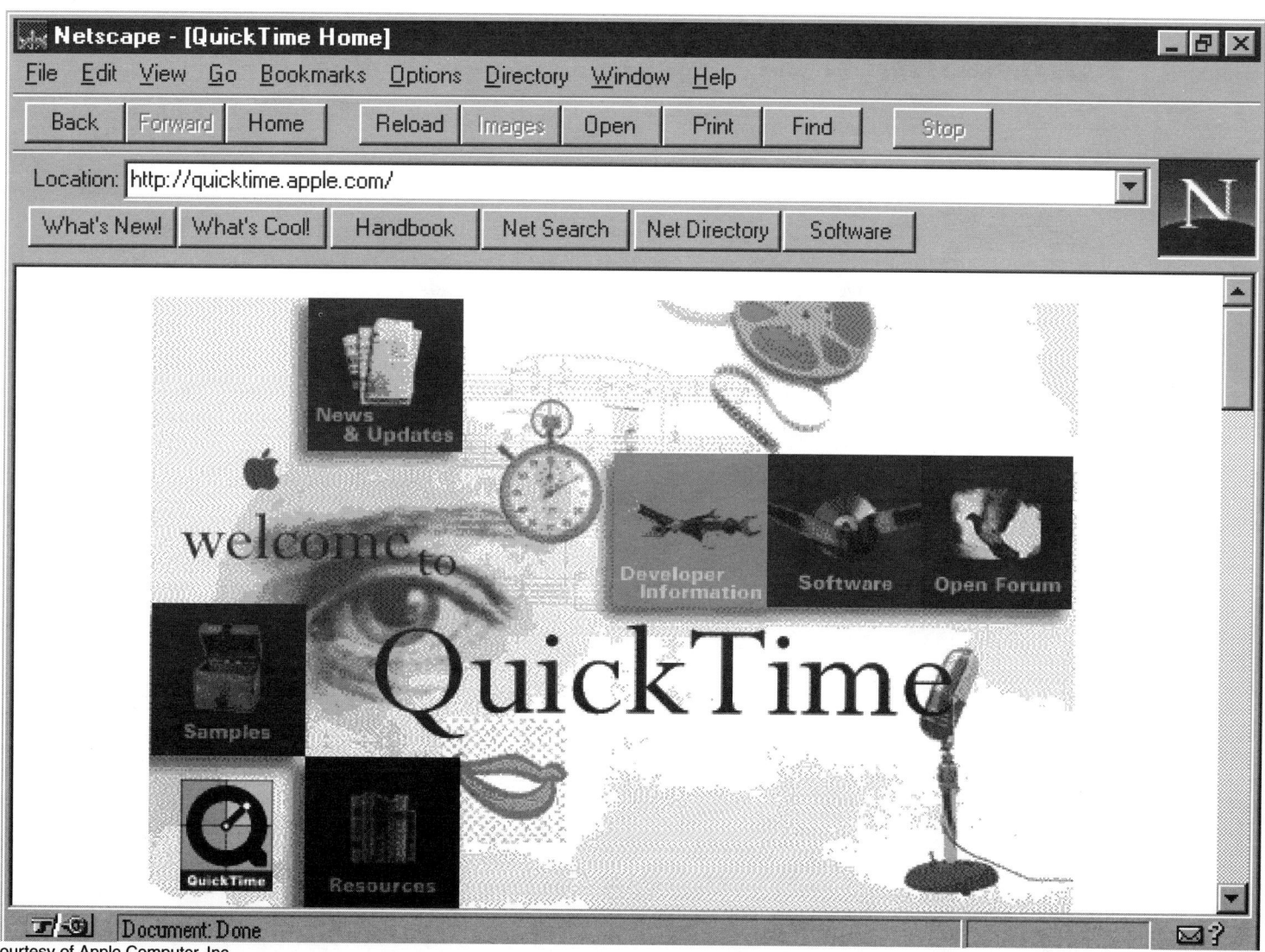

Courtesy of Apple Computer, Inc.

RealAudio

URL: `http://www.realaudio.com/`

Early audio on the Web was mostly in the AU or WAV format and required very large files. Downloading these over modem lines was about as thrilling as waiting for your hair to grow. Audio clips were awaiting a streaming type of delivery. In this new method, the sound is compressed and then sent ahead. When the audio player has enough in the buffer (several seconds' worth), the player starts playing and prays that more will arrive in a timely fashion.

RealAudio from Progressive Networks got in early in this technology and then followed the Internet model by distributing the players free of charge. At the time of this writing there seems to be little competition for audio distribution. Radio and TV stations and sound sites are adopting RealAudio as the system of choice. Players are everywhere and install easily. Even Orson Welles' complete "War of the Worlds" (`http://www.waroftheworlds.com`) can be heard on the Web with the RealAudio player.

Where audio is involved on the Web, we see that RealAudio will continue to be the vehicle that most sites use. RealAudio is continuing to improve their players and encoders to produce better and better quality. Webmasters may need to decide what versions of RealAudio to support

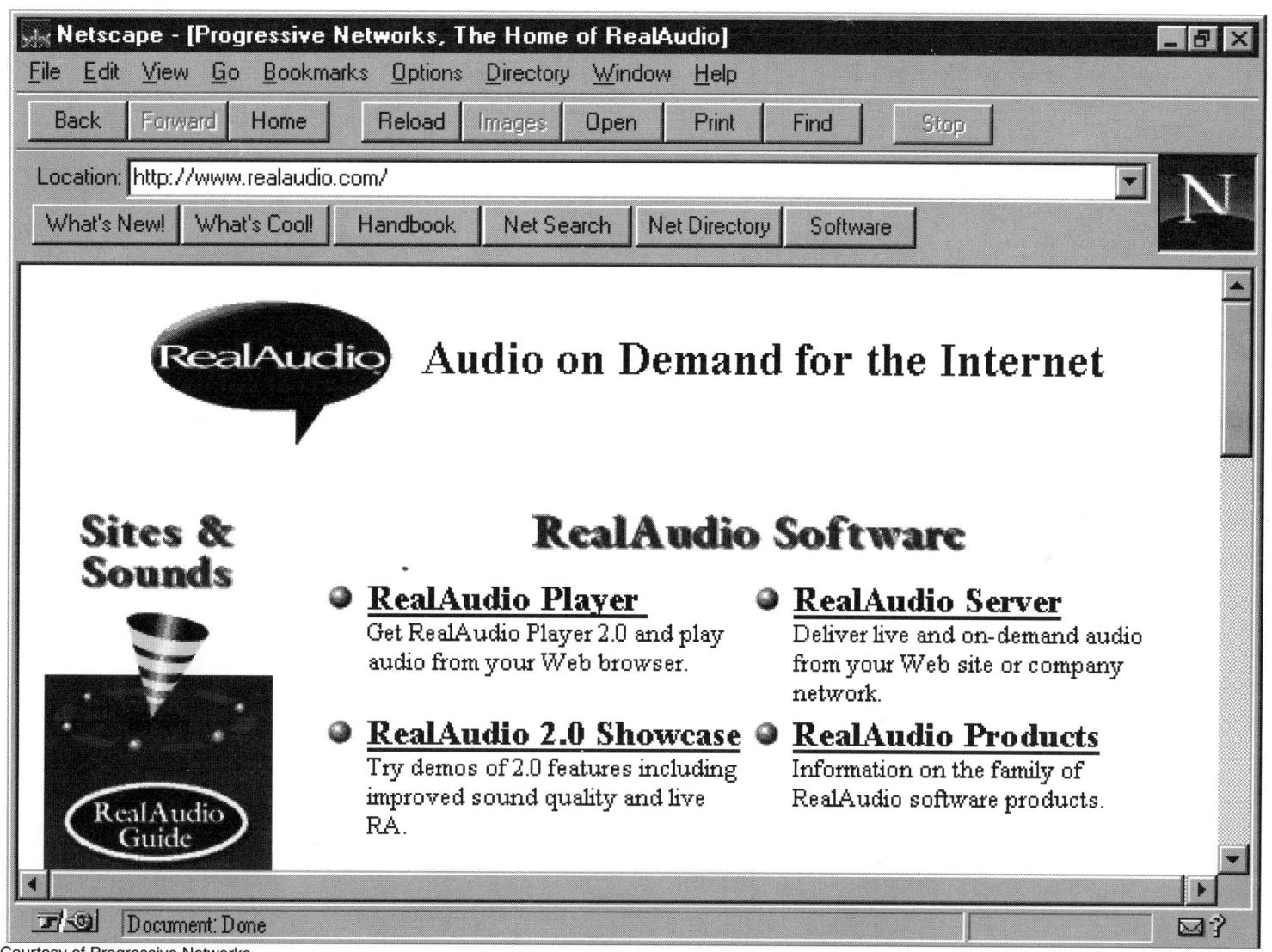

Shockwave from Macromedia

URL: `http://www.macromedia.com/`

Shockwave may be to digital multimedia on the Web what RealAudio is to sound. Using the Shockwave plug-in to Netscape's Navigator browser, visitors to "shocked" sites view, hear, and interact with multimedia animation, sound, and high-resolution digital art. Although "shocked" sites require large files to be downloaded to browsers, the impact and quality of the multimedia are very impressive. As access speed improves on the Web, Shockwave may well become a significant force. Even today, Macromedia offers "Afterburner" as part of the package to compress file sizes. Afterburner is often able to compress file sizes by up to 50 percent. Because of multimedia's larger file sizes, Macromedia is currently placing a strong focus on Intranets where speed (thanks to the higher access speed on Local Area Networks) is less of an issue.

Shockwave is really a set of technologies for Macromedia digital art authoring tools. Shockwave players are available currently for Netscape 2.0 and above. Macromedia also offers a rich family of well-established "backstage" digital and multimedia creation tools. For instance, using Shockwave for Director from Macromedia, Web designers can quickly create interactive multimedia such as animated advertising, online games and highlighted, animated key images and logos. Shockwave is also available for Macromedia's Authorware and FreeHand design tools.

While the authoring tools from Macromedia are licensed programs, the entire collection of Shockwave plug-ins are free to browser users. Licensed users of Macromedia's authoring tools may also download Shockwave free of charge. As we write, the browser user may install either a full set of Shockwave for Authorware, Director, and FreeHand, or a custom set of any combination. Shockwave is available from the Macromedia site URL shown above.

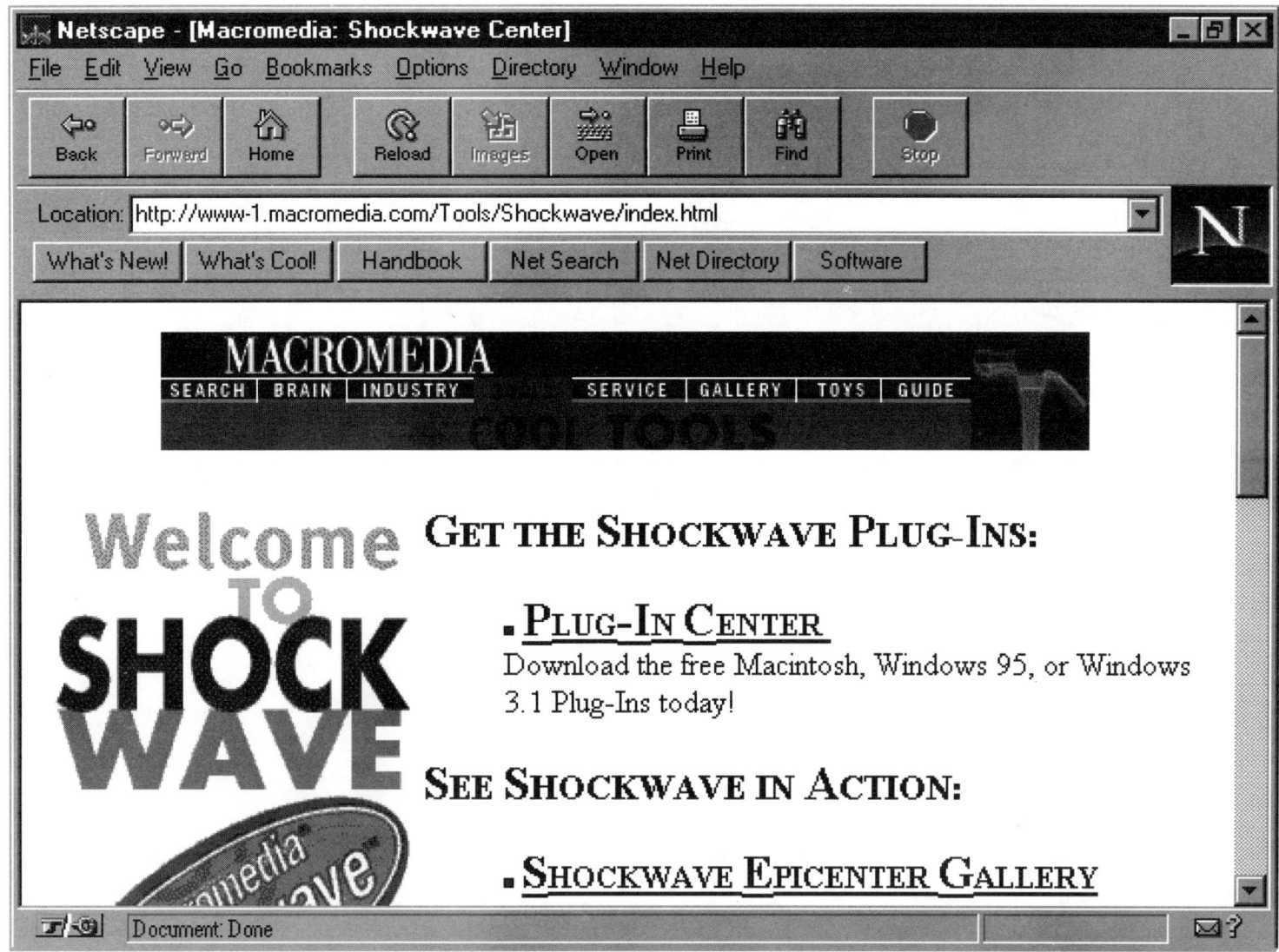

VRML — Virtual Reality Modeling Language

URL: `http://www.ncsa.uiuc.edu/General/VRML/VRMLHome.html`

The next giant step on the Web will likely be VRML or Virtual Reality Modeling Language. But its speed of entry and wide acceptance are not yet clear. At the moment, there are impressive demonstrations and a feeling that we are about to witness a major breakthrough. On the other hand, there is intense competition to be the browser plug-in of choice. As a result, many firms are offering free VRML players and authoring software.

It is also unclear what applications will benefit most from VRML. Will it be computer games, real estate (house tours), medicine, travel (views from hotel rooms), or something more complex? And which VRML viewer can Webmasters assume to be the common (and widely used) one?

VRML cannot be ignored, but it is currently the most difficult of the new and emerging Web tools to categorize or predict. The figure on the facing page is just one of very many sites devoted to VRML. VRML is at the moment a very exciting, if unclear, tool set for a future on the Web.

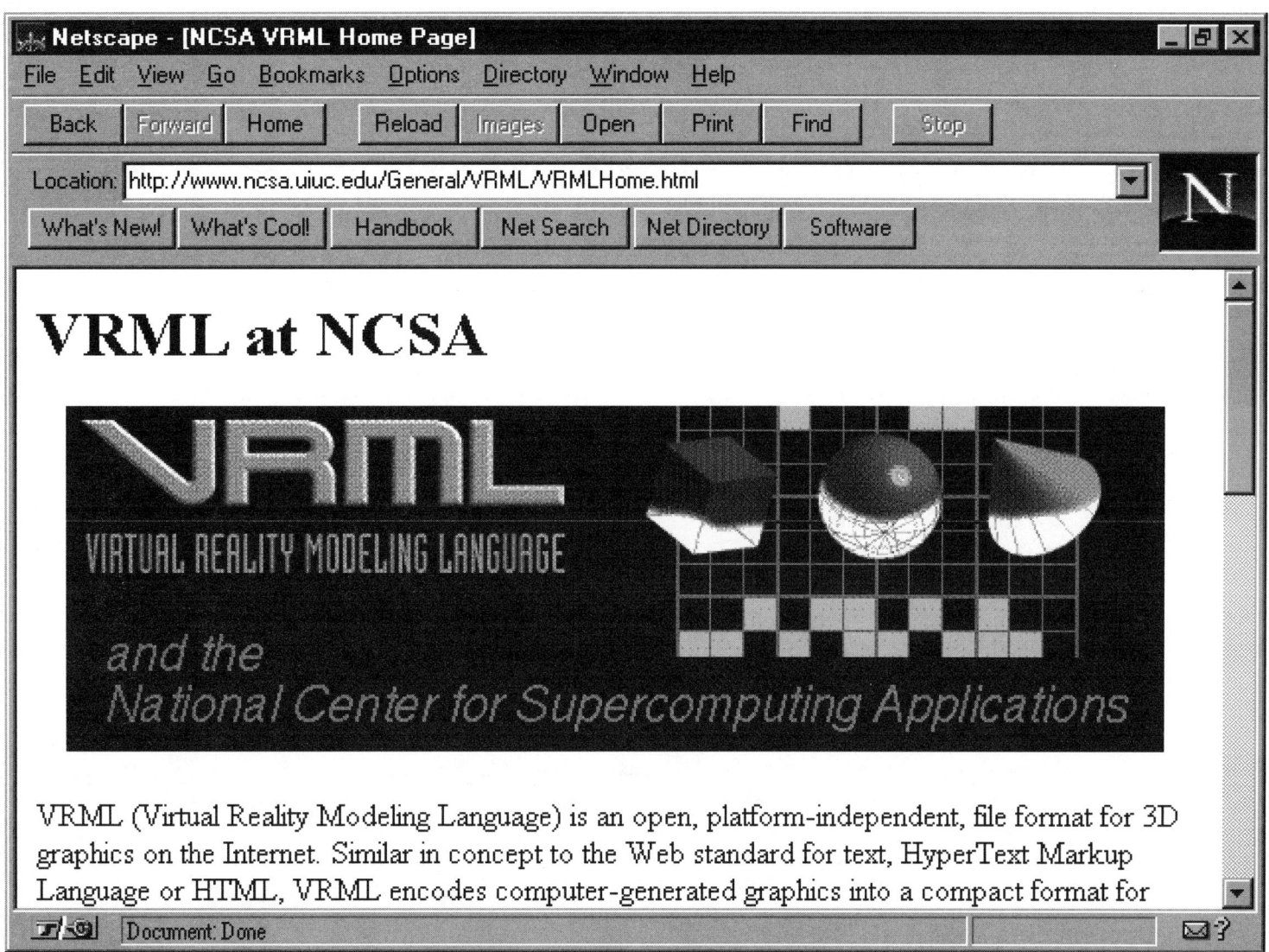

Other Developments to Watch

Web Connection Speeds

Today's Web is limited by only one thing—line speed. Although some people are lucky enough to have connections of 1.5 megabits and above, they are usually shared connections. At peak load times, they are not a lot faster than modems. Most people still connect to the Web via telephone lines and modems. Modems will not get a lot faster than the current 28,800 bps. Integrated Services Digital Network (ISDN) promises up to four times that, but what is really needed are megabits per second. Those speeds are coming, most likely from cable television.

When you have some people on megabit lines from cable and the rest on modems, you will have a severe challenge on Web site content. You may wish to create separate sites for each.

Information and Entertainment Convergence

As cable television begins to deliver Web information, it will become increasingly difficult to differentiate between what is data and what is just fun. Even today, there is a serious age gap developing at Web sites. Older managers may be leaning toward the serious while younger Web-savvy surfers may be leaning toward fun. The cultural collision may be difficult for a few years. Be sure not to get caught in the middle of this family dispute.

Evolution of the Web

Most of the programmers who develop the best browsers will not be 30 years of age for some time to come. Their energy, creativity, and enthusiasm is evident in their products. We do not believe this process will slow at any time in the future. For Webmasters, this means a nonstop job of just keeping up. We really do not know where all this is leading, but the journey is exciting. The only solution is to join the enthusiasm and enjoy the voyage!

Appendix A

Guide to Web Sites

Appendix B

Color Figures

The Color Figures

The figures on the following pages are intended to provide you with a representative sample of the many excellent examples that are included in *The 7 Keys to Effective Web Sites*. Four figures illustrating each of the seven keys and four figures from the New and Emerging chapter have been selected. The figures are intended to represent a particular key well and to provide you with a sense of what you will find within the text in each chapter as we discuss all of the sites and all of the keys in detail. The sites were chosen because they do a good job of incorporating a particular key, not necessarily because they are better than any of the other sites within the same chapter.

Hopefully, the added information that color provides will also give you the incentive to view the sites in this book online. There is much to be gained by viewing sites in color, especially as Webmasters are learning how to utilize their color palettes better.

Courtesy of Condé Net

Condé Nast Traveler   page 32

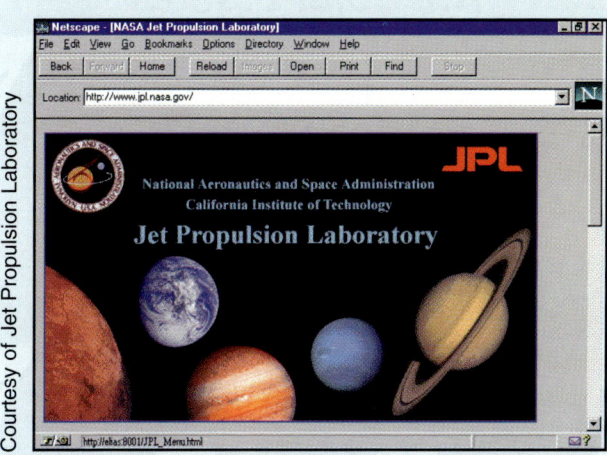

Courtesy of Jet Propulsion Laboratory

NASA's Jet Propulsion Lab   page 38

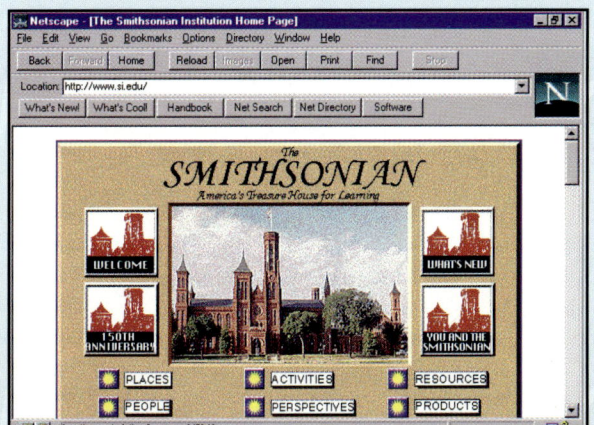

Courtesy of Smithsonian Institution

The Smithsonian   page 50

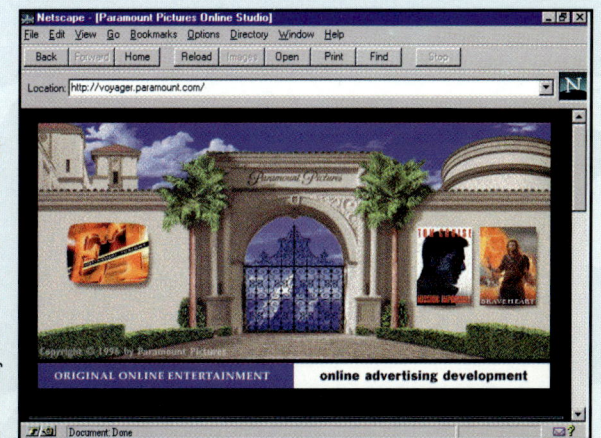

Courtesy of Paramount Pictures

Paramount Voyager   page 56

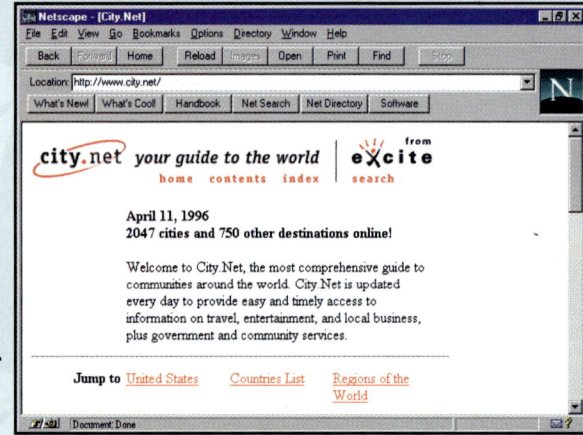

City Net Express' City.Net   page 68

DejaNews Usenet Search   page 72

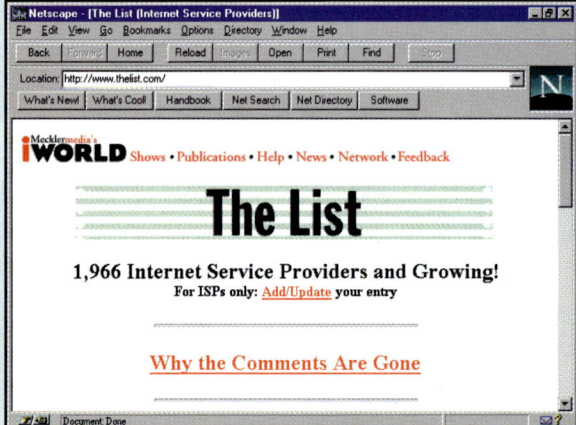

The List   page 84

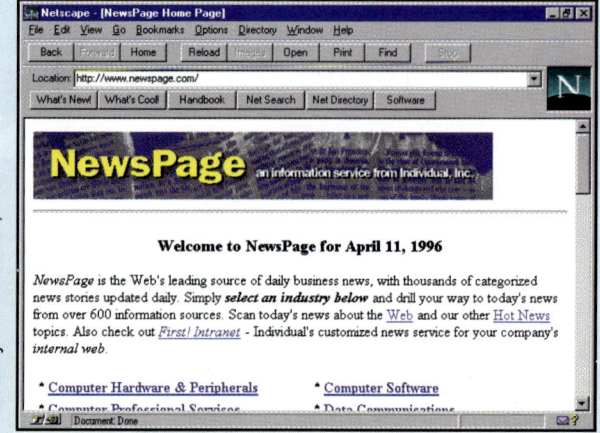

NewsPage   page 86

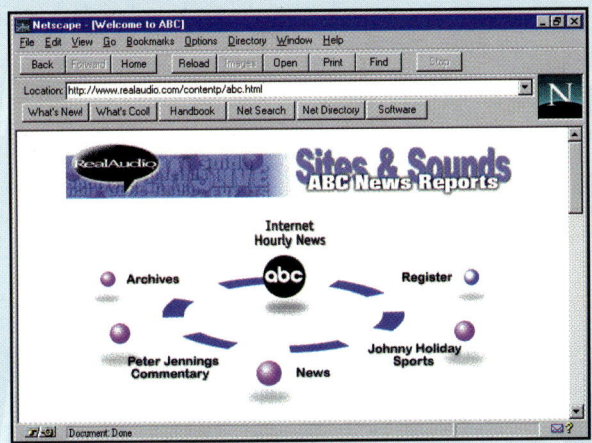

Courtesy of ABC News

ABC's Internet News page 102

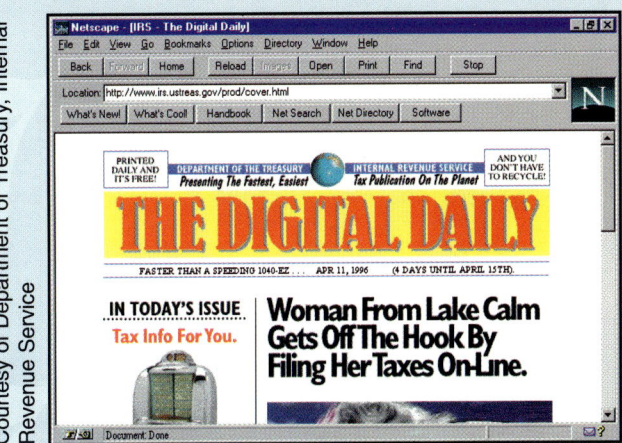

Courtesy of Department of Treasury, Internal Revenue Service

Internal Revenue Service page 112

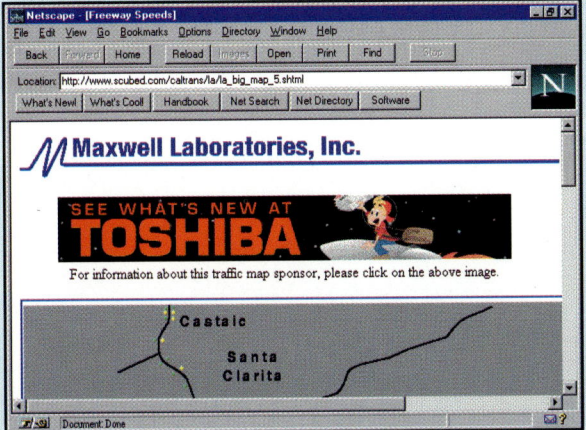

Courtesy of Maxwell Labs

LA Freeway Speeds page 114

Courtesy of Playbill Online

Playbill page 124

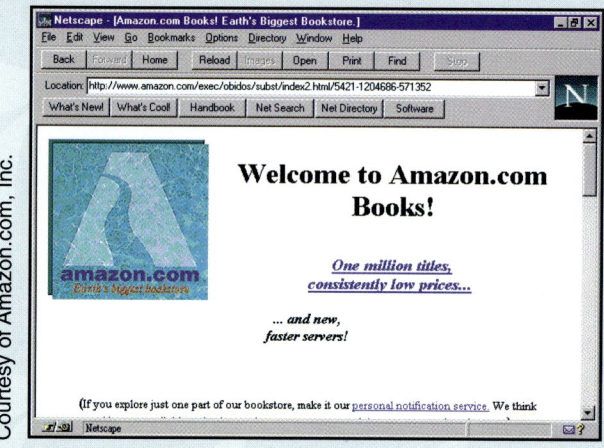

Courtesy of Amazon.com, Inc.

Amazon.com Books   page 142

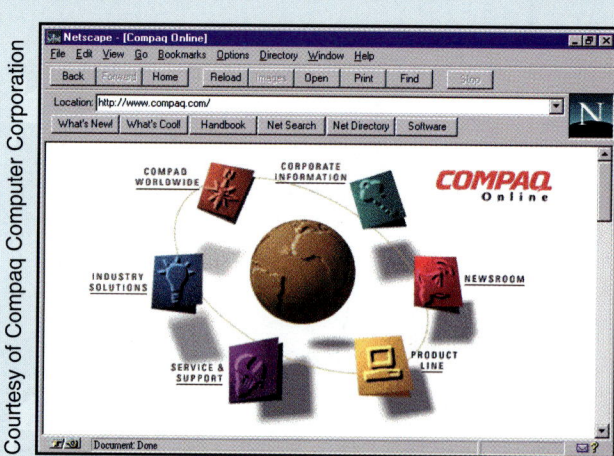

Courtesy of Compaq Computer Corporation

Compaq Computer Corporation   page 148

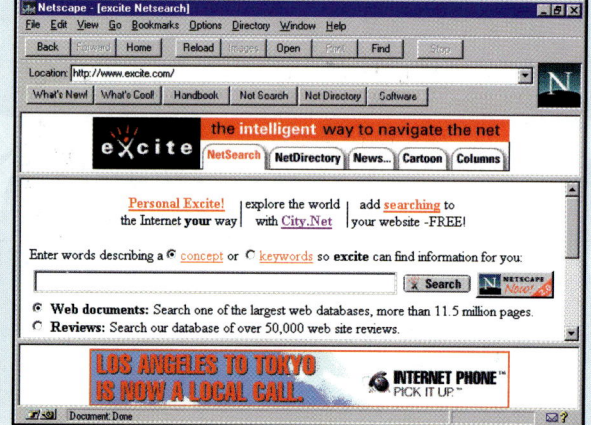

Courtesy of Excite, Inc.

Excite Netsearch   page 152

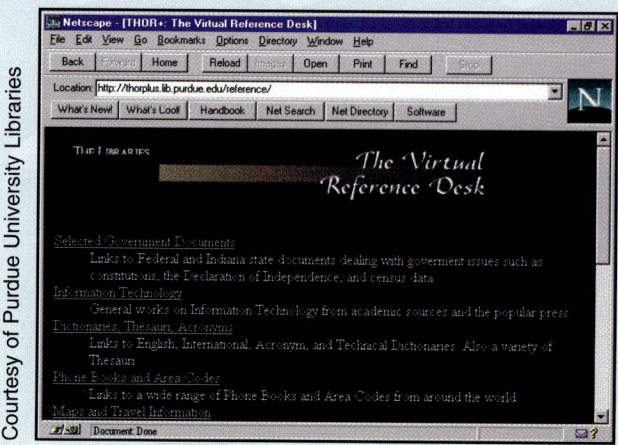

Courtesy of Purdue University Libraries

The Virtual Reference Desk   page 168

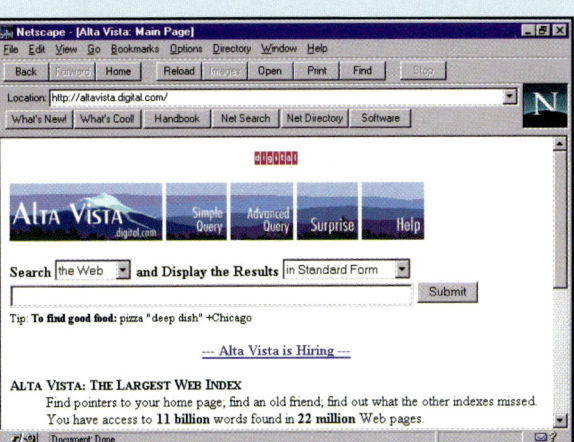

Courtesy of Digital Equipment Corporation. Alta Vista is a trademark of Digital Equipment Corporation

Alta Vista page 178

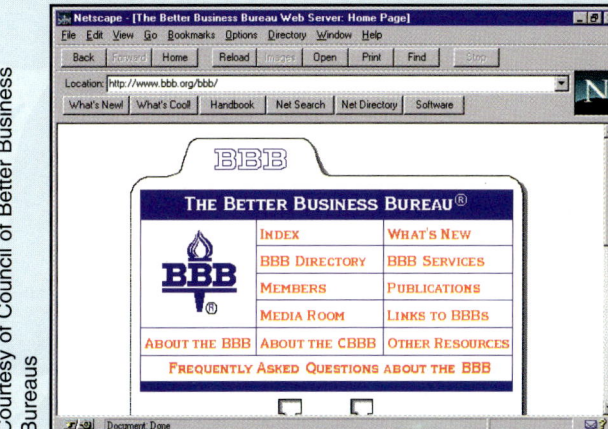

Courtesy of Council of Better Business Bureaus

Better Business Bureau page 180

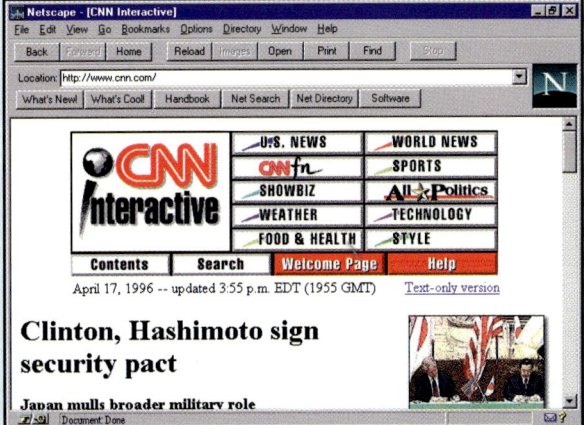

Courtesy of Cable News Network, Inc.

CNN Interactive page 182

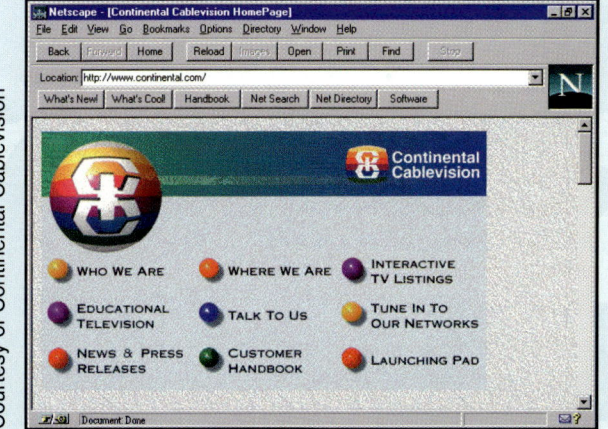

Courtesy of Continental Cablevision

Continental Cablevision page 184

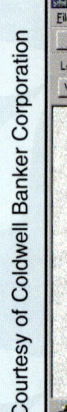

Courtesy of Coldwell Banker Corporation

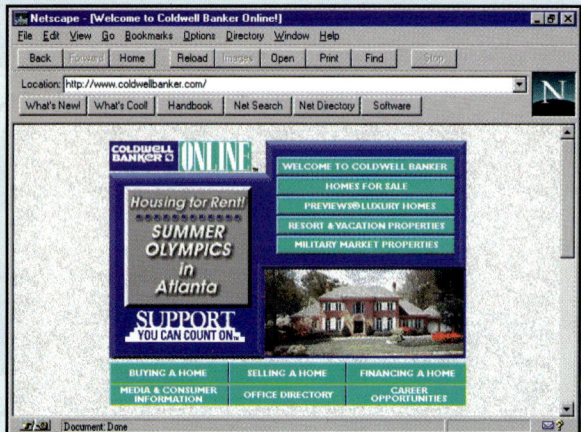

Coldwell Banker Online   page 214

Courtesy of Customer Communications Group, Inc.

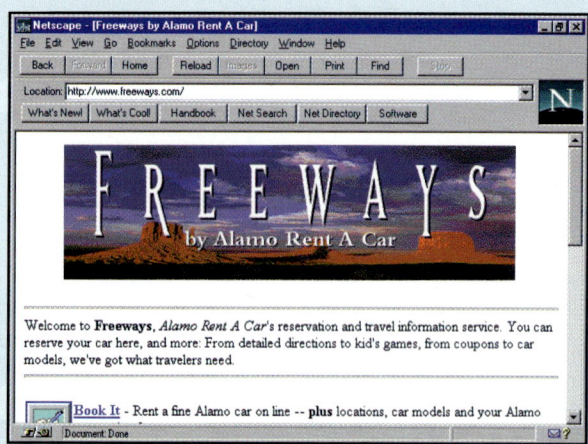

Freeways by Alamo Rent A Car   page 222

Courtesy of Topaz Hotel Services

San Francisco Hotel Reservations   page 232

Courtesy of Windham Hill

Windham Hill Records   page 240

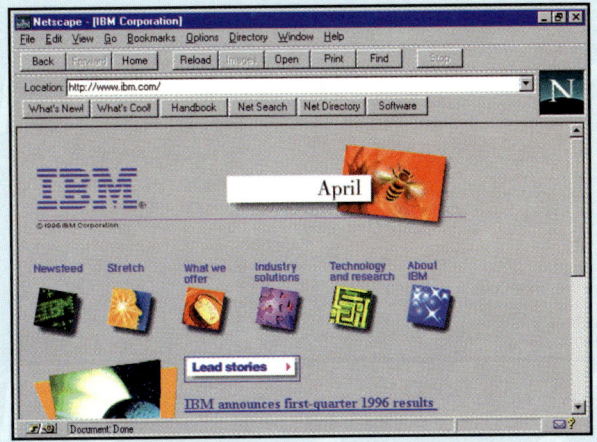

Courtesy of IBM Corporation

IBM Corporation page 256

Courtesy of Lycos, Inc.

Lycos Search page 262

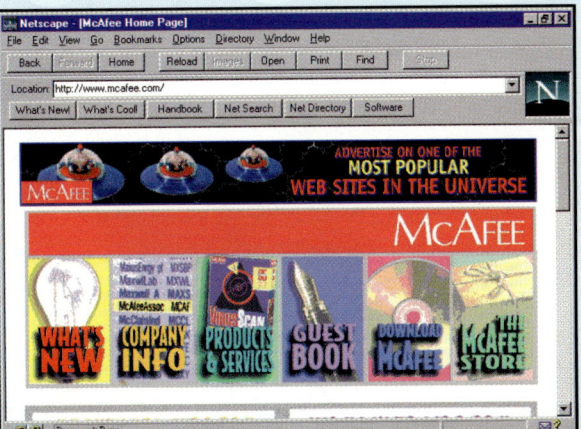

Courtesy of McAfee

McAfee Network Security & Management page 266

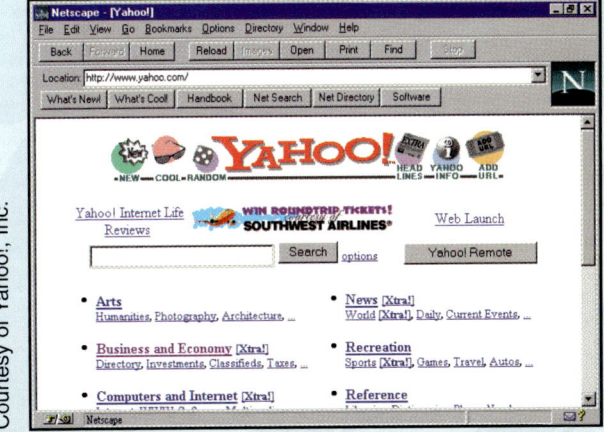

Courtesy of Yahoo!, Inc.

Yahoo Search page 274

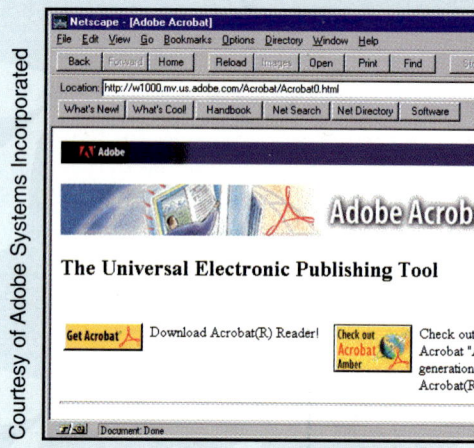

Courtesy of Adobe Systems Incorporated

Adobe Acrobat page 284

Courtesy of Apple Computer, Inc.

QuickTime page 292

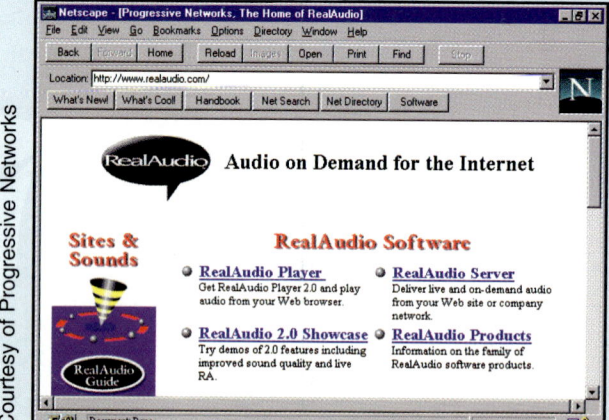

Courtesy of Progressive Networks

RealAudio page 294

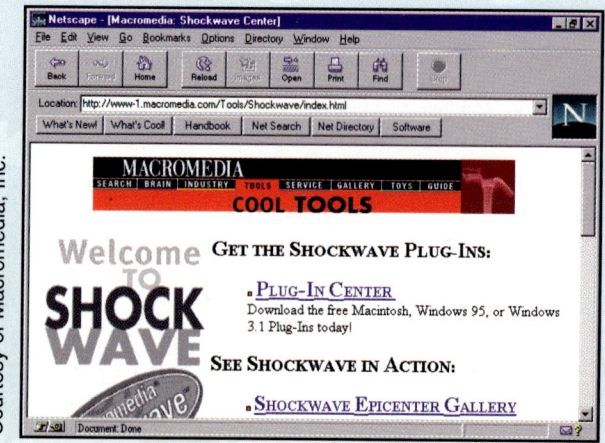

Courtesy of Macromedia, Inc.

Shockwave page 296